The International Labor Organization

The International Labor Organization

An American View

WALTER GALENSON

The University of Wisconsin Press

Published 1981

The University of Wisconsin Press
114 North Murray Street
Madison, Wisconsin 53715

The University of Wisconsin Press, Ltd.
1 Gower Street
London WC1E 6HA, England

First printing

Printed in the United States of America

For LC CIP information see the colophon

ISBN 0–299–08540–6 (cloth)
0–299–08544–9 (paper)

For Daniel

Contents

List of Tables and Figures

Tables

Figures

Preface

Many individuals contributed in one way or another to the preparation of this volume. My greatest debt is to the numerous officials of the International Labor Organization who provided me with material, assisted in arranging interviews in countries in which field work was done, and reviewed critically various sections of the manuscript. I refrain from mentioning their names only because I do not want to implicate them in my interpretations and conclusions. I must name two, however, without whose cooperation my research would have been immeasurably more difficult: Francis Blanchard, present director-general of the ILO, and Bernard Fortin. Their help was unstinting, despite their disagreement with me on particular issues.

Several officials of the United States Department of Labor who are involved in international labor affairs, particularly Donald Avery, Tadd Linsenmayer, and James H. Quackenbush, were very kind in helping me track down key documents and in keeping me up to date on current developments.

A number of scholars who are very knowledgeable about ILO affairs read the manuscript critically and gave me the benefit of their advice. Among them are Professors John T. Dunlop of Harvard University, Ernst B. Haas of the University of California, and John P. Windmuller of Cornell University. Carol Barker and Joshua Nelson of the Twentieth Century Fund staff shepherded the work through its various stages.

Finally, I would like to record my obligation to David A. Morse, the former director-general of the ILO, who initiated me into the mysteries of ILO operations and who shared with me his knowledge of the subject matter involved.

The International Labor Organization

Chapter 1

Introduction

The United States rejoined the International Labor Organization (ILO) in February 1980, more than two years after it had withdrawn from membership. The ILO is the only member of the U.N. family from which the United States has ever resigned, and part of the purpose of this book is to explain why. Other international organizations—including the United Nations Educational, Scientific, and Cultural Organization, the World Health Organization, and the United Nations itself—have come under fire from American interest groups from time to time. The ILO is the only one from which the United States withdrew.

The decision to rejoin does not necessarily mean that all differences have been resolved satisfactorily. Indeed, the Chamber of Commerce, which provided the U.S. employer representative in the past, has declined to continue in this role. A number of problems remain, and it will be some time before it is clear whether the return of the United States will mark a genuinely new era in mutual relationships between the United States and the ILO.

A second purpose of this study is to explore and evaluate the two major purposes of the ILO: the promulgation of international labor standards and the administration of technical assistance to less developed countries. Americans in general know very little about the day-to-day operations of the ILO—or of most other international organizations—and are therefore not in a position to determine whether it is really worth supporting to the tune of 25 percent of its budget.

History of the ILO

The ILO was formed in 1919, a product of the Treaty of Versailles. Representatives of the United States, including Samuel Gompers, president of the American Federation of Labor (AFL), were active participants in the preparatory commission that developed its structure. The ILO's first annual conference was held in Washington, D.C., in October 1919, but the U.S. Senate's failure to ratify the Treaty of Versailles made official U.S. representation at the conference impolitic. The conference was attended by delegations from thirty-nine countries and proceeded to adopt six labor conventions and to develop parliamentary practices that gave life to its formal constitution.

For a number of reasons, the United States did not join the ILO until 1934. Although it would have been technically possible to participate without becoming a full-fledged member of the League of Nations, the anti-League sentiment that prevailed in the United States inhibited successive administrations. So, too, did the fear that ratification of ILO conventions by the federal government would impinge upon the constitutional jurisdiction of the states. The American Federation of Labor, an original supporter of the ILO, backed away when it became evident that the International Federation of Trade Unions (IFTU) would dominate the ILO labor group. The AFL had decided earlier not to join the IFTU because some AFL leaders regarded it as too radical. Employers in the United States were hostile from the start; to them, the ILO was an instrument of international socialism that could endanger the prevailing system of industrial relations in the United States, including the open shop. For its part, the newly established Soviet government denounced the ILO as a capitalist device to oppress working people, and it too remained outside.

During its early years, the ILO concentrated on international conventions and recommendations dealing with standards for hours of work, minimum wages, the labor of women and children, occupational safety and health, freedom of association, and social security. The rise of fascism in Italy, one of the ILO's major founding nations, raised some difficult questions regarding trade union independence which the organization failed to resolve; Italy continued to send worker delegates who were in fact representatives of the state. An even more severe test of the ILO's survivability would have arisen had Nazi Germany not left the ILO in 1934.

With the coming of President Franklin D. Roosevelt's New Deal, U.S. interest in the ILO revived. Frances Perkins, who became secretary of labor in 1933, was the leading figure in the drive for U.S. membership. She persuaded Roosevelt that the United States belonged in the ILO, and enabling legislation was passed in the form of a joint congressional resolution. Opponents of the ILO tried unsuccessfully to have U.S. dues contributions withheld. In 1938, the Senate ratified five ILO conventions relating to seamen's working conditions. Since the federal government clearly had the constitutional authority to legislate in this area, the doctrine of limited federal power had no application. The United States was fully represented at annual ILO Conferences and technical meetings, and in 1939, John Winant, a former governor of New Hampshire, was elected ILO director.[1]

After the United States became a member, the American labor movement strongly supported the ILO. Nevertheless, the internal struggle within the domestic labor movement coinciding with the formation of the Congress of Industrial Organizations (CIO) in 1935, plus the ensuing struggle between the AFL and the CIO for the right to represent U.S. labor in the ILO, hampered full-scale U.S. participation. In the end, the AFL gained the right to represent U.S. labor at almost all ILO conferences and meetings, despite strong CIO protests. This decision on the part of the U.S. government, while political, was correct because the AFL remained the organization "most representative of workpeople" in the United States—the criterion for selection provided by the ILO constitution.

The ILO had little support from employer organizations during this period, however. As a consequence, the Roosevelt administration chose employer representatives from a group of liberal businessmen who shared New Deal views on labor matters, among them Henry Dennison, Henry Harriman, Marion Folsom, and Samuel Lewisohn, none of whom could be described as "most representative of employers" in the United States. It was possible for the administration to choose ILO delegates from such an unrepresentative group only because the antilabor majority of employers lacked the political power to stop it.[2]

In 1934, as part of its new policy of establishing a united front with Western socialists, the Soviet Union also joined the League of Nations, which automatically entitled it to membership in the ILO. The workers' group in the ILO not only raised no objection to sitting with the Soviet worker delegates but welcomed them:

> The Worker's group notes with great satisfaction that, as a result of the entry of the Union of Soviet Socialist Republics into the International Labor Organization, the Organization has taken another step in the direction of universality, which is an important condition for the realization of its aims. The arrival of representatives of the trade unions of the Union of Soviet Socialist Republics is a proof that the work of the International Labor Office is becoming increasingly well understood.[3]

The employer group challenged the credentials of the Soviet employers but did not succeed in barring them from ILO meetings. The question became moot when the Soviet Union stopped sending representatives to ILO meetings after 1937, not to return until 1954.

Since the United States was itself just getting started in the ILO in the 1930s, it played no role in the dispute over Soviet participation. After 1937, the U.S. Communist party had a strong influence within the CIO, and had not the Soviet Union withdrawn, the party might have been in a position to provide some political support for the principle of full Soviet representation in the ILO. By the time the issue came up again, in the 1950s, Communist influence in American trade unions had been virtually eliminated.

By 1939, the ILO had achieved a considerable reputation as

an organization devoted to the improvement of labor standards. It was known especially for its work on various types of social legislation and for its advocacy of shorter working hours. But it had no strong roots in the United States, where "participation was only the activity of a small minority of world-minded Americans. The bulk of the American people and the politicians knew very little if anything of the ILO, nor did they care to know. Except to a very few, the initials 'ILO' meant nothing; and yet those few worked with tireless energy and devotion to making the United States an effective force in the organization."[4]

With the outbreak of war in Europe, Director Winant asked whether the United States would provide a refuge for the ILO. Despite the support of the AFL, the State Department refused; according to one informed observer, "the Administration apparently feared the disapproval of a still isolationist Congress, and 1940 was an election year."[5] Eventually, a small staff transferred the office to Montreal, where it remained for the duration of the war.

The modern history of the ILO began with a conference held in Philadelphia from April 20 to May 12, 1944. Its purpose was to define the future role of the organization and to make recommendations on postwar social policy. The United States took the lead in preparing a broad charter for future ILO activities. Despite a personal plea from Roosevelt to Stalin, the Soviets refused to send a delegation. The results of the conference were embodied in the so-called Declaration of Philadelphia, which has been appended to the ILO constitution as a basic statement of purpose.

At the 1944 Philadelphia conference, President Roosevelt set the tone for a positive American attitude toward the ILO with this statement:

> I see in the ILO a permanent instrument of representative character for the formulation of international policy on matters directly affecting the welfare of labor and for international collaboration in this field. I see it as a body with the requisite authority to formulate and secure the adoption of those basic minimum standards that shall apply throughout the world to the conditions of employment. I see in the ILO an organization which

shall serve the world for investigation and research, for discussion and debate. But more than that, it must be the agency for decision and for action on those economic and social matters related to the welfare of working people which are practical for industry and designed to enhance the opportunities for a good life for people the world over.[6]

When the conference ended, the president invited 150 delegates to the White House and addressed them in a similar vein. In 1948, David A. Morse, who had been undersecretary of labor in the Truman administration, was elected ILO director-general, a post he held until 1970. All signs pointed to an expanding ILO in which the United States would play a leading role.

At the San Francisco conference that established the United Nations in 1945, the ILO was represented only by an observer delegation. There was some fear that the ILO would be supplanted by the United Nations Economic and Social Council, but in 1946, with the firm backing of both Western Europe and the United States, the ILO became a specialized agency affiliated with the United Nations.

On November 1, 1977, President Jimmy Carter notified the ILO that the United States was withdrawing from membership. He stated in part: "Two years ago the United States gave official notice that we would leave the International Labour Organization unless corrective measures were taken to restore that Organization's commitment to its original purposes. Because such measures have not been taken, I direct that United States membership in I.L.O. be terminated. The U.S. remains ready to return whenever the I.L.O. is again true to its proper principles and procedures."[7]

What happened to change U.S. policy from the warm encomia of President Roosevelt in 1944 to the cold letter of withdrawal signed by President Carter in 1977? To gain some insight into the basic issues that were involved, it will be necessary to go into the history of U.S.–ILO relationships in some detail, particularly since the ILO, of all the international organizations, appears to be engaged in activities that are the closest to American ideals—the protection of human rights and the improvement of working conditions for the poorer people of the world. Suffice it to say, at this point, that the United States did not leave the ILO because of momentary pique at not having its own way, but rather because of issues that had been debated for almost a quarter of a century. And to gain some insight into these basic issues, it will be necessary to set out the details of the immediate issues that led to withdrawal and also to provide an evaluation of the work performed by the ILO.

Purposes of the ILO

The preamble to the ILO constitution provides that the organization is to concern itself, *inter alia*, with the following matters:

1. Regulation of working hours, including the establishment of a maximum working day and week
2. Regulation of the labor supply
3. Prevention of unemployment
4. Provision of an adequate living wage
5. Protection of the worker against occupational disease and injury
6. Protection of children, young persons, and women
7. Provision for old age and injury
8. Protection of the interests of those working in countries other than their own
9. Equal pay for equal work
10. Protection of freedom of association
11. Organization of vocational and technical education

These constitutional objectives were amplified by the document adopted at the 1944 Philadelphia conference. Among the additional goals specified were

1. Full employment and increased living standards
2. Provision for migration and training so that workers can be employed at their full skills
3. Effective recognition of the right of collective bargaining, and labor management cooperation in improving productive efficiency

4. Extension of social security to provide basic income and medical care
5. Provision of adequate nutrition, housing, and facilities for recreation and culture
6. Equality of educational and vocational opportunity

These comprehensive and ambitious objectives were further broadened by subsequent activities and programs of the ILO. "Freedom of association" has been enlarged to include a good portion of what is colloquially termed "human rights." Technical assistance programs for developing countries involve a wide spectrum of activities that could not have been foreseen by those who drafted the 1944 Declaration of Philadelphia. That document does state, however, that "it is the responsibility of the International Labor Organization to examine and consider all international economic and financial policies and measures." This coincides with the ILO's fundamental objectives of the pursuit of economic security and equal opportunity.

The ILO's mandate is very broad. It includes jurisdiction over every aspect of the working life of all those who work for a living, whether in the factory or on the farm, whether skilled or unskilled, blue color or white collar, salaried or self-employed. Occasional demarcation disputes have arisen, particularly with the United Nations Economic and Social Council and with the Industrial Development Organization, one of the newest U.N. organizations. Still, the ILO has had plenty of scope in which to operate. The history of its widening activities on an international level mirrors the growth of the functions undertaken by the modern welfare state.

The fact that the ILO is dedicated to the pursuit of those goals to which a substantial majority of Americans would give a high priority makes it difficult to understand why the United States withdrew. In an editorial called "Why Stay in the ILO?" the *New York Times* observed:

> The work of the I.L.O. is changing. Once mostly concerned with labor practices in industrial countries, it now increasingly focuses on pervasive unemployment and underemployment in poor countries. Its Secretariat has done path-breaking work on

development strategies designed to provide employment and meet what have come to be called "basic human needs." The issues raised by these new concerns—rural labor organization, land ownership, women's employment, technology transfer, the roles of multinational corporations—go to the way power is held and wielded in many countries.[8]

A number of the items put forth by the *Times* as self-evident arguments in favor of the ILO are by no means noncontroversial, however. Alternative development strategies are being hotly debated. The issues of land ownership, technology transfers, and the role of multinational corporations raise a host of delicate political and economic problems. No one would argue against the general proposition that "basic human needs" should be met as quickly as possible, but precisely what they are and how to satisfy them are subjects of debate. Much of what the ILO has done, or has attempted to do, in economic development and other areas has generated strong controversy—even when all sides subscribed to the same ultimate objectives.

ILO Structure

What makes the ILO unique among international organizations is its tripartite structure: its legislative and executive organs include representatives from governments, trade unions, and employers alike. Tripartism has been a source of strength because it provides the ILO with a broader clientele than other international organizations can boast and because it enables the ILO to establish direct contact with important interest groups within member nations. It has also been a source of controversy in recent years because of the alleged erosion of the tripartite principle itself.

The General Conference, which is the legislative forum of the ILO, meets for three to four weeks each June. Every member state is entitled to four delegates—two representing its government and one each for employers' and workers' organizations. Each delegate has one vote, and it is not at all unusual, especially among democratic countries, for delegates from one nation to vote differently on various issues. This one man–one vote principle became an increasing problem for the United States. At the

1977 conference, for example, 221 government delegates, 109 employer delegates, and 110 worker delegates were accredited. They represented 113 countries, ranging from India, the United States, and the Soviet Union, on the one hand, to such ministates as Barbados, Fiji, Qatar, and the Seychelles, on the other.[9] The United States had the same voting strength as the Seychelle Islands, despite the great disparity in the size and financial contributions of the two countries. Control of the conference has therefore shifted increasingly to the many states that have joined the ILO in the last two decades.[10]

The conference operates through a series of tripartite committees. Among the most important are the Selection Committee, which nominates members of other committees and arranges the conference schedule; the Credentials Committee; and the Committee on the Application of Conventions and Recommendations. While these and other committees are working behind the scenes, the plenary sessions of the conference provide a forum whereby government ministers—usually ministers of labor—and other distinguished representatives and visitors can extol the virtues and accomplishments of their respective countries. The plenary sessions are almost always poorly attended unless an important vote is being taken or a controversial political issue arises. Representatives of official and nongovernmental international organizations are also allowed to speak. A recent amendment to the standing orders of the conference permits representatives of liberation movements attending the conference to address the membership, provided they have the permission of the conference president.[11] One organization in particular has caused great difficulty: the Palestine Liberation Organization (PLO).

Debates on the report of the Conference Committee on Application of Conventions and Recommendations, which is the ILO policeman on international labor standards, often involve important issues. Over the years, many ad hoc committees have been established, some dealing with substantive issues, others with procedure. Their reports are also submitted to the conference and voted on.

The executive committee of the ILO is its Governing Body,

which meets four times a year and is, in fact, the organization's principal policymaker. The constitutional provisions that were in effect when the United States resigned from the ILO fixed the Governing Body's membership at fifty-six, with twenty-eight of these members representing governments, fourteen representing labor, and fourteen acting on behalf of employers. Of the twenty-eight government representatives, ten were appointed by the states of "chief industrial importance," while the rest were elected by the government delegates to the conference. The states of "chief industrial importance" were chosen by an expert committee and approved by the Governing Body. Employer and worker representatives were elected, respectively, by the employer and worker delegate groups at the conference. As of November 1, 1977, the ten nonelective government seats were held by the United States, the Soviet Union, the United Kingdom, France, West Germany, Japan, Italy, India, Canada, and China.[12]

The nonelective seats were a major bone of contention, and contributed to the U.S. withdrawal. If it were only a question of voting strength, there would probably not be any great problem, since the ten nonelective members of the Governing Body could have been outvoted by various combinations of the forty-six elected members. But in order to amend the ILO constitution, at least five of the ten nonelective members of the Governing Body had to concur, which gave a veto power on constitutional change to six of the nonelective members. Since the less developed countries and the Communist bloc made a number of demands for constitutional change, this constraint became crucial.

The Governing Body prepares the conference agenda, elects the director-general, and supervises the financial affairs of the ILO, including preparation of the budget. Until recently, the major political battles of the ILO were fought within this group. When the non-Western countries were unable to attain their objectives within the Governing Body, they turned to the conference, where the one country–one vote principle gave them greater leverage.

The day-to-day work of the ILO is handled by the International Labor Office, under the director-general, who is the most important individual in the entire ILO structure. He is the ex-

ecutive head of the Office and its liaison with the Governing
Body, and he represents the ILO to the outside world. He also
appoints the staff of the ILO pursuant to regulations approved
by the Governing Body. Assisting him are eight deputy and assistant directors-general. Appointed by the director-general with
the consent of the Governing Body, these individuals need not
necessarily have any expertise in ILO work. The Office is staffed
by some 1,850 officials (1976–77 budget), some of them on permanent status, others with fixed-term contracts. Most are stationed in Geneva, but the ILO has representatives in many other
parts of the world.

The so-called industrial committees have become an increasingly important echelon in the ILO structure. They were first
established in 1945 at the instigation of Ernest Bevin, the British
trade union leader who served as minister of labor in wartime
and became foreign secretary in the postwar Labour government. Their purpose is to bring together labor and management
representatives and public officials operating in specific industries—coal mining, inland transport, steel, textiles, construction, the metal trades, civil engineering, chemicals, and so
forth—for an exchange of information. They make recommendations and establish guidelines for industry action, and they advise the Governing Body on what the ILO should do for the
employees in those industries.

In the industrial committees, there is an equal number of
delegates from each of the tripartite groups. The ILO pays the
expenses of the worker and employer delegates, thus making
possible full delegations from poor countries. The Governing
Body selects the countries to be represented and decides on the
number of seats within each committee. Including delegates and
technical advisers, some 250 to 350 persons attend each meeting.

Regional conferences, which operate similarly to the ILO's
annual June conference but with agendas limited to regional issues, have become increasingly popular components within the
ILO structure. These conferences, each involving an entire continent, are normally held twice during each biennium. Regional
advisory committees, which are smaller affairs, meet once between their respective regional conferences.

Major ILO Activities

A good way to gain insight into the activities of the ILO is by examining its budget. Table 1 contains budget data for 1978–79 for each major program. A substantial proportion of the budget goes for administrative expenses of one kind or another (the ILO is an old bureaucracy and has built up considerable fat over the years). The Governing Body has constantly prodded the Office to decentralize, but while some progress has been made, the ILO remains a fairly centralized organization, operating mainly out of its Geneva headquarters.

The ILO conventions and recommendations, which are the heart of the organization, absorb a substantial proportion of ILO resources. Various technical divisions contribute the basic research essential to the development of the international labor standards set by the ILO. International technical meetings precede submission of these research findings to the Governing Body and the conference for adoption.

During the post–World War II years, particularly since 1960, the ILO has become more and more involved in providing technical assistance to its less developed members. The regional budget gives some idea of the administrative scope of this activity, and most of the technical divisions now devote a substantial proportion of their efforts to this purpose. The regular ILO budget actually finances only a small part of the organization's technical assistance work, most of it allocated to administrative costs. In the 1978–79 biennium, the two major technical assistance categories were financed largely from extra-budgetary sources. Contributions from the United Nations, mainly from its Development Program (UNDP), provided about 26 percent of total ILO expenditures in the 1978–79 budget, while another 8 percent came from special contributions by member nations and private organizations.[13] When these extra-budget funds are set against the regular budgetary provisions, it becomes clear that assistance to developing nations has indeed become a major function of the ILO. The setting of international labor standards has obviously given way to a variety of programs designed to

TABLE 1.:   Expenditure Budget of the International Labor Office, 1978–79, by
            Major Program

	Percentage of total
Policymaking organs	3.3
Annual conference	2.2
Governing Body	0.6
Major regional meetings	0.5
General management	2.6
Technical programs	34.0
International labor standards and human rights	3.2
Employment and development	5.7
Training	4.4
Industrial relations and labor administration	5.3
Working conditions and environment	5.3
Sectoral activities	4.9
Social security	1.8
Statistics and special studies	2.5
International Institute for Labor Studies	0.9
Regional services and relations	20.9
Relations and meetings	4.2
Public information	1.3
Liaison with United Nations	0.5
Management of field programs in Africa	4.2
Management of field programs in the Americas	4.3
Management of field programs in Asia	3.8
Management of field programs in the Arab States	0.7
Management of field programs in Europe	1.9
Service and support activities	35.0
Other budgetary provisions and adjustments	4.6

SOURCE: ILC, *Draft Programme and Budget, 1980–81*, 65th sess., 1979, p. 3.
NOTE: Percentages do not add up to 100 because of rounding.

further economic growth and social development among the less
developed countries.

Several ILO activities are of considerable political or social
importance despite their low standing in budgetary terms.
Among these are workers' education programs, which were set
up to help trade unions (and more recently peasant organizations) in their day-to-day operations. The ILO works mostly

through international seminars and training manuals, although occasionally it will bring in experts to advise unions on specific problems. This program has received strong support from U.S. government and labor representatives. As one official observed, "U.S. interests are served through effective ILO activities which strengthen worker organizations and thus more generally promote democratic institutions."[14]

A second important facet of ILO work has to do with human rights. Although the subject arose in connection with certain conventions that dealt with freedom of association and forced labor, it has tended to go beyond the boundaries of traditional ILO concerns. It is, after all, not always easy to distinguish between economic and political rights. A good deal of controversy surfaced over whether the organization was capable of administering international standards in this delicate area impartially, and in fact, this issue was among the primary causes of U.S. withdrawal from the ILO.

The role of the organization in promoting social security has also been noteworthy. Through conventions, recommendations, and direct technical assistance, the ILO has played a major role in this area in both poor and industrialized nations. In the United States, legislation on unemployment compensation and old-age pensions owes a great deal to early ILO conventions and recommendations, even though the United States did not ratify them. Indeed, John Winant, first chairman of the U.S. Social Security Board, called upon an ILO staff member to advise him on the implementation of the Social Security Act.

A fourth area of ILO work that does not loom large in the budget but has nevertheless affected international working conditions significantly is occupational safety and health. ILO conventions and recommendations that provide for the banning of such poisonous substances as white lead in paints and benzene in dry cleaning are of special importance. So are numerous conventions and recommendations put forth on behalf of the maritime industry, which is a logical area for ILO action because of its international character.

How effective the ILO's actions have been overall is not easy to determine. The United States has ratified only 7 of the 147 conventions adopted, and six of these are concerned with sea-men. And yet the United States operates under labor codes that are in conformance with the great majority of ILO conventions and recommendations. On the other hand, many countries that are frequent ratifiers do not themselves provide good working conditions, freedom of association, or satisfactory industrial re-lations.

Membership and Financing

According to the present ILO constitution, countries are ac-corded membership on the basis of the following criteria: (1) those who were members as of November 1, 1945, automatically continue as members; (2) any member of the United Nations has the right to join the ILO, provided it is willing to abide by the ILO constitution; (3) the ILO Conference may admit members by a two-thirds vote, including two-thirds of the government delegates. Membership terminates only after the expiration of a two-year notice of intent to withdraw.

At the time of the U.S. withdrawal, some 135 nations held membership in the ILO. South Africa, under pressure from the African states, withdrew in 1966, and Albania followed suit in 1967. The People's Republic of China, while nominally a mem-ber, has neither participated in ILO activities nor paid its dues, while the Republic of China (Taiwan) was excluded in 1971 fol-lowing similar action by the United Nations. [15]

Member contributions to the ILO budget are determined by a committee of the Governing Body on the basis of a formula that takes into account each member's ability to pay. The principal variables in this formula are population and national product. The scale of assessments for 1978, as approved by the 1977 con-ference, provided for a minimum national contribution of 0.02 percent, while the maximum of 25 percent was assessed against the United States. Table 2 indicates the scale of assessments by major country groups. Five major Western industrial nations paid for over half the entire budget, and two-thirds of the total was contributed by the developed non-communist countries. The European Communist bloc paid almost 18 percent of the total, while the largest less developed countries accounted for

7.5 percent. The rest of the members, almost 100 out of a total of 135, contributed less than 10 percent among them.

This disparity between financial support and voting rights in ILO representative bodies, not to mention other international agencies, was bound to cause trouble. In the conference, for example, any country that paid the minimum 0.02 percent of the budget had exactly the same voting rights as each of the five major Western powers, though these five nations contributed more than 50 percent among them. The situation was somewhat better in the Governing Body, where the five large Western contributors could block constitutional change, provided they voted together and secured the support of one additional nonelective member. Yet the Western nations could be outvoted if they were

TABLE 2.   Proposed 1978 ILO Dues Assessments by Countries and Groups of Countries

	Percentage of total assessments
Major developed non-communist countries	*51.37*
United States	25.00
Japan	8.62
Germany	7.70
France	5.63
United Kingdom	4.42
Other developed non-communist countries	*15.13*
European Communist countries	*17.86*
U.S.S.R.	13.16
Others	4.70
Major less developed countries	*7.57*
China	5.47
India	0.70
Indonesia	0.14
Pakistan	0.06
Bangladesh	0.04
Brazil	1.03
Nigeria	0.13
All other countries	*8.07*

Source: ILC, *Provisional Record*, 63rd sess., 1977, p. 4/3.

opposed by the Communist countries and a sufficient number of less developed countries.

At a meeting of the Governing Body in March 1977, only nine out of twenty-seven government members were from the Western group. By comparison, fifteen were from the less developed nations and three from the European Communist bloc. The ratios for nongovernmental delegates were somewhat more favorable to the West: six, eight, and zero for the employers, and seven, six, and one for the workers, respectively.[16] Thus, while Western strength was greater in the Governing Body than in the conference, particularly since employers' delegates from less developed countries often voted with the industrial nations, the parallel that is sometimes drawn between the ILO Governing Body and the Security Council of the United Nations is not appropriate. The Governing Body was able to restrain the forces in the ILO that were seeking to make radical changes in the constitution, but there was no veto right on other matters.

At the 1944 session, where the Declaration of Philadelphia was produced, forty-one countries, most of them industrialized, were in attendance. The ILO was then an organization that represented the West primarily. With the admission of new states, Western influence was gradually eroded, although the financial burden continued to be borne by the industrial nations. The culmination of this trend came in 1977, when a united West was defeated on two key issues by the combined votes of the so-called Group of 77 (the less developed countries) and the Soviet bloc.[17] These votes were deliberate challenges to Western control, and even had the United States not withdrawn, it was abundantly clear that a new dispensation would prevail in the ILO.

The following chapter deals with the major issues that have divided the United States and the ILO over the years. They are not all of equal importance. For example, the fear by American employers that the ILO was actively engaged in promoting socialism has been dissipated. The rest of the issues are still very much alive, although they differ in terms of what can be done about them. For example, the United States has expressed concern that the tripartite structure of the ILO is being eroded be-

cause of the presence of Communist worker and employer delegates who are, in fact, subservient to the state. Only withdrawal
of the Communist states could alleviate this problem. On the
other hand, the ILO can take action to meet certain U.S. charges
against the Soviet Union and other Communist countries. These
include violation of commitments on freedom of association and
employment discrimination, which the United States contends
have not been prosecuted with as much vigor as those levied
against non-Communist nations—the so-called double standard.
It is also possible to prevent condemnation of nations in a manner that violates the ILO's own constitution—the issue of due
process.

Chapter 3 attacks some of the problems inherent in the ILO
structure and operation, specifically those that have caused friction with the United States. Among them are the composition
and operation of the ILO's executive council—the Governing
Body—and its annual conference. A major problem is the degree
to which the countries that are paying most of the costs of ILO
work are able to exercise authority in the determination of its
operations. ILO staffing and research policies have also given
rise to U.S. complaints.

Chapter 4 analyzes the events that finally led to the U.S.
withdrawal from the ILO in 1977. This course of action was not
a unanimous one by any means, and the story provides an interesting example of foreign policy formulation when government
is acting under constraints imposed by the presence of powerful
private interest groups that have veto power over administrative
decisions. If the ILO had not been a tripartite organization, with
trade union and employer participants officially represented, it
is highly probable that the United States would never have withdrawn.

The focus of the study then shifts to an analysis of the two
major functions of the ILO: technical assistance to less developed
countries and the promulgation and policing of international labor standards (Chapters 5 and 6). The degree to which the
United States should compromise on the issues of principle that
brought about its withdrawal depends in part on the quality of
the services rendered by the ILO. If the organization is assisting

poor countries effectively, or if it has been efficient in promoting human rights and working conditions through its conventions, then it might be plausible for the United States to make greater concessions on other issues, certainly more so than if the reverse were true. The ILO devotes most of its energies to these two basic fields of endeavor, and yet they scarcely figured in the U.S. decision to withdraw. In fact, very little is known about them in the United States. The major purpose of Chapters 5 and 6, therefore, is to make available to decisionmakers and to the general public material that may assist them in future considerations of the U.S. position.

Chapter 7 describes ILO events subsequent to the U.S. withdrawal, and the final chapter presents my own views on what the United States might reasonably demand of the ILO as conditions for continuing its membership.

To the general reader, some of the detail concerning the divisive issues, on technical assistance, and on international labor standards may appear excessive. These chapters represent, however, the result of a drastic condensation of a great mass of relevant material. It would have been possible to summarize the historical material briefly, but the reader would then have been left with only a superficial view of the difficulties involved. Knowing something about the persistence of the various issues over many years, and the attempts that have been made to deal with them, is essential to an understanding of why the United States left the ILO, not to mention the obstacles that must be overcome before this country's return to the organization can be thought of as permanent.

Chapter 2

The United States and the ILO: The Issues in Conflict

Many of the major overt issues of conflict that have arisen in the course of the relationships between the United States and the ILO—or more properly, between the United States and groups of ILO member nations—are closely intertwined. It is useful, however, in trying to gain an insight into actions taken by the U.S. government, as well as by American labor and management representatives, to consider these issues separately as far as possible. The emphasis has changed over the years; some issues declined in importance, some grew. But it is interesting to see how many of the problems persisted, despite numerous efforts to solve them.

The conflicts are due largely to the ILO's tripartite structure. The U.S. government has rarely played an active role in ILO affairs. Moreover, the division of responsibility between the State, Labor, and Commerce departments in the determination of U.S. governmental policy led inevitably to bureaucratic struggles. In all three departments there was a constant turnover of responsible policy officials. State and Commerce devoted very little of their personnel resources to monitoring the ILO, while Labor's Bureau of International Labor Affairs gave priority to its other responsibilities. As a result, the U.S. government tended to move one way or another in direct response to pressures generated by labor or management.

This passivity stood in sharp contrast to the positive positions taken by the government delegations of other nations, notably, France, Italy, and the United Kingdom. Their work at the ILO was integrated with their overall foreign policy, something the United States failed to do. In 1970, a former ILO assistant director-general published a list of those "whose work on the Governing Body in more recent years will be specially remembered"; the list did not include a single U.S. government delegate.[1] Indeed, the only U.S. name on the list was James D. Zellerbach, an employer delegate in the 1940s.

Did the United States neglect the ILO more than it did other international organizations? The answer to that question would take us too far afield. A 1977 report of the Senate Committee on Government Operations suggests that the ILO was by no means unique in this respect.[2] But the fact that in the case of the ILO there were official nongovernmental delegations with strong views on policy and considerable domestic political influence undoubtedly contributed to governmental reticence.

Interestingly enough, within the ILO American labor and management generally took similar positions with regard to the issues in conflict, even though these groups occasionally voted differently for reasons of group solidarity. This is remarkable in view of the fact that the organizations from which the labor and management representatives were selected—the AFL-CIO and the U.S. Chamber of Commerce—did not see eye-to-eye on many of the questions normally considered by the ILO. The U.S. government was often a reluctant dragon, pushed into positions it might have preferred not to take. Had the ILO conformed to the usual structure of international agencies, with government representation only, the United States would probably never have withdrawn. There have been difficulties with UNESCO and the World Health Organization (WHO), but withdrawal was never a serious possibility.[3]

Finally, the issues in conflict had very little to do with the day-to-day operations of the Office. The large technical assistance program conducted by the ILO raised few problems as far as the United States was concerned. Most of the conventions and recommendations, and their implementation, were noncontroversial, particularly those of a technical nature. The substantive issues that did give rise to dispute were primarily those of little concern to the Office, as distinct from the organization. It was possible for an ILO official in Geneva to do his job effectively over the years without being aware of the battles that were raging above his head.

This was not true of the director-general, of course. He was always directly involved and was usually trying to put out fires and keep the organization going. Much credit should be given to David A. Morse, who was the director-general from 1948 to 1970—by far the longest tenure in the history of the ILO—for his role in defusing potentially explosive situations. His successor, C. Wilfred Jenks of the United Kingdom, lacked Morse's political skills and exacerbated the difficulties, if anything. Jenks died a few years after taking office, and his successor, Francis Blanchard of France, was unable to avert the eventual schism, despite his heroic efforts to bring about a compromise. By the time Blanchard took office, the damage was simply too great to be repaired.

The fact that the "modern" history of U.S.–ILO relationships can be dated from 1954 offers an immediate clue to a major cause of the problems: the hostility of U.S. labor and management within the ILO context toward the Soviet Union. Both were deeply opposed to the ideology and the system of government represented by the Soviet Union. They could never reconcile themselves to its presence in an organization that they believed was dedicated to the protection of human rights and the promotion of social advance. The last U.S. worker delegate to the ILO, Irving Brown, once commented that the Soviet entry into the ILO marked a decisive turning point in the history of the organization.[4] That may not have been the only reason for U.S.–ILO differences, but it was an important one.

The reasons behind the late entry of the United States into the ILO, especially after the United States had played such a substantial role in its creation, were quite different from those

that affected the country's postwar relationships. They had more
to do with domestic conservatism and the prevalent American
isolationism than with any specific events that occurred in Geneva.[5] Before the Great Depression, management and labor
were equally opposed to joining the ILO. It was the Roosevelt
administration, and particularly the efforts of Secretary of Labor
Frances Perkins, that finally succeeded in inducing the United
States to join.

With the exception of "creeping socialism"—which proved to
be an evanescent controversy but did have a permanent impact
on U.S. financial contributions to the ILO—the issues to be examined in this chapter are those specified in the 1975 U.S. letter
of intent to withdraw. All of them involved fundamental principles that had been debated time and again. In fact, apart from
tripartism, which is unique to the ILO, the principles embodied
in the letter of intent might well serve as a guide to U.S. participation in any international organization. The United States is not
in a position to require other nations to conform to constitutional
practices within international agencies, but it can and should insist upon such conduct as a condition for its membership and
support.

Not all U.S. participants consistently supported the code of
conduct they espoused. Under the influence of momentary political passions or for tactical reasons, U.S. delegates occasionally
sanctioned deviations from established procedure. The United
States was more insistent than any other member nation, however, that the ILO constitution be adhered to, and it was alone
among the nations of the world in its willingness to take the ultimate step of withdrawal. Far from being a quixotic gesture, this
action administered an effective warning to the international
community that continued erosion of normal operating rules
might lead to the eventual realignment of the pattern of international organization. UNESCO and WHO have already prof-
ited from this warning.

"Creeping Socialism"

The ILO constitution provides that labor and management
delegates and advisers to the annual Conference shall be nomi-

nated by member governments "chosen in agreement with the industrial organizations, if such organizations exist, which are most representative of employers or workpeople, as the case may be, in their respective countries." From 1945 to 1948, the U.S. employer delegate was J. D. Zellerbach, who was selected on the recommendation of Eric Johnston, then president of the U.S. Chamber of Commerce. Zellerbach was a liberal, internationally minded businessman who felt that the ILO represented the same philosophy as that embodied in the American New Deal.

As long as Zellerbach remained the U.S. employer delegate, matters proceeded smoothly. But in 1949, Zellerbach was replaced by Charles McCormick, whose attitude toward the ILO was less positive. The Cold War was in full swing, and domestic labor affairs had become increasingly tense. The enactment of the Taft-Hartley Act in 1947, despite President Truman's veto, had greatly sharpened labor-management animosities, and there was inevitably some spillover into the ILO forum.

The first cause of U.S. employer complaint on the ILO was the adoption by the 1948 ILO conference of Convention No. 87 on freedom of association and protection of the right to organize. This was followed in 1949 by Convention No. 98, which dealt with the right of workers to organize without employer interference and to bargain collectively. Although these conventions are now among the basic ILO weapons for the protection of human rights, at the time of their adoption they were viewed with some alarm by U.S. employers as possible ways to circumvent the restrictive provisions of the Taft-Hartley Act. Many employers apparently believed that the ILO had been taken over by European socialists who were attempting to use the organization as a lever to weaken American capitalism. William L. McGrath, who had been involved with the ILO for several years and became the U.S. employer delegate in 1954, explained these fears as follows: "Here is what has happened in the ILO, as I see it. For some years the 'more power for government' boys had been itching to switch the ILO from an international labor organization to an international government organization. They pulled it off at the ILO Convention in Philadelphia in 1944."[6]

Earlier, in 1951, the ILO conference had considered a draft convention designed to set minimum standards for social insurance, which was adopted in 1952 as Convention No. 102. This move was regarded by U.S. employers as further evidence of socialist tendencies in the ILO. The report of the employer delegation to the 1951 conference contained the following comment: "It becomes clearer that the effort of the present ILO government-labor majority to impose centralized government control is being allowed to take precedence over its primary goal of raising standards of living. The goal of providing greater opportunity for the individual is being replaced by a passion for imposing government-dictated 'welfare' upon the people."[7]

The employers also felt that the cards were stacked against them in the ILO and that U.S. government delegates tended to work closely with trade unions. They believed that the Department of Labor was prolabor, even during the administration of Dwight Eisenhower (1952–60), and that it had too much influence over the choice of government delegates. Although their objections were somewhat blunted by the appointment in 1953 of Irving Ives, a Republican senator from New York, as head of the U.S. delegation to that year's ILO conference, the admission of the Soviet Union to the ILO in 1954 led to increased friction.

The prevailing sentiment among employers gave rise to a constitutional amendment introduced in the U.S. Senate in 1952 by John W. Bricker of Ohio. If passed, it would have provided, *inter alia*, that "no treaty or executive agreement shall vest in any international organization or in any foreign power any of the legislative, executive or judicial powers" of any branch of the U.S. government. In Senate hearings on the amendment in 1953, George Delaney, the U.S. worker representative to the ILO, defended the organization, pointing out that ILO conventions would have to be approved by Congress before they could be ratified. The Bricker amendment was supported by both the American Medical Association (AMA) and the American Bar Association, on the ground that it was essential to prevent undue encroachment upon the American governmental system by international organizations. The AMA, moreover, was concerned lest the ILO provide an entering wedge for the introduction of socialized medicine in the United States. The amendment died when the Senate failed to act on it.[8]

But Senator Bricker refused to give up the fight. In April 1956, the Senate Committee on Foreign Relations sent to the floor of the Senate a bill that would have raised to $3 million the existing ceiling of $1,750,000 on the U.S. contribution to the ILO. This ceiling had been imposed in 1950, and then represented 25 percent of the total ILO budget. The United was also contributing 33.5 percent of the budget of the United Nations and over 30 percent for all the major U.N. specialized agencies. Senator Bricker introduced the following amendment to the committee bill:

> Provided, however, that no sum in excess of $1,750,000 shall be appropriated to defray the expenses of the International Labour Organization, for any calendar year after the calendar year 1956, if during the preceding calendar year delegates allegedly representing employers and employees in the Union of Soviet Socialist Republics or in any nation dominated by the foreign government controlling the world Communist movement are found by the State Department to have been permitted to vote in the International Labour Conference or in any other meetings held under the auspices of the International Labour Organization.[9]

The Senate adopted the amendment by a vote of 43 to 40, but the entire bill, including the proposed increase in the ceiling, was defeated in the House of Representatives. Another attempt was made to raise the ILO ceiling in 1957, when the Senate Foreign Relations Committee proposed an increase to $2 million. The possibility had arisen that unless the United States paid its assessed share of the ILO budget it might lose its voting rights. The Senate agreed with its committee, but the House failed to act. In 1958, the Eisenhower administration asked the Congress to eliminate the ceiling and approve "such sums as may be necessary for the payments by the U.S. of its share of the expenses of the Organization, but not to exceed 25 percent of such expenses." The Senate, through Senator Bricker's urgings, eliminated this language and inserted a ceiling of $2 million. The House-Senate Conference Committee then deleted the dollar limitation but retained the 25 percent maximum.[10] This percentage remained in all U.S. appropriations legislation right up to the time of the U.S. withdrawal.

During this period, the employers were alone in their criticism of the ILO. The AFL-CIO gave it strong support, not least because the unions liked the freedom of association and social insurance conventions, and they continued to defend it even after the admission of the Soviet Union. George Delaney, who represented the AFL-CIO at the time, wrote: "The [Communist] motive is abetted by division in the Western ranks and by the intrusion of anti-ILO, anti-United Nations attitudes by isolationists posing as the spokemen of free employers or free workers. Now, more than ever, while the Communist bloc in the International Labour Organization and the United Nations remains small, it is up to the free governments and to their organizations of free employers and free workers to strengthen the ILO's hand."[11]

The Eisenhower administration, despite pressure exerted by the employers, remained basically pro-ILO. It appointed a mixed business-academic committee, headed by Joseph E. Johnson, president of the Carnegie Endowment for International Peace, to look into the dispute. The Committee emphasized that, rather than trying to evaluate the work of the ILO, it was concentrating on U.S. participation in that organization. Its conclusions were generally supportive of the ILO. The committee pointed out that the ILO was beginning to move toward providing technical assistance to developing nations, and it recommended that the United States pay more attention to ILO programs. And while it favored decreased emphasis on conventions and recommendations, the committee urged that when these instruments were under consideration by the ILO conference the U.S. position should be determined on the basis of substance, not on how difficult U.S. ratification might be.

The committee's principal recommendation was that the U.S. government should improve its own internal organization for dealing with the ILO. It pointed to "a serious lack of coordination and communication between the interested government agencies, as well as between these agencies and employer and worker delegates, in the formulation of positions to be taken in ILO meetings." The importance of the continuity of representation personnel was stressed. The committee was "impressed by the evidence presented to it of the effectiveness of representatives [both governmental and nongovernmental] from other countries who have served for a number of years." Washington staffing for the ILO was deemed inadequate, and the committee further urged that the State Department, in collaboration with Labor and Commerce, clarify and elaborate "the place of United States participation in the International Labour Organization in furthering our broad foreign policy objectives."[12]

These points were repeated during the next two decades. The committee deserves credit for initiating criticism of the U.S. government for its failure to take the ILO seriously and for not providing the resources necessary to prepare for its participation in ILO affairs. The committee failed to come to grips, however, with some of the basic issues that had already emerged while its study was under way. For example, the future of the tripartite structure of the ILO had already been called into question. The committee recommended that the United States help maintain tripartism and "utilize this structure to demonstrate the advantages resulting from the activities of free employers and free workers." While it concluded that Communist worker and employer delegates could not be denied seats, it urged "relentless American attacks" on their seating until such time as constitutional means could be found to bar them.

It would have been useful had a more searching analysis been made of the difficulties arising out of the presence of the Soviet Union and its satellites in the ILO, as well as the growing number of non-Communist dictatorships in which there were no free trade unions and sometimes no independent employers. Representation problems had already arisen before the war concerning Fascist Italy, as well as the Soviet Union. If the United States had faced the problem head-on at that time, the future might have been changed significantly. Even though a solution might not have been readily available, better advice could have been given to the American employers responsible for raising the issue than simply to exercise "ingenuity and imagination . . . to circumvent many of the difficulties."[13]

This first phase of U.S. discontent with the ILO, centering on employer concern with its "socialist" proclivities and the threats they posed to the capitalist system, came to a close by the mid-1950s. That was before the full impact of the Soviet presence could be felt. In 1955, W. L. McGrath recommended to the National Association of Manufacturers and to the Chamber of Commerce that they break all ties with the ILO. Both organizations passed resolutions early in 1956 calling upon the administration and the Congress to investigate the ILO in terms of future U.S. participation. Congressional hearings were conducted by a subcommittee of the House Foreign Affairs Committee, but nothing further was done. The administration's response was to establish the Johnson Committee, which came down firmly against withdrawal from the ILO. Indeed, that committee's final recommendation was that "the United States Government make vigorous and sustained efforts to call the attention of the American people to the purposes, objectives, and activities of the International Labour Organization, emphasizing that it is the sole specialized agency of the United Nations devoted to improving management and labor standards throughout the world."[14]

The U.S. government, in response to these recommendations, issued a policy statement that was endorsed by the Departments of State, Commerce, and Labor. Its premise was that the ILO represented an important forum for explaining the free processes of the American political, economic, and social systems and that it was "an important means of furthering U.S. foreign policy objectives, which seek—in essence—the preservation of peace."[15] The three departments agreed that State would exercise primary responsibility for foreign policy issues in the ILO; that efforts should be made to improve consultation with employers and workers; that an attempt should be made to provide for continuity of representation at ILO meetings; that ILO technical assistance and research would be supported; and that efforts would be made to encourage more U.S. citizens to accept positions in the ILO. Worker and employer advisory committees were appointed to increase consultation between the government and its ILO partners.

And so the first round had concluded in a manner favorable to the ILO. The U.S. government committed itself to renewed efforts on behalf of improved participation in the ILO; the financial picture was clarified, although not entirely to the satisfaction of the ILO; the U.S. trade unions were now firmly behind the organization; and the employer attack had been blunted. But this apparent victory for the pro-ILO forces was deceptive. The issue on which the employer complaints had been based—"creeping socialism"—was disappearing as a result of the decline of the strident anti-Communism that had prevailed in the United States in the early 1950s. Employers and the American public alike had grown more sophisticated about the differences between socialism and Communism. It had become clear to them that the establishment of socialist governments in Europe did not mean the demise of private enterprise and democratic freedoms. But before this issue could be laid to rest, new ones arose, and they proved less tractable.

Tripartism

To the Western European nations that had founded the ILO, tripartism reflected the manner in which each one approached its own social and economic problems. Independent trade unions, even as they struggled for full recognition in post–World War I Europe, had become a reality. In some countries, such as France and Italy, it would be many years before employers would accept collective bargaining as the means of determining labor conditions. But even to these employers, the concept of worker representation in an international labor organization seemed harmless compared to the radical political currents that were sweeping across Europe.

From the very beginning, the concept of tripartism could not be maintained as an unalloyed structural principle. The ILO constitution does not specifically require that worker or employer representatives be *independent* of government; it merely provides that they are to be chosen by the government "in agreement with the industrial organizations, if such organizations exist, which are most representative of employers or workpeople." The possibility that tripartism might not always be feasible was recognized by the stipulation in the ILO constitution that if one nongovernment delegate failed to be nominated, the other could not vote at the annual conference. Moreover, of the forty-four nations that became members of the ILO in 1919, perhaps twenty lacked any effective independent trade union organizations.[16] These countries were admitted to full participation, however, presumably because the founders were anxious to bring as many nations as possible into the organization.

Trouble was not long in coming. At the 1919 conference, the credentials of worker delegates from Argentina, Japan, and South Africa were all challenged because they did not derive from the "most representative" organizations. These objections were turned down. The first serious problem arose in 1927, when the Italian worker delegate to the conference was challenged on the ground that Italy's Fascist-controlled unions could not possibly represent the working people, since these labor groups were merely administrative organs of the state. The Italian delegate was seated, nonetheless, and the Governing Body subsequently amended the procedural rules (or standing orders) of the conference to provide that, should a delegate fail to be nominated by his group (workers or employers) to sit on any conference committee, he could appeal to the Conference Selection Committee, which was empowered to place him on one or more committees.

This was the first time the problem of how to deal with a modern totalitarian state had come before the ILO. Accommodating the oligarchies of Latin America was one thing; they usually made some pretense of independent unionism, even if the reality was different. Moreover, there was always the possibility of legitimate trade unions emerging. The fluctuating fortunes of trade unionism in countries like Argentina, Brazil, and Chile provide good examples of this process.

The governmental structure of totalitarian states, however, made no provision for independent trade unions or employer associations. The organizations established by Fascist Italy, Nazi Germany, or the Soviet Union to represent workers and employers were completely subservient to the state. The provision of the ILO constitution that "every delegate shall be entitled to

vote individually on all matters which are taken into consideration by the Conference" cannot be honored where worker and
employer delegates are part of the government bureaucracy.
Worker and employer delegates presumably represent the interests of their constituents, and there is little logic in tripartism
when those interests are *always* identified with those of the
state. This is the basic dilemma that has not been resolved and
that continues to plague the ILO.

The Soviet Union, which had labeled the ILO part of a capitalist plot to oppress workers, joined the League of Nations in
1934 after it had adopted its United Front policy. This automatically entitled the Soviet Union to membership in the ILO, although the appearance of Soviet delegates at the 1937 conference led to strong protests by some workers and by the employer
group. The workers who challenged the Soviet Union maintained that since the All-Union Central Council of Trade Unions,
the only labor federation in the Soviet Union, was completely
subordinate to the Communist party, which also controlled the
government, the delegates could not claim to represent the independent interests of workers. The Credentials Committee rejected this challenge on the ground that since there was no other
labor organization for the Soviet government to consult in choosing its delegates, it had conformed to the ILO's constitutional
obligations. The employers, meanwhile, argued that Soviet employers were in fact representatives of the government and that
their presence in the ILO was incompatible with the tripartite
principle. But a legal analysis prepared by the ILO Office concluded that the Soviet Union had acted in full conformity with
the ILO constitution.[17]

A motion made in the Standing Orders Committee of the
Governing Body to bring this question before the League of Nation's Permanent Court of International Justice was defeated by
a vote of 8 to 7.[18] A brief report submitted by the Office to the
1938 conference merely confirmed that the Governing Body had
not made a decision.[19] When the Soviet Union did not put in
appearances at either the 1938 or 1939 conference, however, this
entire issue became moot.

Following World War II, challenges based on the "most representative" clause of the ILO constitution continued to be made against certain Conference delegates from a number of countries, but almost all were rejected by the Conference Credentials Committee, which contended that it could not possibly undertake detailed studies of the situation prevailing in each and every country. The first test in what became a new phase of this problem occurred in 1953, when the employers objected to the seating of an official of the Czech Ministry of Heavy Engineering who claimed to represent the employers of that country. The majority of a tripartite committee set up to solve this problem concluded that the Czech government had conformed to the constitutional requirements by appointing a person whose functions most closely resembled those of an employer. But an employer argued for the minority that the Czech delegate in question was merely a government representative. The majority view prevailed at the conference, in which the U.S. employer voted with the minority, the U.S. worker with the majority, and the U.S. government abstained.[20]

Before 1953, the Soviet Union had not availed itself of its right, as a member of the United Nations, to participate in the ILO. The death of Stalin, in 1953, may have been among the factors that led to a changed attitude, for in November 1953 the Soviet government informed the ILO that it was prepared to join. It expressed reservations, however, about provisions in the ILO constitution referring constitutional disputes to the International Court of Justice and disputes over the interpretation of conventions to a tribunal appointed by the Governing Body (Article 37). The director-general replied that such reservations were not possible under the ILO constitution, whereupon these objections were withdrawn, and the Soviet Union, plus Byelorussia and the Ukraine, became active members.[21] The remaining countries of Eastern Europe were either in the ILO already or activated their membership soon thereafter.

Problems were not slow in coming. The Soviet Union, of course, was designated as a state of chief industrial importance and therefore was entitled to a nonelective seat on the Governing Body. Brazil, which was ranked lowest on the list of chief industrial states at the time, objected to being displaced. A compromise resolution was adopted by the Governing Body whereby Brazil received an elective seat. The U.S. government abstained from voting on this resolution, "on the ground that it considered it anomolous to place on the Governing Body at that time a nation which not only had no recent or extended experience of the organization but which, as was well known, had taken an exceedingly antagonistic attitude toward the ILO and its objectives."[22]

At the 1954 conference, the employers' group challenged the credentials of employer delegates from seven Communist countries. Also, several international trade union organizations objected to the presence of Soviet and Czech worker delegates because they were creatures of the state. Again, these objections were not upheld. The employers returned to the attack at the next meeting of the Governing Body. When the Soviet government delegate, in his first appearance at a Governing Body meeting, complained that the Communist nations were being discriminated against in appointments to industrial committees, the British employer delegate observed that "the Committees were supposed to be tripartite, and Poland and Czechoslovakia, under their present constitutions, were incapable of sending a tripartite delgation in the normal sense of the word."[23] By a vote of 27 to 13, the Governing Body then agreed to add one seat to each of the industrial committees, presumably from among the Communist delegates, to be filled by a secret ballot of the Governing Body itself. Only two government delegates (from the United States and Taiwan) and one worker delegate (from the United States) were opposed to this resolution of the problem. Thus ended the first of many efforts by European governments and trade unions to reconcile the basic idea of tripartism with the realities of Communist societies.

The employers' next move was to urge an amendment to the ILO constitution establishing the principle that worker and employer delegates should be *independent* of government control. Rather than confront the difficult problem of a constitutional amendment, the Governing Body decided to ask the director-general to arrange for a report "regarding the extent of the freedom of employers' and workers' organizations from Government domination or control," to be prepared by a committee of independent persons. Arnold D. McNair of the United Kingdom, a former president of the International Court of Justice, was appointed chairman of the committee. The other members were Pedro de Alba, former president of the Mexican Senate, and Justice A. R. Cornelius of the Federal Court of Pakistan. This marked the first time that the ILO had faced the issue of tripartism in a comprehensive fashion. The committee sent questionnaires to all member governments, inviting them to provide a list of relevant laws and regulations and to submit such comments and analyses as they wished. The replies were assembled in "monographs," one for each responding country, and these provided the basis for the committee report.[24]

The committee's approach was to find out what opportunities were available to each government to exercise control over its employer and worker organizations, and what safeguards were available to prevent them from doing so. The committee noted that during the preceding two decades there had been a general increase in government participation in economic affairs but that in the leading industrial states "there is not much opportunity for government domination and control." In the case of the Soviet Union, it conceded that employers' organizations did not exist in the same sense as in the capitalist nations, but still, the committee concluded, "it appears from the information supplied by the U.S.S.R. that, within the sphere of a particular industry or part of an industry, these managers have extensive powers and discretion and responsibilities and that a great deal is left to their independent judgment within the limits of the over-all economic plan, so that it is evident that by reason of their experience they are capable of making a distinctive contribution to the work of the organization."[25] On the worker side, the committee found that the Soviet trade unions were indeed very powerful, since their memberships included 90 percent of all Soviet workers: "The documents give the impression that the organization of workers in their hierarchy are well able to look after themselves and not likely to be subject to domination and control by the government. The question which is more difficult to answer, and which does not lie within our terms of reference, is how far both the government and the trade unions themselves are subject to the domination of the Communist Party." Justice Cornelius of Pakistan concluded that while the Soviet employers were dominated by their government, "the trade unions clearly possess a status in the life of the country, of which all potentialities and powers in the country must necessarily take notice."[26] In other words, they were presumably *not* government dominated.

At the 1956 ILO conference, the British employer delegate announced that the report documented the fact that the ILO was no longer a tripartite organization. It was, he insisted, a hybrid— part tripartite and part intergovernmental. "Let us therefore have no more nonsense about retaining or maintaining the tripartite structure. We have already lost it. Our task is to regain it." He felt that the principles of tripartism and universal membership could not be made compatible and promised that his fellow British employers would throw their weight in favor of tripartism. He concluded on a prescient note: "It may well be that ultimately the only real solution is for the free countries to withdraw from the present set-up and to establish an I.L.O. of their own. Do not let us forget that that is what happened in the international trade union movement."[27]

The U.S. employer delegate agreed that tripartism and universality could not be reconciled, and he too warned that the ILO would have to choose between them. The U.S. government delegate, after pointing out that there were no free trade unions or employer associations in Communist countries, urged the Governing Body to face squarely the question of whether both the Soviet government and the trade unions were dominated by the Communist party. Pierre Waline, the French employer delegate and one of the most influential participants in ILO activities throughout the organization's history, stated flatly: "In Communist dictatorship countries there are no directors of undertakings or trade unions independent of their governments, and the government is of course controlled by the Communist Party."[28]

The debate continued at the next meeting of the Governing Body, at which, it was expected, some decision would be reached. The employers' group formally proposed an amendment to the constitution to ensure that only independent workers' and employers' representatives could participate in the ILO.

This position was vigorously supported by the U.S. employers.
The U.S. workers' delegate, George Delaney, on behalf of the
workers' group in the Governing Body, acknowledged that in
view of the governmental opposition there was no realistic possibility of amending the ILO constitution along those lines. He
was critical of the McNair Report because it was confined to an
analysis of legislation and gave only half the picture. As a way
out of the dilemma, he proposed that the ILO set up machinery
to make periodic factual inquiries, including on-the-spot investigations, to determine whether freedom of association was indeed a reality in member countries.

The French government delegate argued that the McNair
Report showed "that it was not possible to draw a clear-cut distinction between countries which respected freedom of association and other countries which did not."[29] Over the years this
theme became a favorite one for those who were advocates of
universality of membership. A familiar variant of that theme held
that as the government economic sector of Western countries
grew, along with the "inevitable" tendencies toward democracy
in Communist states, there would occur an eventual conver-
gence of the two systems, leading to harmonization of tripartism
and universality.

Somewhat unexpectedly, the U.S. government representative took a soft line. He also felt that the employers' proposal had
no chance of enactment, but he added: "Not only would such a
proposal probably lead to involvement in legalistic issues but
those who believed in the purposes of the United Nations would
be reluctant to see one of its specialized agencies, the I.L.O.,
shrink in membership, losing perhaps those very member states
whose people most needed the example and help of the I.L.O."[30]
This was to be the line of influential voices in the United States,
led by the State Department. This group had never been ena-
mored of tripartism and was more concerned with the "purposes
of the United Nations," which to them implied universality.

The Soviet government representative expressed satisfaction
with the McNair Report and with its reception at the conference.
He also supported the workers' proposal for investigative machinery, thus marking one of the few times that representatives

of the AFL-CIO and the Soviet Union saw eye-to-eye. The employers' proposal was defeated by a vote of 29 to 11, whereupon a resolution was adopted calling upon the director-general to submit a report on the practicability of some kind of permanent machinery to examine the facts relating to freedom of association.

In retrospect, it was a mistake for the U.S. government and worker representatives to accept a compromise on tripartism that made no progress whatever toward a resolution of the basic issue. Never was there a better time for the U.S. delegation to take a principled stand against the proposition that the labor market institutions of totalitarian states differed only in degree from those of the social democratic welfare countries. Considering the reluctance of most Western governments to risk a split in the organization, the chances of carrying the employers' proposal were admittedly not great. Still, the debate took place not long after the Hungarian revolt, and a firm stand by the United States might at least have signaled that no easy solutions to reconciling tripartism with universality of membership existed. By accepting a compromise, the United States made it more difficult to take a strong line on later issues of importance.

Despite this setback, the employers persisted in their efforts to disassociate themselves from Communist employer representatives. In response to Soviet complaints that their employer delegates were still not being placed on conference committees, the Governing Body set up a committee to find a solution. The committee recommended that, with certain exceptions, a delegate who felt aggrieved at not being appointed to a committee with full voting rights could appeal to an impartial board of three members chosen by the conference and with full authority to act. A voting procedure was tacked onto the proposal whereby a conference group, employer or worker, could cast a vote on behalf of the entire group if a two-thirds majority was obtained. It was also proposed that the impartial board could add a maximum of two voting delegates to each committee.

The employers' group adamantly opposed this proposal, calling it an infringement of group autonomy. But it was adopted by a vote of 27 to 12, with the U.S. government voting no and most

Western European and Communist governments casting their
votes in favor. The proposal then went to the 1959 conference
for final approval. The employers urged that it be sent to the
Committee on Standing Orders so that its constitutionality could
be considered in detail. Cola Parker, the U.S. employer delegate, strongly supported this course of action. He was seconded
by the U.S. government delegate, this time with no equivoca-
tion:

> The question before us is whether an administrative agent—
> whether he is called an employer or a worker—of a monolithic
> state without the right to act on his own authority can be con-
> ceived as being an employer or a worker as that title has been
> conceived in the functioning of this Organization. . . . The
> United States is committed to the preservation and strengthen-
> ing of the tripartite structure of the I.L.O. and the preservation
> of the rights of the Employer and Worker groups to designate
> who shall sit as spokesman for their viewpoint.[31]

The few workers' delegates who spoke on this issue were in
favor of the Governing Body committee's proposal. Unlike the
employers, the workers' group had seated Communist trade
union delegates in their conference committees with full voting
rights. European trade unions, led by the British, appeared uneasy about supporting the viewpoint of private employers, and
they referred to the ILO as "a bridge between East and West,
because we had one common objective no matter what political
philosophy we were living under."[32] The employer proposal was
rejected, and after some attempts at amendment, the committee
proposal was adopted by the conference. The U.S. delegation
was split: the government and the employer delegates were opposed, while the worker delegate voted in favor. Why he did so
is not clear. The AFL-CIO never modified its antipathy toward
trade union representatives of Communist countries, and thus,
it was expected to lead the movement for group autonomy. Several worker delegates from the West, including France and the
Netherlands, voted against the proposal, so there was no question of loyalty to a group decision.

The closeness of the vote indicates how deeply the ILO was
divided on this issue. Voting with the U.S. government were the

governments of Belgium, Germany, the Netherlands, and the United Kingdom, all of whom had apparently decided that it would be better to send the whole matter back to the Governing Body for further consideration. The alignment of all but a few worker delegates, as well as the governments of Scandinavia, France, Italy, and Japan (and Israel!), with the Communist bloc was a strange one not destined to survive.

As a result of the resolution, eleven Communist employers were added to conference committees, causing the employer group to withdraw from all further participation in the proceedings of those committees. At the next meeting of the Governing Body, the employers reacted angrily, and the U.S. employer delegation, among others, withdrew from the committees whose membership had been augmented by the 1960 conference. The battle, however, had already been lost. The Communist nations had won the right to be seated in the worker and employer groups of committees selected by the conference.

Until 1968, this new mechanism was used each year to place Communist delegates on employer committees; thereafter, the employers' group selected these delegates. Up to the time of the U.S. withdrawal, however, the employers successfully resisted efforts by the Communist bloc to secure the election of an employer member to the Governing Body. But in 1966, the worker group elected a Soviet worker delegate to the Governing Body, and this precedent has been effective ever since.[33]

The next formal debate on tripartism occurred at the 1971 conference in connection with a resolution sponsored by the Western industrial nations. It called upon the Governing Body to ensure that the tripartite principle was applied to all ILO activities, including standard-setting and technical assistance. The resolution, which was given top priority, requested the director-general to remind member states of the constitutional requirement that members of tripartite delegations be able to act in full independence of one another.[34]

Again, a sharp conflict arose between the United States and the Soviet Union, with the U.S. worker delegate this time carrying the burden of the attack. He emphasized that genuine tripartism should be considered a dominant principle of ILO organization. While there might be other international agencies that were universal, he pointed out, only the ILO was tripartite: "Unless the ILO is a tripartite organization it has no reason for being. It is a tripartite organization representing these three groups, and if [the Communist] delegates think that in some way universality is impossible with tripartism, then I say we must put tripartism in the first place."[35]

The delegates of the Soviet Union attacked the resolution on several grounds: (1) that it merely repeated old statements; (2) that in actual practice tripartism always redounded to the advantage of employers and to the disadvantage of the trade unions; (3) that tripartism represented artificial opposition to universality; (4) that the purpose of the resolution was to strengthen the monopolistic position of private employers and of the International Confederation of Free Trade Unions; and (5) that it was "a sort of warhorse in the fight against communism."[36] The resolution was adopted by an overwhelming vote, and the Communists suffered a clear defeat.

Because it is germane to the issue of tripartism, a note on the general voting strength of the Communist bloc at ILO conferences should be included. Eleven countries from Eastern Europe (plus Cuba) have been represented at recent conferences, including Byelorussia, the Ukraine, and Mongolia. The delegations from all these countries were "tripartite," but since it is virtually unknown for those worker or employer representatives to vote against their governments, this meant that forty-eight votes were automatically available for any position taken by the Soviet government. By contrast, U.S. employers and workers often took positions quite different from that of their government, perhaps more often than any other country's delegation. This difference in practice clearly reflected the gulf that existed between the United States and the Soviet Union in their conceptions of what tripartism was all about.

The tripartism issue surfaced once again in the 1975 letter explaining why the United States was giving notice of withdrawal. The statement on this issue is worth quoting, for it represents a good summary of the U.S. position:

The ILO exists as an organization in which representatives of workers, employers, and governments may come together to further mutual interests. The constitution of the ILO is predicated on the existence within member states of relatively independent and reasonably self-defined and self-directed worker and employer groups. The United States fully recognizes that these assumptions, which may have been warranted on the part of the western democracies which drafted the ILO constitution in 1919, have not worked out everywhere in the world; in truth only a minority of the nations of the world today have anything resembling industrial democracy, just as only a minority can lay claim to political democracy. The United States recognizes that revising the practices and arrangements of the ILO is not going to restore the world of 1919 or 1944. It would be intolerable of us to demand that it do so. On the other hand, it is equally intolerable for other states to insist that as a condition of participating in the ILO we should give up our liberties simply because they have another political system. We will not. Some accommodation will have to be found. But if none is, the United States will not submit passively to what some, mistakenly, may suppose to be the march of history. In particular, we cannot accept the workers' and employers' groups in the ILO falling under the domination of governments.[37]

These were brave words, but they came twenty years too late. It is difficult to imagine what the ILO could have done in 1975 to restore genuine tripartism, a fact that the statement itself recognized. The analysis given by Charles H. Smith, Jr., the last U.S. employer delegate, may have been less philosophical, but it was more to the point: "Some nations have been admitted to membership with an economic and political system that precludes the naming of non-Government delegations to represent employers and workers. When government representatives are allowed to participate in the meetings and conferences of the ILO as representatives of either workers or employers, it destroys the tripartite relationship that makes this organization unique among international organizations."[38] The AFL-CIO reaction to the letter was that the ILO would have to determine "whether the founding principle of tripartism lives in fact as well as in form, or continues to be smothered in the suffocating spirit of accommodation with totalitarianism of the left or right."[39]

The U.S. position had less support from Western European governments in 1975 than it might have expected two decades earlier. Shortly after the United States gave notice of its intent to withdraw, Alexandre Parodi, long a representative of the French government, called a meeting of the government members of the Governing Body representing the industrial market economies. Parodi questioned the U.S. arguments relating to tripartism and "asked in what manner the ILO was not respecting tripartism. He noted Eastern European support for the conference resolution on strengthening tripartism and alleged that the Third World had also accepted the principle of tripartism."[40] Roberto Ago, Italian government representative and one of the principal architects of the various compromises on group autonomy, felt that the threat to tripartism came not from Eastern Europe but rather from the Third World, "where many countries have one-party governments and no understanding of a free trade union movement."[41] The views expressed by these influential men persisted right up to the time of the U.S. withdrawal and exemplified the unwillingness of Western European nations to face up to this fundamental problem of ILO structure, undoubtedly because of their foreign policy imperatives.

By 1977, the requirements of tripartism in the ILO were satisfied merely by sending delegates labeled "employers" and "workers" to the ILO conference, regardless of the degree of domination by their governments. That was the practical implication of the attitudes adopted by virtually all government and labor representatives except those of the United States and the beleaguered private employers of the industrialized nations. Whenever the United States raised the issue of tripartism, the oft-repeated response of Western European representatives was that the world had changed and that the concept of tripartism must change with it to accommodate the many member states which for institutional or practical reasons could not nominate independent labor and employer delegates. Over the years, the United States had more or less adjusted to the type of tripartite representation sent by the Communist countries, and it is unlikely that it would have withdrawn because of that issue alone.

If the United States were to insist, as a condition for ILO membership, that the ILO require full independence for worker and employer representatives, the organization that emerged would have a considerably more limited membership than now. However, group autonomy in the ILO is not dead by any means, and there remains a possibility in many countries for advancing the cause of independent worker and employer organizations through the ILO machinery.

Selective Concern for Human Rights

The U.S. notice of withdrawal from the ILO cited as the second basic reason for its action the following:

> The ILO Conference for some years now has shown an appallingly selective concern in the application of the ILO's basic conventions on freedom of association and forced labor. It pursues the violation of human rights in some member states. It grants immunity from such citations to others. This seriously undermines the credibility of the ILO's support of freedom of association, which is central to its tripartite structure, and strengthens the proposition that these human rights are not universally applicable, but rather are subject to different interpretations for states with different political systems.[42]

The "states with different political systems" are, of course, the Communist countries, especially the Soviet Union. This has been a long-standing complaint, one that has been pursued with consistency.

ILO procedures (which are dealt with more fully in Chapter 6) require every member state to report periodically on the measures it has taken to conform to the provisions of each convention it has ratified. These reports are reviewed by a committee of experts, consisting mainly of high court judges of the member nations.[43] The committee submits its findings to the tripartite Conference Committee on the Application of Standards, which in turn reports to the annual conference. Government delegates of countries found to be in default of their obligations are given an opportunity to explain their position. The conference committee report has a special listing of countries that are in serious and persistent noncompliance, and may even devote "special paragraphs" to their transgressions. No country likes to be singled out in this manner, the Soviet Union in particular.

In addition, any association of workers or employers may file a complaint with the Governing Body alleging that a member state has failed to honor its obligations under a convention. The same may be done by any member state or by any delegate to the conference. In the case of human rights the relevant conventions, all ratified by the Soviet Union, are No. 29, Forced Labor; No. 87, Freedom of Association; and No. 98, Right to Organize and Collective Bargaining. Special machinery has been developed to deal with complaints specifically involving freedom of association. Worker or employer organizations may file against a government even if it has not ratified the relevant conventions. The Governing Body has established the tripartite Committee on Freedom of Association to hear such complaints and to make recommendations for action.

The 1956 McNair Report carefully skirted the question of whether freedom of association of workers and employers prevailed in the Communist countries. It concluded merely that trade unions existed in the Soviet Union and that individuals performed certain technical managerial functions. When the report was received by the Governing Body, the U.S. labor delegate proposed, on behalf of the worker group, that the Office set up machinery to obtain "not just the legal but the real facts about conditions in each member State, and that the Governing Body ask the director-general to recommend a specific form of action to accomplish this."[44]

At the same 1956 meeting of the Governing Body, the Committee on Freedom of Association submitted its report on a complaint brought by the International Confederation of Free Trade Unions (ICFTU) against the Soviet Union. The committee raised questions about various aspects of the Soviet labor scene. Was it possible to organize unions independent of the Soviet All-Union Central Council of Trade Unions? Were social security preferences accorded on the basis of union membership discriminatory? Were wages determined by a State Plan that barred any deviation? Were Soviet workers aware that no legal prohibitions pertained against strikes, as alleged by the Soviet government? Were the trade unions controlled by the Communist party? Was the chairman of the All-Union Central Council appointed by the government and the Communist party? And why had no congress of the Russian trade unions been held in seventeen years, despite the fact that their constitution called for one every four years?

The Soviet government delegate answered these questions as follows: Anyone could organize a union; only in the case of medical insurance was there discrimination; wages could be altered by the unions; Soviet workers were fully aware of their legal right to strike, but chose not to; the Soviet government could not be held responsible for constitutional oversights by the trade unions; Soviet workers were grateful to the Communist party and followed its advice willingly. The Soviet government, its delegate continued, "was prepared to discuss all aspects of freedom of association in a friendly spirit, but it could not agree to being placed in the position of an accused party accepting certain conditions under threat."[45] He counterattacked by pointing out that those countries that had not ratified Convention No. 87 (e.g., the United States) ought not to criticize the Soviet Union, which had ratified it. The committee's recommendation that the charges be referred to a fact-finding and conciliation commission was adopted with only the Soviet Union dissenting. Since the Governing Body could not make such a referral without the consent of the Soviet government, this ILO censure amounted to little more than a light tap on the wrist. Nevertheless, the Soviet Union expressed its resentment over the matter.

The next controversy arose in 1957 in connection with a report by the Ad Hoc Committee on Forced Labor, which had been established in 1955 to examine various charges. All the Eastern European Communist countries, along with China and a few others, were in the dock. In the case of the Soviet Union, the committee confined itself to quoting the famous speech delivered by Premier Nikita Khrushchev at the Twentieth Congress of the Soviet Communist Party, and expressed the hope that things were changing and that the relevant legislation would be revised.[46] The U.S. labor delegate urged that the report be given wide publicity and worldwide distribution, while the Soviet government delegate termed it a bad report, arguing that the "sole concern of the members of the Committee had been to whitewash capitalist exploitation."[47] The Governing Body eventually agreed to submit the report to the conference and to bring it to the attention of workers' and employers' organizations around the world. This was a clear victory for the United States.

Thanks to continued pressure from the West, freedom of association and forced labor continued at the top of the ILO agenda. In October 1957, the Governing Body debated a proposal to set up continuous fact-finding machinery for the purpose of monitoring freedom of association. Although the U.S. government delegate offered only lukewarm support, the U.S. worker delegate left no one in doubt about his position: "Freedom of association could not be interpreted in different ways in the United States on the one hand and in the U.S.S.R. on the other; it must mean the same thing to all people and must be applied in the same way. . . . The ILO must not confine itself to investigating allegations of violations of freedom of association; it must develop programs and initiate ideas that would really further the development of freedom of association wherever it did exist."[48] The Soviet government representative responded in characteristic fashion. He argued that too much emphasis had been placed on protecting employers, who did not need protection; he talked of gangsterism and racial discrimination in American trade unions and asserted that "the trade unions in the Soviet Union had more rights than in any other country, including the United States of America."[49] This acrimonious debate ended with a directive to the director-general to bring in a revised proposal at a future meeting.

This session of the Governing Body then returned to the issue of forced labor. A convention on forced labor (No. 105) had just been adopted by the conference, and the U.S. worker delegate proposed that the life of the ad hoc committee responsible for it be extended. This proposal was supported by both the employer group and the U.S. government. The British government opposed it, however, on the ground that adequate machinery already existed, and so did the Soviet government representative, who charged that "everyone was aware that the Committee on Forced Labor had so far been an instrument of the cold war and a device to disguise certain discreditable situations, in particular in countries whose representatives were the most eloquent defenders of freedom."[50] Nevertheless, the ad hoc committee was extended by a vote of 35 to 3.

This same meeting of the Governing Body, which marked one of the peaks of U.S.–U.S.S.R. discord at the ILO, still needed to take up some unfinished business on freedom of association left over from previous meetings. When the Soviet case came up, the Soviet delegate delivered a long, rambling ideological speech in which he asserted that the Committee on Freedom of Association had ignored Soviet statements; that the workers' group had rejected invitations to visit the Soviet Union and see for itself how matters stood there; that the ILO was becoming "a political and propaganda battleground instead of dealing with technical questions with a view to the improvement of the conditions of life of the workers throughout the world."[51] The British worker delegate replied that he had no desire to visit the Soviet Union because of the propaganda purposes it would serve: "He had seen the results of similar visits, and the tendentious and lying statements that had been made about them. He had also seen the reports of trade union delegations which had visited the United Kingdom and the calculated falsehoods they contained about the situation in the trade unions there."[52] If similar sentiments had been expressed by European trade union representatives two decades later, the United States would never have left the ILO. In any event, the committee's report, including the criticism that had caused the debate in the first place, was adopted with only a few countries dissenting.

In March 1958, Director-General Morse presented to the Governing Body, as it had requested, a proposal to set up permanent machinery for monitoring freedom of association. Morse advocated the establishment of an independent conciliation commission on freedom of association, to which alleged infringements of trade union rights could be referred from any source.

The commission would work closely with an accused country in an effort to settle disputes; while it could put forth its own proposals, if necessary, it was not empowered to render any judgments. This proposal was received coolly by government representatives, who feared that the new commission might create diplomatic problems. Morse reluctantly withdrew it, commenting that "the proposed conciliation machinery would have strengthened the moral position of the ILO; it was not sufficient for an organization like the ILO to deal with the problem of trade union rights solely by grinding out quasi-judicial opinions, even though some good might result from that process."[53]

A second part of the proposal, calling for a factual survey of freedom of association, was accepted by the Governing Body. Broad in scope, it provided for survey missions by ILO staff members upon proper authorization by the Governing Body. Before the survey machinery could get into action, however, another contretemps took place. The report of the Committee on Freedom of Association on the ICFTU complaint against the Soviet Union, which had been considered by the Governing Body several times before, came up again at its next meeting, in the spring of 1958. The Governing Body had asked the Soviet Union to agree to have certain charges against it referred to an ILO fact-finding and conciliation commission on freedom of association. Such a referral could not take place without the consent of the country concerned, and the Soviet Union had refused. Several members of the Governing Body then suggested that their committee's findings be published. This led to a slashing attack by the Soviet delegate, who charged that the committee's verdict had been decided in advance.[54] The matter was held over until the following meeting, when the Governing Body finally voted to give publicity to the report of its Committee on Freedom of Association.[55] While the U.S. government delegate had not displayed any great interest in pushing this matter, he supported the decision in deference to the strong positions taken by the worker and employer delegates.

The issue had been somewhat defused when the Soviet Union agreed that a factual survey of its trade union situation could be conducted through the recently authorized Office survey procedure. The United States requested that its own labor practices be surveyed, anticipating that the two studies would show clearly the great differences in freedom of association prevailing in the two countries. But matters did not turn out as expected.

To understand these reports, the reader needs to know something of the structure and functions of Soviet trade unions. These organizations, which were originally promoted by the Social Democratic Workers party, the precursor of the Communist party, were led by political activists from the start. Until 1917, they were relatively powerless, but they grew rapidly following the overthrow of the Russian czar. Some union leaders advocated a syndicalist solution, in which the unions would be vested with the task of industrial management. But the Leninist concept of the unions as a "transmission belt" for selling the decisions of the Communist party to the rank-and-file workers prevailed. When Stalin gained absolute power, Mikhail Tomsky, head of the trade unions and an advocate of union independence, was arrested and disappeared.[56]

Soviet trade unions are industrial in form. All workers in an enterprise, regardless of their individual crafts, are members of the same union. At the organizational apex stands the All-Union Central Council of Trade Unions (AUCCTU), which meets about twice a year. The AUCCTU then selects an executive committee, which meets at frequent intervals, and a small secretariat to supervise the daily operations of the organization.

Heading up to the AUCCTU are national industrial unions, their jurisdictions corresponding to those of the industrial ministries. These unions are in turn subdivided into republic, regional, and district unions. The basic unit of organization is the factory local and its central committee (*fabkom*). A labor-management disputes committee (KTS) handles grievances at the shop or factory level.

There is no labor ministry in the Soviet Union, where trade unions perform most of the tasks allotted to the ministries in non-Communist countries, including administration of the social security system. Wages are determined centrally by the State Planning Commission and the industrial ministries, although the trade unions are allegedly given an advisory role. The collective agreements entered into at the factory level in Russia have little resemblance to those of the West. Much of their content is devoted to specifying the production obligations of the workers, since one of the major functions of Soviet trade unions is to exhort workers to increase productivity.

How independent are Soviet trade unions? A study published a decade ago, not long after the ILO survey was made, concluded that "the union central committees and the Central Council of Trade Unions, led by trusted communists, function as agents of the Communist Party and the state, more like sections in a governmental department of labor than as independent trade union centers."[57] There may be more independence at the local level, though here there has been considerable variation over time and from factory to factory. One thing is clear, however: all top officials of Soviet trade unions, and often even the lower-echelon members of the factory committee, are members of the Communist party and subject to its discipline. The notion that Soviet trade unions, or any other Soviet institutions for that matter, are exempt from Party control has no factual basis in the reality of the Soviet governing structure. To cite one example of Party–trade union relationships, the chairman of the AUCCTU for a period of years up to 1975 was Alexander Shelepin, whose training for the job had been as head of the KGB, the Soviet spy agency, and also as a member of the Politburo, which runs both the Communist party and the government. Shelepin was removed from his party and trade union positions while visiting Great Britain in 1975 as head of a bilateral exchange mission with the British Trade Union Council, a visit marked by a great deal of unpleasantness because of public protest against his presence.[58]

Soviet workers are not required to join unions, but since dues are low, and nonmembership deprives them of access to facilities controlled by the unions, including vacation resort hotels, the overwhelming majority are members. Soviet spokesmen have often asserted that workers are free to form rival unions if they are dissatisfied with the official ones, but this is contrary to reality.[59] The Soviet constitution guarantees the right to strike, but officially called strikes are unknown, and the few spontaneous ones that have been reported over the years were suppressed by the government. In sum, Soviet trade unions share little but their name with their counterparts in the West.

It was against this background that ILO survey missions were dispatched in 1959 to the Soviet Union and to the United States "to provide a full picture of the actual conditions in each country which affect the extent to which freedom of association is respected." The report on the United States[60] was fairly accurate, though uninspired and a bit too kind on the issue of corruption. It revealed nothing not already available in numerous books and articles, to say nothing of newspaper headlines.

The Soviet report[61] was another matter. Its publication was greeted with indignation and dismay by the American labor movement. The executive council of the AFL-CIO adopted a resolution that concluded: "The Mission's report on freedom of association in the USSR is not objective. It has failed to make clear the very issues which occasioned its survey. Under cover of 'neutrality' it shut its eyes to the Soviet Communists' continuous contempt for and flagrant violation of freedom of association."[62] These strictures were largely justified. It was not so much what was said, but what could be fairly inferred from the many cryptic statements in the report. The mission made such strenuous efforts to be "objective" that it managed to avoid almost all direct reference to the subject of its inquiry, freedom of association. The few firm statements that appear raised grave doubts either as to the competence of the officials who prepared it or as to their political motivation.

For the most part, the report simply repeats statements made by Soviet spokesmen or paraphrases Soviet trade union dogma. But even in its attempt merely to set forth the Soviet position, some peculiar things emerged. Take for example the statement that in 1929 "some leading officials of the trade union movement were relieved of their functions so as to retain only persons who were faithful to the Party line. From 1930 onward, there was no further fundamental disagreement concerning the respective roles of the Party and the unions."[63] This reference to one of the most crucial episodes of Soviet trade union history is a masterpiece of understatement; it fails even to hint at the impact of the Stalinist purges on the trade unions. Again, "links between the trade unions and a political party are not peculiar to the Soviet system,"[64] which suggests that there was some basic similarity between the Soviet situation and, for example, the British Labour Party–Trade Union Council (TUC) relationship. The mission admitted that it had no opportunity to study the guiding Soviet principle of "democratic centralism" in any detail, but nonetheless, it recorded its impression that union officials "were fully conscious and responsive to the problems affecting union members."[65]

Only in the final few pages does this report of 136 printed pages approach, in a gingerly fashion, the focal point of the investigation: the degree to which freedom of association prevailed. Some of the conclusions it drew were very odd. On the question of whether workers were free to establish unions of their own choosing, it stated that "it is hardly likely that organizations could be set up outside the established framework, because of the principles enunciated in Article 14 of the rules of the Trade Unions of the U.S.S.R. that 'all persons employed in the same factory or office belong to the same union.'"[66] The reader is left with the impression that Article 14 was the major barrier to rival unionism in Russia; just amend it and new unions might begin to proliferate.

The report went on: "Nor is any stress placed in the U.S.S.R. on the right of workers to strike." The absence of strikes is ascribed largely to close cooperation between management and labor in pursuit of a common objective and to the absence of political differences between unions and government. But the report, recognizing that spontaneous strikes might occur, noted that if they did, "the necessary machinery for dealing with the problem is immediately set in motion."[67] The Soviet labor code provides no machinery to set in motion, and moreover, the Soviet government has steadfastly denied the occurrence of even a single strike. In sum, this report must be ranked as one of the worst ever published by the ILO, even from a purely technical viewpoint.

In addition to its surveys for the Soviet Union and the United

States, the ILO wrote reports for Britain, Sweden, Malaysia, and Burma. When the survey program was reviewed by the Governing Body in 1963, there was a notable lack of enthusiasm for continuing it except among Communist representatives. The Soviet delegate praised the ILO mission for its "sincere effort to find out what was happening and to convey their impressions honestly." He added: "Anyone who read the report on the trade union situation in the U.S.S.R. carefully would understand what the true situation was in that country and would come to the same conclusions as were contained in the McNair Report—namely that trade unions in the U.S.S.R. were able to defend their interests and were free from government control."[68] (Surprisingly, there was no comment by the U.S. government representative.) The surveys on freedom of association were discontinued.

After this fiasco, the Governing Body decided to adjourn debate on the issue. This moratorium, which lasted for some years, was apparently due largely to an informal agreement within the workers' group to let matters rest. Beginning in the mid-1960s, the non-Communist unions of Western Europe began changing their attitude toward contact with Soviet trade unions. A decade earlier, in 1955, the executive board of the ICFTU had adopted a policy of strict noncooperation with Soviet trade unions lest the Communists gain by (1) winning moral respectability and legitimacy for their state company unions; (2) misleading the workers of the free world into identifying these organizations, which were run by the Communist party, with bona fide free trade unions; (3) facilitating Communist infiltration and subversion in the free world; (4) promoting the expansionist interests of Soviet imperialism.[69]

Although there had been absolutely no change in the character of Soviet unions by the mid-sixties, détente between Western Europe and the Soviet Union led to a modification of these views. In 1966, the German Federation of Labor began contacts with the Soviets, proceeding slowly at first, but gaining momentum within a few years, a consequence of the new Social Democratic *Ostpolitik*. The British Trade Union Council followed the German lead and embarked upon a series of bilateral exchanges with the Soviet AUCCTU—this despite the fact that its then general secretary, Victor Feather, had written in 1973, when he was assistant general secretary:

> The fact is that no person who expresses opposition to Soviet Government control can be elected to office in a union. No one dare advocate a strike, and an individual who absents himself from work as a mild private protest against a personal injustice can be imprisoned by the State. When the State is the employer and also controls the unions, the worker has no protection left. The right to work becomes an obligation to suffer exploitation. . . . And when exploitation and injustice must be suffered without protest, man has not even the status of a machine; he has only the status of a slave without hope.[70]

Most of the remaining Western European labor federations, which in the 1950s could have been counted on to support U.S. attacks on the Soviet Union, joined in the exchange programs, which the Soviet government was pushing hard. Why they did so is a complicated matter, and part of the answer lies in the growing influence of the Communists and of New Left groups within the traditional social democratic parties.

Governments and trade union leaders also discovered that, following visits by Soviet trade union delegates, their internal problems with leftist militants diminished. It was recently observed that "it takes a particularly clear-sighted and ideologically committed trade union leader, with ample political support from within his union, to overcome the obstacles placed in his way by the Western politicans who have initiated and supported the détente policy."[71]

In 1969, the growing breach between the American labor movement and the Western European unions led to the formal withdrawal of the AFL-CIO from the International Confederation of Free Trade Unions. Immediately after World War II, the then-independent Congress of Industrial Organizations (but not the American Federation of Labor) joined a newly established World Federation of Trade Unions. Within a few years, this body had fallen under Soviet domination. In 1949, the non-Communist unions seceded and, with AFL participation, established the ICFTU.

During its first decade, this new international body was firmly anti-Communist, but with the emergence of East-West détente, it began to weaken in its commitment to face up to Soviet pressures. As a result, rather than work through the ICFTU, the AFL-CIO resorted increasingly to its own programs in the less developed countries as a means of promoting independent unionism. Since the ICFTU was the coordinating body of the worker group within the ILO, the AFL-CIO decision to go it alone weakened the American union's ability to influence events in Geneva.

Neither before nor after the American labor movement left the ICFTU did it waver in its firm opposition to Communist trade unionism. It kept up continual pressure, in the ILO and elsewhere, to deny legitimacy to Communist-dominated trade unions, but without the backing of Western European labor it was not able to keep the issue in the forefront. When the controversy erupted again in the 1970s, it was in the context of events that enabled the AFL-CIO to bring about unilateral U.S. action against the ILO, despite the reluctance of the U.S. government to back it.[72]

In 1974, the ILO itself played a role in helping bring about a rapprochement between the labor unions of Eastern and Western Europe. The occasion was the second ILO European regional conference (the first took place in 1955), a device that had been set up so that nations could meet periodically in their own areas and discuss common problems. Given the existence of the OECD and the Common Market, such an ILO conference was hardly necessary for the Western industrial nations. It was the Soviet Union that was very much in favor of reviving the European conference as a means of furthering East-West contacts.

When the European conference report was debated by the Governing Body, opinions were sharply divided on its achievements. The U.S. government representative expressed doubt that the conference recommendation to study trade union structure under various economic and social systems of Europe would lead to better results than the disastrous studies of 1960. He insisted that any such studies "should be based on the assumption that the trade union situation in all countries, whatever their economic and social system, should be judged by the same criteria, namely, the requirements of Convention No. 87."[73] The U.S. worker representative declared that while Western delegates had discussed their problems in an open manner, the Communists had simply boasted of their achievements and glossed over their problems. He concluded that if ILO resources were to be devoted to the fulfillment of the recommendations, all countries would have to show equal candor.[74]

But almost everyone who had attended the European conference appeared to be satisfied. The spokesman for the workers' group, Joseph Morris of Canada, reported that the labor representatives agreed that the proceedings were friendly, relevant, and productive. The Soviet trade union delegate observed that the conference "had brought together trade union leaders from different European countries for the first time since just before the Second World War; they had held a frank exchange of views on matters of common concern and decided to meet again regularly in the future."[75] The Soviet trade union movement had now achieved the respectability it had so long sought. As a consequence, the United States found itself almost completely isolated.

At the 1974 ILO conference, the United States succeeded in having the Committee on the Application of Standards place the Soviet Union on a special list for having failed to implement fully a forced labor convention. Among other things, the report of the Committee of Experts to the ILO had cited Soviet legislation against "idlers" and "parasites" as leading to possible prison sentences at hard labor. An acerbic debate in the committee resulted in a 3 to 1 vote against the Soviet Union.[76] Following this vote, the Soviet government delegate declared his complete lack of confidence in the impartiality of the Committee of Experts, and he accused the Conference Committee on the Application of Standards of returning to "cold war" procedures.

The debate continued after the committee report had reached the conference plenary session. Soviet representatives denied the existence of forced labor in their country and asked that the accusation against the Soviet Union be voted on separately from the remainder of the report. Under the existing rules of procedure, an immediate objection by the United States made this impossible. A spokesman for the U.S. government then charged the Communist countries with having attempted to filibuster the work of the committee; he further condemned the Soviet Union for refusing additional collaboration with the Committee of Experts. He pointed out that thirty-seven other countries had been placed on the list of violators and concluded: "The question now before the Conference is whether we apply a standard to the weak and the small that is different from the standard which we apply to the high and mighty. How this body answers that question carries implications for the future of this Organization, the importance of which cannot be overstated."[77] The U.S. worker representative added: "The real issue . . . is whether a double standard is going to be permitted to continue under which the Soviet State can set its own rules of conduct and compliance after ratification of Conventions."[78]

The outcome was not favorable for the United States. Representatives of the governments of Britain, the Netherlands, Belgium, the Scandinavian countries, France, and Italy, as well as trade union delegates from some of these countries, all indicated their opposition to including the offending paragraph. Some abstained from voting on the report; others voted for it with an explanation. The final result was 123 in favor, 0 against, and 156 abstentions. Since there was no quorum, under ILO voting rules the report failed of adoption.[79] As a result of this unprecedented conference refusal to adopt the report of one of its key committees, the United States now stood virtually alone, deserted by its European allies. A U.S. worker delegate warned the conference just before the voting that if the report was altered to suit the Soviet Union, "we must accept the fact that we are proclaiming to all the world that certain countries are going to be permitted to operate under different standards than apply to the rest of us."[80] The debate on the report, and the vote on it, clearly indicated that Western Europe, at both governmental and trade union levels, was prepared to acquiesce in a double standard in the interest of détente.

The Soviet Union subsequently supplied some information on its employment legislation to the 1975 conference committee, but the U.S. government representative on the committee found that this was insufficient. The committee refused to cite the Soviet Union, however, and instead asked the Soviet government to respond to the issues raised in the debate.[81] In the plenary session, the U.S. government representative decried the failure of the committee to call attention to the continued existence of forced labor, but again his was a voice crying in the wilderness.

The 1976 report of the Committee of Experts noted that while Soviet legislation relating to a parasitical way of life had been repealed, another law that had previously applied to persons engaged in vagrancy and begging had been extended to cover "persons leading over a prolonged period of time any other parasitic way of life." The committee also pointed out that previous observations on freedom of association in the Soviet Union had not been answered satisfactorily; specifically, it expressed doubt that Soviet laws permitted the formation of unions rivaling the official ones or that it was legally possible for unions to be independent of the Communist party.[82] The conference committee devoted a special paragraph to the forced labor issue, asking for clarification of the "parasitism" legislation, but it omitted any reference to freedom of association. The committee report was adopted with little debate. The Soviet failure to object was probably due to the very polite manner in which request for further information was made.[83]

The climax to the years of charges and countercharges came at the 1977 conference, with the U.S. notice of withdrawal providing the backdrop against which the proceedings took place. The Western Europeans were only half convinced that the United States would carry out its threat if the double standard, among other things, continued to prevail. The Soviets appeared unconcerned about the possibility of a U.S. exit.

The Committee of Experts set the stage by noting that the Soviet penal code, while it provided definitions of "systematic vagrancy" and "begging," did not define the crime of "leading any other parasitic way of life," except to state that criminal proceedings on that count could not be brought against minors, invalids, pregnant women, or women with children under eight years of age.[84] It asked the Soviet Union for clarification. On freedom of association, the committee reiterated its earlier conclusion that Convention No. 87 carried with it an obligation to permit the establishment of rival unions, if so desired by the workers, but that this did not seem to be possible in the Soviet Union. The committee was also dissatisfied with the Soviet response on the dominating role played by the Communist party. The Committee of Experts finally came out squarely on the double standard issue: "The Committee has made no assumptions about capitalist, socialist or Third World countries. It applies to all, impartially, the same test of conformity to the obligation undertaken by each country under ratified conventions. Furthermore, the Committee has no indications which might lead it to consider that its observations concerning socialist countries did not reflect the actual situation."[85]

The conference committee debate on this report was very tense. While meetings of the Committee on the Application of Standards are open to the public, they are normally sparsely attended. But in 1977, there was standing room only. The Soviet representative spoke at great length in opposition to the conclusions of the Committee of Experts. He claimed that the offense of "leading any other parasitic way of life" applied only to fortune-telling. His credibility was hardly enhanced when, in response to a question raised by the Canadian government delegate about why it was necessary to exempt pregnant women et al. from the operation of the law, he replied that fortune-telling and begging by these people were illegal but that they would not be prosecuted. He added: "That was proof of the humanitarian nature of the legislation and the case-law of the U.S.S.R., taking into account the concrete nature of the offender."[86] The central issue, of course, was the application of the laws of "vagrancy" and "parasitism" to Soviet dissidents. The explanation by the Soviets was disingenuous, to say the least.

There were more fireworks over the issue of freedom of association. The Soviet representative claimed that the Committee of Experts had misconstrued the Soviet labor code and that the Russian text "extended trade union rights to *any committee which could be created*, although there existed only one in practice" (italics supplied). As for the role of the Communist party, he continued,

> The guiding role of the Party had not been imposed on the trade
> unions; the tie between trade unions and the Party was volun-
> tarily created even before the October Revolution of 1917. The
> Committee of Experts, by refusing to take into account the spe-
> cific conditions existing in a country, especially the historical cir-
> cumstances, could be led to incorrect conclusions. . . . The
> guiding role of the Party was not the result of Legislative mat-
> ters but had come about on a voluntary basis. . . . The guiding
> role was exercised only by one voice: by the members of the
> Party who at the same time were members of the trade union
> and acted within the framework of internal democracy of the
> trade union. Their sole means was persuasion. . . . The auton-
> omy and the independence of the trade unions were totally pre-
> served and the Party possessed no means of coercion even if in
> fact its influence was great, as was that of the trade unions within
> the Party.[87]

The U.S. government representative reaffirmed his belief
that the unions were Party-dominated, while the German government member expressed the view that the committee would
be unable to do anything about changing the Soviet system.
Nevertheless, the committee voted to devote a "special paragraph" to the Soviet Union on both forced labor and freedom of
association, expressing the hope that the Soviet Union would examine the report of the Committee of Experts "to see whether
changes could be made to bring the legal position more closely
into conformity with the Convention."[88]

The denouement came at the conference plenary session
when the report of the Committee on the Application of Standards was considered. A U.S. worker delegate appealed to the
conference to accept the report in the name of human rights,
pointing out that 70 percent of all the cases chosen for discussion,
covering many countries, involved such matters. The Soviet government delegate replied that socialist and developing countries
could not be judged from the point of view of "bourgeois legal
systems" and that the committee could not sit in judgment upon
countries by putting them on special lists—denying, in effect,
the validity of long-standing ILO practice. Finally, he asserted

that countries that had not ratified the relevant conventions (e.g., the United States) could escape supervision themselves even as they used the conventions to make extensive criticism of others.

The final vote was complicated when an issue involving Israel arose and drew the opposition of the Arab states.[89] Perhaps the outcome would have been different without this issue, but the final result was clear: 135 votes in favor of accepting the report, none opposed, 197 abstentions. The report was therefore defeated for lack of a quorum. The record reveals that 87 of the affirmative votes came from the OECD countries, which were almost solidly lined up behind the U.S. position this time, while the remainder came from a few less developed nations, including Kenya, Honduras, Surinam, and the Cameroons. The opposition garnered 47 votes from the Communist bloc (the vote of the Yugoslav worker delegate was not recorded) and 56 from the Arab states. Among the less developed countries, Indonesia, Pakistan, the Ivory Coast, and Panama voted unanimously against the report. Most other less developed nations also voted against the report, but not with unanimous delegations.

In a postmortem speech, the U.S. worker delegate, Irving Brown, commented on the action of the conference:

> I feel that Monday, 20 June, what Cyril Plant has called the dark day in the history of the ILO, has badly damaged, has badly tarnished that mechanism [of the Committee on the Application of Standards and the Committee of Experts] and whether it can be repaired and be respected is gravely in doubt. . . . In answer to the question whether this Session of the Conference has strengthened or weakened the ILO, my answer is, especially on the basis of the results of Monday, 20 June, that the ILO has been badly weakened and its basic machinery badly damaged and perhaps damaged beyond repair.[90]

Every delegate present at this crucial session of the conference was well aware that a negative vote added to the possibility that the United States would leave the ILO. In effect, the United States had asked for a vote of confidence, and none was forthcoming. The Communist bloc appeared unconcerned about the prospect of a U.S. withdrawal; as for the Arabs, the fight against

Israel counted for more than any action the United States might take with respect to the ILO. The votes of the less developed countries, the so-called Group of 77, are less understandable. Perhaps they feared alienating the Arabs, while at the same time they resented U.S. economic power. Also, the proposed New International Economic Order was in the wind at that time.

Although Western Europe supported the United States, it did so without any great enthusiasm. Apart from a few delegates who made sentimental pro-U.S. speeches—notably the British worker and Dutch employer delegates—the Western Europeans maintained a low profile. They were clearly unhappy at U.S. insistence on keeping alive an issue that they had resolved for themselves more than a decade earlier. The United States was to them a kind of Don Quixote, tilting at the windmills of freedom of association and forced labor in the Soviet Union, with predictable results. The conventional wisdom in the corridors of the conference building in Geneva held that the United States seemed unaware that the world had changed and that, principles or no principles, international organizations must change with it.

Some of the delegates who refused to support the report may have believed that the U.S. threat was a bluff and that a compromise would be worked out, as had been done in the past. But there was nothing in the behavior of the U.S. delegates to the conference that would have sustained this belief. Despite the negotiations that ensued, the die was cast on June 20, 1977, and no one should have expected a different result. One more controversial issue remained, that of disregard of due process, but its outcome was clearly forecast by the final resolution of the double standard problem.

Disregard of Due Process

The U.S. letter of withdrawal from the ILO defined "disregard of due process" in the following manner:

> The ILO once had an enviable record of objectivity and concern for due process in its examination of alleged violations of basic human rights by its member states. The Constitution of the ILO provides for procedures to handle representations and complaints that a member state is not observing a convention which

it has ratified. Further, it was the ILO which first established fact-finding and conciliation machinery to respond to allegations of trade union rights. In recent years, however, sessions of the ILO Conference increasingly have adopted resolutions condemning particular member states which happen to be the political target of the moment, in utter disregard of the established procedures and machinery. The trend is accelerating, and it is gravely damaging the ILO and its capacity to pursue its objectives in the human rights fields.[91]

The best way to elucidate this issue is through an examination of some critical cases in which normal ILO procedures were not followed.

South Africa

Perhaps the first occasion in recent years on which the regular procedures of the ILO were seriously challenged involved South Africa.[92] The 1961 conference had, on the initiative of the Nigerian government, adopted a resolution calling upon South Africa to withdraw from the ILO because of its apartheid policies. The U.S. and Western European governments were in favor of that portion of the resolution which condemned apartheid, but they opposed putting pressure on South Africa to leave the ILO, since it was constitutionally entitled to ILO membership and because they believed that it might be easier to influence South Africa if it remained a member. The U.S. worker representative, however, supported the resolution in full, and it was subsequently adopted.[93] The South African government simply brushed the resolution aside.

At the 1962 conference, the director-general was asked to include in his annual report to the conference information regarding action taken on previous conference resolutions. The target of this demand was the South African resolution.

The conference the next year, 1963, turned out to be one of the most disorderly in the history of the ILO, and the focus of the storm was South Africa. Nigeria's minister of labor was elected president of the conference, thus becoming the first African to hold that post. The South African employer delegate was scheduled to speak on the afternoon of June 12. The Nigerian

president failed to appear, and the vice-president of the conference, the Ukrainian government delegate, presided. When the
South African speaker arose, a point of order was made, asking
for a legal opinion on his right to speak. After the ILO's legal
counsel had confirmed the right of the South African delegate to
speak, a broadside of speeches condemning apartheid followed.
Although they were clearly out of order, the speeches were permitted by the presiding officer. The meeting adjourned in disarray.

Before the next sitting convened, the Nigerian president declared himself unwilling to preside if a South African were permitted to speak. Therefore, the conference officers decided that
the U.S. labor delegate, Rudolph Faupl, who was the worker
vice-president of the conference, should preside. Faupl declared
that he had no choice "but to rule that Mr. Hamilton [the South
African employer delegate], as an unchallenged delegate duly
accredited to this Conference, has a right to be heard by those
who wish to hear him."[94] A demonstration ensued,[95] and the African, Arab, and Communist representatives all departed. To
prevent the conference from breaking down completely, Director-General Morse tried to bring the African bloc back through
a resolution calling upon the United Nations to address the problem of apartheid. He was told that the Africans would not return
if the South Africans were present; "Morse thereupon met the
South African adviser, Oxley, and advised, on a confidential basis, the South African delegate to withdraw from the Conference.
Oxley said he would give his reply after consulting Pretoria, but
the reply received that night was that South Africa would not
withdraw."[96]

After several days of negotiation, the conference resumed
with the Ukrainian vice-president in the chair. The director-general was to be recognized so that he could explain the results of
attempts at mediation. Instead, the Nigerian president was given
the floor, and he proceeded to denounce South Africa and Faupl,
and also the ILO for its failure to act. Morse then rose to explain
why it was impossible to accede to the African request without
violating the ILO constitution. "Any breach of this constitutional
law would open the way for arbitrary, vicious rule which today

may be turned against one party but tomorrow will be turned against another party."[97]

The debate continued for several days. Beginning on June 20, members of the Soviet bloc attempted to halt the work of the conference by making one motion after another, but without success. Faupl attacked the Soviet tactics in the following manner: "It is not only a question of South Africa; it is a question of human rights in other parts of the world. . . . Millions of people behind the 'wall of shame' are being suppressed by those who claim that they are bringing a new type of democracy to the I.L.O. If this democracy is so successful, why do they have to have a wall? A system which wants to conquer the world should not have to shut itself up in brick walls."[98] After settling some problems having to do with adoption of the budget because of the lack of a quorum, the conference finally resumed its routine business and adjourned.

Even though constitutional niceties were preserved in the end, the breakdown of orderly procedures at the 1963 conference was a serious blow to the ILO. What happened after that did not improve matters. At the Governing Body meeting held immediately after the conference, the director-general proposed that South Africa be excluded from all meetings convened by the Governing Body. "Morse was fully alive to the danger inherent in tampering with the principle of universality by excluding any Member State from the Organization. However, this step had to be taken with regard to South Africa to avoid political trouble in the long run."[99] The workers' group proposed a constitutional amendment to allow the expulsion of South Africa, while the employers favored a broader amendment permitting the expulsion of all states that violated human rights. It was decided to bar South Africa from all ILO meetings except the conference and to send a tripartite delegation to meet with the secretary-general of the United Nations to find out if South Africa could be expelled legally from that organization.[100] At that meeting, the secretary-general pointed out that no government had proposed the expulsion of South Africa from the United Nations and that even if such a course of action were to be proposed its chances of success were minimal.[101]

At the first 1964 session of the Governing Body the following proposal was made: that the ILO adopt a declaration calling upon South Africa to abolish apartheid; that the ILO adopt a constitutional amendment enabling it to expel or suspend a country against which similar action had been taken by the United Nations; and that the ILO adopt a second constitutional amendment allowing the conference to suspend from participation in any of its activities a country found by the United Nations to engage in racial discrimination. Some delegates felt this response was too weak; they proposed that the constitution be changed to permit the ILO to take appropriate action against South Africa whether or not the United Nations acted. But the U.S. government, among others, felt that this was a political matter and that the United Nations should take the lead. U.S. delegates pointed out that the ILO constitution "had worked well in the past and constituted a safeguard thanks to which the Organization's technical work . . . could proceed unhindered by the intrusion of disruptive political problems."[102] With the support of the United States and others, the initial recommendation was eventually accepted.

After it was made clear to South Africa that the credentials of its delegates to the 1964 conference would be challenged, and probably with success, it resigned from the ILO, without the required two years' notice. South Africa's letter of withdrawal pointed out that it was being asked to eliminate apartheid on the basis of conventions it had not ratified; that countries which *had* ratified the conventions, and were not honoring them, had not been subject to the same type of action now being used against South Africa; and that the ILO action constituted interference in the internal affairs of a sovereign state.[103]

The director-general responded that there had been "scrupulous respect for due process of law in all actions taken to deal with the problem" in this case. It is unlikely, however, that an American court of law would have ruled that the combination of acts taken by the ILO constituted due process under the ILO's own constitution. The ILO Office had naturally been anxious to get rid of this disruptive issue, and universality had given way to political expediency. Meritorious though the case may have been, a precedent had been established whereby a state could be driven out of the ILO through political pressures exercised outside the normal complaint channels. It should be noted that the AFL-CIO delegate made no objection to the procedures.

Notwithstanding South Africa's withdrawal, the 1964 conference acted upon the Governing Body recommendation. In the Resolutions Committee, the Soviet Union attempted to strengthen the proposed resolution by inserting a clause stating that apartheid in South Africa "constituted a serious threat to international security." This was opposed by the United States and other Western governments on the ground that it involved the ILO in a political area in which it had no competence. Compromise language was adopted to the effect that apartheid "is seriously disturbing international peace and security."[104] The conference adopted the resolution by acclamation.

A conference committee considering the two proposed constitutional amendments quickly reached agreement on the first, enabling the ILO to expel a country that had been voted out of the United Nations. But on the second proposed amendment, which would, in effect, have made it possible to deprive a country of representation at the conference, there was a serious division of opinion. The United States opposed this amendment again on the ground that political issues should be left to the United Nations. Nevertheless, the conference committee approved both proposed amendments, and they were presented to the plenary session and adopted, the controversial second amendment barely obtaining the requisite two-thirds majority. The U.S. delegation was split; the worker delegate voted in the affirmative, the government delegates in the negative, while the employer abstained.

This entire controversy was mere political shadow-boxing; in order to become effective, the amendments had to be approved by at least six of the ten permanent members of the Governing Body. Six of those states opposed the controversial second amendment and had voted against it, and in the end, neither amendment was ever approved.

Portugal

A similar, but less explosive, issue involved Portugal, which at the time was under the Salazar dictatorship. It began in February 1961, when Ghana filed a complaint alleging that Portugal was violating its obligations under the forced labor convention in its African colonies. The Portuguese government agreed to the establishment of a commission of inquiry, marking the first time this procedure has been employed.[105] The commission made an extensive investigation, including visits to Angola and Mozambique, where it was given complete freedom to see what it wanted.[106] While it concluded that certain questionable practices existed, the committee report essentially rejected the charges. Both Ghana and Portugal accepted this decision, and the U.S. representative on the Governing Body declared: "The ILO had once again demonstrated its effectiveness and the service it could render to the international community by using machinery based on due process of law which the other international organizations did not possess and by redressing wrongs they had as yet been powerless to rectify."[107]

Although the matter appeared to have been resolved, it was raised again at the 1965 conference by the African bloc, with strong support from the Communists. Egypt filed a resolution condemning Portugal for using forced labor in Africa, and this became an excuse for a general attack on colonialism, not an ILO concern. The Western nations argued that, while forced labor should be condemned wherever it was found, the ILO commission had failed to sustain the specific charges against Portugal.

The Committee on Resolutions reported out a resolution "condemning the Government of Portugal on the Grounds of the Forced Labor Policy Practiced by the Said Government."[108] In opposition, the employer group maintained that Portugal had made great efforts to eliminate all forms of forced labor and that, even if some vestiges remained, it was unreasonable to conclude that this was the result of a deliberate policy. The workers' group supported the resolution, however, and it was adopted. The U.S. worker delegate favored the resolution, despite its irregularities, in an apparent gesture of solidarity with the workers' group. The employer abstained, while the U.S. government cast two of the eleven votes against the resolution.[109]

Passage of this resolution was a clear violation of due process. Portugal had been the first country—and one of the last—to submit to a searching examination by an ILO commission of inquiry. It had cooperated fully with the commission, and while it had not received a clean bill of health, it had made a commitment to eliminate some remaining practices that the commission found objectionable. This degree of compliance with the ILO's enforcement of standards was unusual, particularly in human rights cases.

A similar resolution against Portugal, one which also clearly violated due process, was adopted by the 1972 conference, again with the support of the U.S. worker representatives.[110] This resolution served as a model for a subsequent one that condemned Israel.

A later reference to the Portuguese incident was included in a U.S. government study in 1976:

> The US Government was consistent in refusing to accept this outright disregard of ILO procedures. The US workers were prepared to condone it, presumably for political reasons. Whatever the provocation, departure from legality contributed to a weakening of the ILO fibre. A recent evaluation concluded that this action, which reflected the political frustrations of the Africans over their demand that independence be granted to the Portuguese Territories, did more damage to the ILO and its objectivity and respect for due process than to Portugal.[111]

Chile

Soon after the overthrow of the Allende government, Chile became a target of attack in the ILO, as elsewhere. The Governing Body Committee on Freedom of Association had taken cognizance of the situation as a result of complaints filed by a number of trade union organizations, but indicated in an interim report to the Governing Body in November 1973 that it had not yet been able to ascertain sufficient facts to reach any conclusions regarding Chilean compliance with freedom of association.

Debate in the Governing Body focused on the question of whether a fact-finding and conciliation commission should be set in motion. This could be carried out only with the consent of the Chilean government, since Chile had not yet ratified the relevant conventions. The workers' group favored immediate action, a position supported by the U.S. workers. Other Western governments and employers were more cautious, preferring to give the Committee on Freedom of Association time to establish the facts. A representative of the Office pointed out that, in the past, "the Committee on Freedom of Association normally examined the merits of referral to the Commission and made its recommendations to the Governing Body."[112] The Governing Body decided to go ahead and determine whether Chile would accept a fact-finding commission. While this was an unusual action, it conformed to constitutional procedures.

A full-scale debate on the issue took place at the next meeting of the Governing Body. The Committee on Freedom of Association had made some inquiries, and the chairman of the workers' group stated that "although the Chilean Government had given answers that were precise, brief and to the point to the questions put to it by the Committee on Freedom of Association, there were nevertheless some gaps in the information provided."[113] Soviet representatives called for immediate action in the form of demands on the Chilean government, but the U.S. government and employer delegates advised the Governing Body to adhere to its regular procedures. The decision was made to follow the recommendations of the Committee on Freedom of Association: that the Chilean government be asked to agree to having the matter submitted to a fact-finding commission and that meanwhile the director-general make preparations for such a submission.[114]

The Chilean government agreed in May 1974 to the establishment of a fact-finding commission. Nevertheless, the 1974 Conference Committee on Resolutions adopted a resolution calling upon the Chilean authorities to "close down the concentration camps in which workers, militant workers, and trade union leaders are interred for political reasons" and also "to put an end to the torturing of trade union militants and leaders and punish those who were responsible for such inhuman activities." The committee further instructed the Governing Body to set up a commission of inquiry to study possible violations of the ILO conventions on hours of work and job discrimination, conventions that Chile had ratified. [115]

It is difficult to find in the history of the ILO a conference resolution that made such specific judgments in the absence of a prior investigation. The resolution against Chile was supported by the Communist bloc and virtually all of the worker members of the committee, including the U.S. worker representative. It was also backed by the governments of the Scandinavian countries, Belgium, Italy, the Netherlands, and Britain. The U.S. government abstained, [116] along with the governments of Germany, Canada, France, and Japan. Most of the remaining abstentions came from employer delegates. [117] Except for the Chilean representative himself, no votes were cast against the resolution. In the plenary debate that followed, the U.S. delegate stated: "We have serious reservations about making pronouncements concerning violations which are to be investigated by a Commission of Inquiry at some later date. In our view, the assertive language in the resolution unnecessarily prejudices the situations which the Commission of Inquiry is supposed to investigate. . . . Therefore, despite the positive elements in the resolution, the United States Government delegates regret that they must abstain in the voting on this resolution." [118]

This action was a clear violation of due process. The 1975 U.S. letter of withdrawal might have been more persuasive had the AFL-CIO joined with the U.S. government in abstaining on the 1974 Chilean resolution.

The Governing Body decided to entrust the fact-finding commission, which had already been established, with the additional inquiries mandated by the conference. The commission proceeded to hold hearings, although it was criticized for its dilatory pace by the Soviet Union, which apparently believed that it was the ILO's responsibility to solve all of Chile's internal political problems. [119] After spending three weeks in Chile (November–December 1974), the committee's interim report was submitted at the Governing Body's meeting in March 1975.

The report was sharply attacked by the Communist members, as well as by non-Communist worker members, for being too mild—even though no conclusions had been reached by the committee regarding violation of conventions. The employers, on the other hand, found the interim report satisfactory. The U.S. government member said he "hoped that the concerns expressed by the representatives of the Governments of Bulgaria, the USSR, Poland, and the Ukraine over the delay in the Commission's work was an encouraging sign of their solicitude for trade union rights."[120]

The final report of the fact-finding commission was submitted to the Governing Body in May 1975 and was warmly received by those who had earlier been critical of the commission's lack of progress. A resolution was adopted calling upon Chile to implement the recommendations of the commission; it also recommended that the report be widely publicized. On the motion of the employers, the resolution was amended to include a paragraph calling attention to the fact that Chile had responded favorably to the establishment of a fact-finding commission. A second proposed amendment, again requested by the employers, read as follows: "To express the hope that ILO Member States will when similar cases occur in future accept the requests and recommendations made by the Governing Body concerning human and trade union rights, in the same way as the Government of Chile is being called upon to do on this occasion."[121] A Soviet member objected to the reference to "similar cases." In his mind, that wording suggested "the violent overthrow of lawful governments and the rape of democracy in other countries besides Chile." The U.S. delegate found the clause reasonable as an expression of confidence in ILO procedures. But the employers withdrew their second amendment, leaving only the U.S. and Canadian governments in support of it.[122]

The debate continued at the 1975 conference, where the employers continued to express their unhappiness during a debate on a workers' resolution.[123] Acrimonious words were exchanged at the next meeting of the Governing Body, with the Communist bloc attacking Chile, and Chilean representatives, in turn, defending their government.[124] The Communists claimed that matters were getting worse and that the Chilean government was paying no attention to the ILO recommendations; the Chilean government insisted that improvements had been made in the situation.[125] A 1977 report to the Governing Body did indicate progress. The Soviets, however, asserted that "the recent release of trade unionists and the statements about the closing of camps was [sic] mere window dressing, since there were 6,000 political prisoners still in concentration camps." They demanded that the ILO help promote a complete boycott of the Chilean regime.[126] The Soviets also criticized the forced exile of Chileans, to which an employer delegate replied: "The Employers fully supported the Committee's views on forced exile. This applied not only to Chile, but to any country which imposed exile on its citizens. Mention had, for instance, been made of the case of Luis Corvalán [the Chilean Communist leader], but the country which in exchange for Corvalán had imposed exile on another individual should also not be forgotten."[127]

And thus the matter rested as the United States made its departure from the ILO. During this entire affair, U.S. worker delegates had stood alongside the other worker delegates in the ILO, despite all the legal irregularities that were involved in that stance. The U.S. government took a more consistent position in opposing deviations from constitutional procedures, but in general, it had maintained a low profile. The burden of upholding due process was borne by the employer group. Whatever their motives, they emerged as the only group prepared to fight for the principle, even while many of them expressed strong dislike over events in Chile.

Israel

Whereas the U.S. workers were prepared to accept political pressure against Chile, which had become a pariah for the Communists and could not be defended by non-Communists without embarrassment, Israel was another matter entirely. For the five years prior to the U.S. withdrawal, the Israeli case was a matter of great concern to the United States, and it became a major factor in the decision to leave the ILO, even though the formal letter of withdrawal did not specifically mention Israel.[128]

A full-fledged attack was launched against Israel at the 1973 conference by means of a resolution introduced by the Iraqi employer delegate. This resolution condemned Israel for racial discrimination, violation of trade union freedoms, and impairment of the basic human rights of the Arab peoples. It requested the Governing Body to set up a committee empowered to make on-the-spot investigations of these transgressions, and it asked the director-general to take immediate steps to put an end to them.[129] This was despite the fact that Israel had offered to receive an impartial ILO investigator to look into earlier charges, and further, that the Committee of Experts had found no Israeli violations of the freedom of association conventions.

In the committee debates, the Arab and Communist representatives repeated these broad charges against Israel. Unlike Chile, however, Israel had some staunch defenders. The AFL-CIO had long enjoyed close relationships with Histadrut, the Israeli trade union federation, and its ILO representative declared that adoption of the resolution "would bring nothing but shame on the ILO." The U.S. government member "could not agree with a proposal to condemn racial discrimination and violation of trade union freedoms without having ascertained the facts of the situation and prior to the establishment of a committee of investigation." The U.S. employer delegate observed that "if the ILO was serious in its function of mediation it could not begin by issuing a harsh public rebuke before ever initiating an inquiry."[130] The U.S. delegates repeatedly pointed out that the resolution against Israel dealt with matters outside the ILO's jurisdiction.

Debate in the conference plenary session revolved around the same points. The U.S. worker delegate countered the Arab charges in an impassioned speech in defense of Israel. In his closing address to the conference, Director-General Jenks made a strong plea for adhering to due process: "For the Conference first to condemn and then to call for an inquiry, the terms of reference of which would be to confirm such condemnation, would be to offend the principle of due process on which all our work relating to the implementation of Conventions rests."[131] By the time the resolution was to be voted on, the conference was almost at an end, and many delegations had left. The resolution was therefore defeated for lack of a quorum, and the conference ended in disarray, having engendered only bitterness.

A similar resolution was adopted by the Resolutions Committee once again the following year, after an attempt by the Western countries to substitute a more neutral draft had been held nonreceivable. This led to a scathing attack in the plenary session by the U.S. worker; he called the action of the Resolutions Committee the replacement of law by anarchy. Nevertheless, the resolution was adopted by a large majority, the Communist and Arab blocs having secured the support of the less developed nations, with the Western bloc united but in a minority.[132]

The Governing Body was the next arena of combat. When it met half a year after the conclusion of the 1974 conference, the director-general was strongly attacked by the Arabs and Soviets for having failed to take immediate action. It was proposed that the director-general officially communicate the resolution to the Israeli authorities and that documentation of the charges be given wide dissemination. A compromise was worked out whereby the ILO was to provide "the widest dissemination of ILO documents concerning the exercise of civil liberties and trade union rights."[133]

Yet complaints against lack of action continued. The director-general was accused, among other things, of failing to circulate relevant ILO documents to the Palestine Liberation Organization and of being dilatory about ILO obligations toward Arab workers.[134] The Office had been doing precisely what it had been directed to do: communicating with the government of Israel, collecting information, and disseminating documents.

A preliminary Office report presented to the Governing Body in March 1976 was received with the same impatience by the Communist and Arab blocs. In previous Governing Body meetings, the U.S. government representative had spoken only briefly on the issue, if at all. At this meeting, he warned the ILO that the United States was serious in its threat to withdraw:

> [He] considered it a most serious matter that the Governing Body was discussing a particular question now before it . . . because it had originated in a violation of due process. . . . The

present question—unfortunately—arose out of the kind of impatience often manifested where important political problems of vital concern to particular regions also had international implications. . . . The comments made by previous speakers, particularly regarding the slowness of the procedure, reflected the practical implications for the Governing Body, and for the Director-General of having to follow up a resolution which had violated due process and bypassed existing machinery.[135]

An even clearer warning was given by the U.S. worker representative:

If the attempts to force the Governing Body to issue a condemnation without due process persisted, the United States trade union movement would not long be able to stay in the Organization. . . . If the Governing Body were to persist in the course advocated by some members in violation of due process, the crisis would not be in the Middle East but in the ILO.[136]

The U.S. position received *pro forma* support from the Western European governments. The Communist view was well summarized by the representative of the government of Yugoslavia when he declared that he "could not accept the reasoning according to which a resolution could not be properly adopted until an investigation had taken place"[137] (though the resolution was one of condemnation).

For the United States, the final act in this drama took place in the spring of 1977. The director-general had engaged T. Opsahl, professor of international law at the University of Oslo and a leading figure in the human rights movement, to work with the Office in its study of the problem. In June 1976, after arrangements were under way for Opsahl to visit Israel for the purpose of making an on-the-spot investigation, the Office was informed by a representative of the Arab nations that such a visit could not be approved unless they (including the PLO) were notified in advance and gave their consent.[138] The motives of the Arab countries were not clear, but it is highly likely that they suspected that any investigation into the labor conditions of Arab workers in Israel would have found those conditions to be satisfactory. The director-general, concluding there was nothing more he could do, asked the Governing Body at its March 1977 meeting to accept his documented report on the factual situation as final.

The Arab governments apparently changed their minds, however, and asked the director-general to resume his efforts. This move was opposed by the Western members of the Governing Body, who argued that any further pursuit of the matter should be made through the normal constitutional channels of the ILO. The Governing Body then decided to relieve the director-general of any additional responsibility for pursuing the question. [139]

The 1974 conference resolution had asked that the ILO determine whether Israel was fulfilling its obligations under Convention No. 111, which covered employment discrimination, with particular reference to the occupied territories. Israel had submitted a long statistical report to the ILO dealing with this question. When the matter arose in the 1977 meeting of the Conference Committee on the Application of Standards, the Soviets argued that since Israel had no administrative rights in the occupied territories, the committee had no jurisdiction. [140] Although this position was in direct contradiction to the 1974 conference resolution, the Arabs supported the Soviet motion. When the committee voted to continue its deliberations on the case, the Arabs withdrew from further participation. [141] The committee then decided that the Israeli document constituted a sufficient reply and should be referred to the Committee of Experts for examination.

In the plenary debate, the Israeli delegate complained that "in 1974 Israel was condemned for violating Convention No. 111. Now that the question of the application of Convention No. 111 was to be handled by objective experts, we are being told that we may not apply that Convention." [142] His argument fell on deaf ears, however, and the Arabs voted with the Communists to help defeat the committee report.

Article 17 of the Standing Orders

In a final effort to pacify the United States on the due process issue, the Western nations attempted in 1977 to modify the clause in the annual conference procedural rules, Article 17, wherein an open-ended possibility for introducing resolutions was provided. The Governing Body considered the problem at length in March 1977.

What emerged was a detailed proposal to amend the standing orders of the conference so that resolutions condemning or criticizing a member state would be screened by the Committee of Experts, with appeal possible to the officers of the conference. If the charge made in the resolution was determined to be unfounded, the resolution could not be considered by the conference.[143]

The purpose of this amendment was to prevent circumvention of the constitutional procedures of inquiry through the device of conference resolutions, as had been done in the case of Israel. Some worker members of the Governing Body were uneasy about the possibility of cutting off quick action by the conference, but the U.S. worker member argued that "its sole aim was to ensure that the Organization fully respected law and due process, even if that entailed certain delays."[144] The Soviet government member termed the recommendations pernicious, "since they sought to curtail the prerogative of the ILO's constituents to submit resolutions in defense of workers' rights."[145] Other Communist speakers argued that it was impossible to separate "political" from "technical" matters and that all resolutions should be submitted to the conference on an equal footing. Despite these objections the Governing Body decided to forward the proposal to the conference.

This action was welcomed by the Western bloc as a harbinger of success, for it provided the United States with some evidence that the ILO might at last satisfy one of its major demands. But trouble soon developed at the 1977 conference. The opponents of the amendment wanted it to be referred to the Conference Committee on Structural Change, which had been considering far-reaching constitutional changes.[146] Its proponents wanted the amendment referred to the Standing Orders Committee, where they believed they had a majority. The U.S. government delegate pointed out that "the only procedure which has been followed through the years had been that the standing orders committee, the very committee created to consider changes of the

Standing Orders, consider the subject."[147] The U.S. worker delegate made a strong plea for amending the procedures:

> I think it is time that some people began to understand what a democratic procedure is. . . . We must have due process, we must have adherence to a democratic procedure . . . and to help to make this a functioning organization, not just a talk fest, not just a Conference where people can talk, talk, talk, and there is no implementation. . . . The resolutions procedure . . . has to be changed so that we will not get resolutions that stop the functioning of this Organization, that prevent us from dealing with the real technical problems and with the problems that affect the masses of the workers and the people of this world.[148]

Despite these strong statements, the conference voted to send the amendment to the Committee on Structure, which refused to give it priority and linked it to basic structural changes desired by the anti-Western forces. A U.S. government delegate stated that the committee report constituted "a determination that there would be no substantive consideration of Article 17 at this Conference, that it be wrapped up with intractable, difficult, important problems about which there was no question of any solution and no expectation of any solutions in this Conference. It was made a bargaining counter with respect to other matters."[149]

Coming on the heels of U.S. defeat on the "double standard" issue, this action made U.S. withdrawal a virtual certainty. To the present writer, who was at the conference, there is very little doubt that the Communist bloc, at least, welcomed the event and did all they could to bring it about. Whether the less developed countries would have taken so intransigent a line had they accurately evaluated the credibility of the U.S. threat is not at all certain. There were possibilities of compromise, and efforts were going on constantly behind the scenes to prevent an overt confrontation, but they were rejected. Immediate action was the watchword, regardless of the innocence or guilt of the accused.

Sadly, the denigration of ILO procedures and the emergence of a kangaroo court as a substitute achieved nothing. In none of the cases did any observable progress flow from ILO action. Apartheid continues in South Africa, the lot of Chilean trade unions has not greatly improved, and Israel still occupies some

Arab territory. Only in Portugal has there been any change, and that had nothing to do with the ILO.

The Increasing Politicization of the ILO

The final reason given for withdrawal in the 1975 U.S. letter was as follows:

> In recent years the ILO has become increasingly and excessively involved in political issues which are quite beyond the competence and mandate of the Organization. The ILO does have a legitimate and necessary interest in certain issues with political ramifications. It has major responsibility, for example, for international action to promote and protect fundamental human rights, particularly in respect to freedom of association, trade union rights and the abolition of forced labor. But international politics is not the main business of the ILO. Questions involving relations between states and proclamations of economic principles should be left to the United Nations and other international agencies where their consideration is more relevant to those organizations' responsibilities.[150]

This point in the U.S. letter of intent to withdraw is less precise than the others and is therefore more difficult to document. Nevertheless, a few examples cited in various U.S. government documents serve to illustrate the nature of the complaint.

The Palestine Liberation Organization (PLO)

The ILO was the last of the U.N. agencies to grant observer status to the PLO. The PLO had requested the right to participate as an observer at all ILO conferences and meetings in May 1974. The first response from the ILO came in the form of a statement by the 1974 conference president, who noted that the officers of the conference had discussed the issue and decided that, since the standing orders of the conference made no provision for invitations to liberation movements, the matter would have to be handled by the Governing Body.[151] At the Governing Body meeting in November 1974, a proposal was made to draft certain changes in the standing orders so that a decision could be taken at the next meeting. Although the Communist and Arab delegates wanted immediate action, the decision was delayed.

Shortly after the Governing Body meeting, the U.N. General Assembly invited the PLO to participate in its work as an observer, and indicated that the PLO was entitled to participate in all international conferences convened by the United Nations. While this decision was not binding on the ILO, it provided a strong argument for PLO supporters. In March 1975, the Governing Body agreed that several different changes in the standing orders should be submitted to the next conference and also that the PLO should be represented there, provided observer status was granted.

Soon after the 1975 conference opened, the Committee on Standing Orders recommended procedural amendments that would permit liberation movements recognized by the Organization of African Unity and the League of Arab States to participate in the work of the conference. In the ensuing plenary debate, seven workers' delegates, including the U.S. worker, offered an amendment to the proposed changes in which all references to the OAU and the Arab League were deleted. A proviso was added stating that attendance at future conferences would be conditioned upon assurance that "the liberation movement in question fully recognized the principle of the ILO and its Constitution and the rights of all member States to continue in existence and participate in the work of the Organization."[152] This restriction would have barred the PLO, which refused to recognize Israel's right to exist. The U.S. labor representative launched a fierce attack on the PLO, accusing it of "despicable terrorist murders." He was supported by a U.S. government delegate and the U.S. employer delegate, who referred to the recent hijacking of American planes and the murder of American diplomats. The U.S. tripartite delegation was firmly united on this issue.

Nevertheless, the PLO advocates won by a lopsided margin. The Western workers' amendment failed, by a vote of 74 to 0, with 305 abstentions, for lack of a quorum. The governments of France, Italy, and Britain all abstained. The only Western delegates who voted solidly with the United States were those of Germany, Austria, Canada, New Zealand, the Netherlands, and the Scandinavian nations.[153] After the vote, the U.S. labor delegation announced that it was withdrawing from all further participation in the conference, whereupon the U.S. government delegation left the hall temporarily. The PLO representative was immediately ushered into the meeting hall and invited to address the conference. He did so by launching a strong political attack on Israel.[154]

The PLO issue arose once more in 1976 in connection with the World Employment Conference.[155] A PLO request for observer status at that meeting was opposed strongly by U.S. representatives in the ILO Governing Body. Despite threats of disruption if the PLO were not admitted, the Governing Body voted, 24 to 23, with one abstention, not to accredit the PLO.

When the vote was appealed, the ILO legal adviser held that it could not be challenged. But a week later, according to the *New York Times*, "after interminable wrangles, in which the ILO parliamentarians were called on for dozens of constitutional interpretations, the Palestinians were in, not out, and the American victory had slipped away on a flood tide of legalisms. The same parliamentarians who had originally declared that the first vote was not subject to either review or appeal had no difficulty in deciding that 'new elements' in the situation justified bending the rules to authorize a new ballot."[156] The Arabs, having succeeded in rounding up absent African delegates, won the new vote for the PLO, 31 to 23.

PLO admission to ILO meetings thus became a major factor in the U.S. decision to withdraw. While the U.S. government was apparently prepared to tolerate the PLO presence in the ILO, as it had in other international organizations, the AFL-CIO was not. President George Meany, in his concurrence with the U.S. letter of intent to withdraw, later referred to the series of crises leading to that decision: "Those developments reached a culmination at the last annual Conference of the ILO in June [1975], with the admission of the PLO—the leading symbol and practitioner of terrorism and race hatred in the world today—as an official observer and participant in the affairs of the Organization."[157]

Other Aspects of Politicization

A U.S. Department of Labor ILO position paper prepared in 1975 included the following statement, under the head of "irrelevant political attacks":

> There is a continuing failure in the [ILO] Conference to apply the "rule of relevancy" to the debate on the Director-General's Report which is used as a vehicle for polemics and political attacks on member states of the Organization on issues irrelevant to the competency or work of the ILO. While the United States was the principal subject of such an attack at the time of the last U.S./ILO crisis, the level of these attacks has been reduced substantially since our departure from Vietnam and since the immediate right of reply was at last recognized [as a result of U.S. pressure on Director-General Jenks and the withholding of U.S. payments to the ILO]. However, other countries experience such attacks, which are disruptive and heighten the political atmosphere and the politicization of the Conference.[158]

As this statement makes clear, the United States was under constant attack on purely political grounds during the Vietnam War. At the 1967 ILO Conference, for example, twenty-five speakers from Communist countries mentioned the United States by name during the debate on the director-general's report. This debate extends throughout the conference whenever committees are not reporting, and it ordinarily provides a forum in which visiting dignitaries can extol the virtues and accomplishments of their countries. In addition, five African nations criticized the United States without specifically mentioning it by name. Attempts were made by members of the U.S. delegation, either on points of order or in their own speeches, to answer these criticisms.[159] In 1968, twenty-eight interventions were made against U.S. policy in Vietnam, twenty-nine against Israel, and twenty-nine against Portugal, Rhodesia, and South Africa. These attacks did not go unanswered, although U.S. government policy was generally one of not counterattacking. This low profile line was not followed by the U.S. labor representative, who replied that the United States sought to maintain Vietnam's independence, in sharp contrast to an unnamed member state "which recently sent its troops into a neighboring country to staunch a political transformation. In that member state . . . trade unions were a subservient arm to the Communist Party. Slave labor camps existed in that country, thousands have been imprisoned there.[160]

Perhaps because of Soviet sensitivity about Czechoslovakia, the anti-American political rhetoric in 1969 was comparatively mild, but it picked up again later. The U.S. government delegate took the floor in 1971 to defend U.S. action in Vietnam. His speech, which admittedly involved "extraneous political issues," came in response to repeated attacks by Communist speakers.[161] In 1972 the United States adopted a new policy of immediate response on points of order. When a Cuban delegate raised the subject of Vietnam that year, the United States immediately objected to his "irrelevant and scurrilous" remarks. When the Cuban persisted, he was ordered by the president to sit down, a rare event in ILO meetings.[162] Thereafter, such direct political attacks trailed off.

However, spokesmen for the Soviet and Arab blocs continued with unabated diatribes against their public enemy list of the year, without regard to ILO competence on the issues. Their tactics were designed to annoy and enrage; speaker after speaker would rise to repeat the same themes. Government, labor, and management delegates from the Soviet Union, the Ukraine, Byelorussia, Eastern European satellites, Cuba, Algeria, and other adherents of the bloc would simply repeat identical phrases as if by rote. Those among the U.S. delegates who were professional diplomats could shrug off these attacks, since they were inured to them by experience in other forums. But labor and employer delegates, not accustomed to routine slander, reacted sharply and virtually forced the government representatives to take harder lines than they would have otherwise done. The perception that one got from attendance at these ILO conferences was that the U.S. government was a reluctant dragon, being pulled along by incensed labor and employer representatives.

One additional incident at the 1977 conference, on the eve of the U.S. decision against remaining in the ILO, is worth citing. The workers' group at the conference had nominated Irving

Brown, the AFL-CIO European representative and head of its
ILO delegation, as vice-president of the conference (there are
three vice-presidents, on a tripartite basis). Notwithstanding the
fact that the government group had nominated a Polish delegate
as its vice-president, the Soviet worker representative took the
floor to denounce the Brown candidacy on the grounds that the
AFL-CIO was responsible for the crisis in the ILO and that there
was no logic in electing someone from a country that had indicated its intention to leave the ILO a few months later. He also
questioned the voting in the workers' group because no record
vote had been taken.

Brown was elected to the post, but this objection, coming at
an early stage of the conference, was a clear signal that the Soviets and the left-wing Arabs, at least, were not only not prepared to make any concessions to the United States, but were
doing what they could to exacerbate the situation and make it
difficult to reach compromises. Nothing could have been better
calculated to harden the attitude of the AFL-CIO than this open
attack upon one of its leading functionaries by representatives of
Communist trade unions.

These, then, were the substantive issues specified by the United
States in its notice of withdrawal. Far from being dreamed up at
the last moment to justify a political decision, they represented
long-standing complaints of considerable merit. The U.S. delegation was not entirely consistent in adhering to the principles.
The labor unions in particular were prepared on occasion to con-
done departure from regular procedures under the impact of political pressures. Nevertheless, it would be impossible to point
to any other country with an ILO voting record equal to that of
the United States on matters relating to the basic integrity of the
organization. One is hard put to quarrel with most of the points
raised by the United States. An international organization must
rely on moral force; the very least it can do, therefore, is honor
its own constitution. Violation of due process, excursions into
areas that are *ultra vires*, failure to act against powerful nations
while smaller ones are being routinely condemned—these are
practices ill designed to provide the moral authority required to

make an international organization effective. The ILO has done some commendable work in technical assistance and in helping to improve labor standards throughout the world, but these accomplishments were inevitably compromised by the highly visible defaults that have been outlined. In this writer's view, the United States was fully justified in withdrawing from the ILO; and it is regrettable that other democratic nations failed to follow its lead.

Chapter 3

Structural and Operational Problems of the ILO

Apart from the formal charges brought by the United States against the ILO, a number of issues relating to the structure and operation of the ILO created dissension as well. Among these were the composition and authority of the Governing Body, the organization and procedure of the conference, and the operation of the Office. This chapter deals with these issues.

Composition of the Governing Body
States of "Chief Industrial Importance"

The original ILO constitution stated that the Governing Body should consist of twenty-four members, with twelve representing governments and six each acting on behalf of the workers' and employers' organizations. All were to be nominated by the separate groups of conference delegates, except that eight government representatives were to be appointed by "members of chief industrial importance." As the number of member nations grew, the size of the Governing Body increased. At the time of the U.S. withdrawal in 1977, there were fifty-six voting members, with the same tripartite distribution as before, but the number of nonelective seats had been raised to ten. In addition, there were eighteen nonvoting government members, and fourteen each from among employers and workers. The substantial decline in the proportion of nonelective seats might have satisfied the aspirations of the new members had it not been for Article 36 of the constitution, which required the concurrence of at least five of the ten nonelective members of the Governing Body to amend the constitution.

Great Britain and France have always held nonelective seats on the Governing Body, as have the United States and the Soviet Union during those periods when they were members. With some interruptions during and after World War II, Germany, Italy, and Japan have had permanent seats. India has held a seat since 1922, while China was awarded one after World War II. Canada has had a nonelective seat since 1937; Belgium and the Netherlands have alternated and shared one seat. Brazil lost its seat in 1954, when the Soviet Union reentered the ILO.[1]

The bloc of less developed nations—the Group of 77—came out strongly in recent years in favor of abolishing the nonelective seats. They argued that the very concept of nonelective seats was undemocratic. There was no logic, they claimed, in awarding a few governments such prerogatives when their own workers and employers did not enjoy them. Moreover, they took the position that the weighting system under which the permanent seats were allocated was inequitable and tended to favor rich countries.[2] They pointed out that no similar system existed within the executive bodies of other specialized U.N. agencies.

The United States consistently opposed any tampering with the concept of nonelective seats. As the U.S. government member of the Governing Body explained in 1976, "It seemed indispensable that the States which had the greatest responsibility toward the Organization because of the size of their active population (and for whose service the ILO had been created) and because of the financial support which they gave to its activities, should be represented on a continuing basis. There was nothing antidemocratic in this. The principles of universal suffrage could not be simply transposed from the level of individuals to the level of States."[3] The United States also argued that there were parallels among international agencies—the Security Council of the United Nations and the executive boards of the World Bank and the International Monetary Fund are cases in point—and that since the ten permanent seats were held by states that contributed about 75 percent of the ILO budget, "it was therefore normal to give them certain guarantees as regards their special interests arising out of this situation in the activities of the ILO."[4] Representatives of the Group of 77 replied that the United Nations has a unique political role that might justify the composition of the Security Council and that the Bank and the Fund were financial institutions in which it might be logical to give the donors of funds larger representation, but that none of this applied to the ILO.

Similar arguments were made with respect to the "veto" right inherent in Article 36 of the ILO constitution. The status quo was defended by most of the industrial nations, especially the United States. When a U.S. employer delegate pointed out that the states of chief industrial importance had never blocked an amendment to the constitution, spokesmen for the less developed nations replied that the constitutional provision was abnormal and that "there was no justification for those who paid more to have more rights than others."[5]

A working party on structure, which was established by the 1974 conference to explore these issues, was unable to resolve them prior to U.S. withdrawal. But the tide was running strongly against the United States. When meetings of the Working Party scheduled for the spring of 1977 were cancelled at the request of the U.S. government, some members of the Group of 77 were infuriated. The Committee on Structure, in its report to the 1977 conference, refused to consider changes in conference resolutions procedure that were advocated by the United States separately from these structural problems. The worker group indicated its readiness to accept changes in the veto rights of Article 36.[6]

Was the United States justified in holding fast to its negative position, or should it have been more flexible by agreeing to some amendments in exchange for other reforms it desired? While most Western European countries supported the U.S. position, some were unhappy at what they regarded as its excessive rigidity. It was highly likely, they felt, that the governments of the major industrial nations would be elected to the Governing Body under any system of selection. Moreover, it had become virtually impossible for six of the ten permanent members to stand in the way of a constitutional amendment, which required a two-thirds majority of the conference and ratification by two-thirds of the members of the ILO. Conceivably, a concession on the permanent seats and the veto right could have been exchanged for a reform in conference procedure. This hypothesis is strengthened by the fact that the 1977 Conference Committee on Structure tied the issues together. No evidence exists, however, that the possibility of a compromise was given any serious consideration by the U.S. government.

Size and Geographical Distribution of Governing Body Membership

A closely related issue involved the size of the Governing Body and the weight given to regional representation. The developing nations persistently demanded that the Governing Body be enlarged so that more of them could be given seats and that greater attention be paid to regional balance. In response to this pressure, the size of the Governing Body was increased by a constitutional amendment in 1972 to fifty-six members. The number of countries present at Governing Body meetings was also raised by the inclusion of nonvoting deputy membership. Still, the demand for more seats continued.

The United States opposed expansion of the Governing Body. In 1975, the U.S. worker delegate argued that "the size of the Governing Body should not be enlarged so as to render it ineffective."[7] The U.S. government sounded the same theme: "The Governing Body would become more unwieldy, less effective and more costly; continuity of representation would in no way be strengthened; the present system already afforded scope for ensuring continuity within the electoral process, provided that there was a genuine will to do so."[8] The United States was concerned that the Governing Body, which had always been more or less under the control of the Western nations, would be transformed into a replica of the conference, where each member country had the same vote. Nevertheless, the addition of new members from among the less developed countries gradually eroded Western control, culminating in the events that took place during the June 1976 meeting of the Governing Body. There, U.S. efforts to bar the PLO from the World Employment Conference were defeated by a vote of 31 to 23, suggesting that the non-Western nations could put together a comfortable majority on any highly political issue.

A closely allied question concerned the geographical distribution of seats. Table 3. shows the distribution as of March 1977, the year of the U.S. withdrawal. Western Europe had over 20 percent of the total number of seats, but if the Group of 77 and the Communist bloc voted together, they could command a two-thirds majority.

The less developed nations and the Communist nations have consistently urged the allocation of Governing Body seats along regional lines. Partly an attack on the nonelective principle, this also reflects a desire on the part of the smaller nations to share in the Governing Body membership on a rotational basis. The Scandinavian countries, for example, have urged that it was "just and urgent that the Nordic Governments, like other Members,

TABLE 3. Geographical Distribution of Voting Members of the ILO Governing Body, March 1977

	Govern-ment	Labor	Employ-ers	Total
Africa	5	2	2	9
Asia	3	2	2	7
Australia	1	1	0	2
Central America and Caribbean	3	1	1	5
Eastern Europe	3	1	0	4
Middle East	3	1	3	7
North America	2	2	1	5
South America	2	1	1	4
Western Europe	5	3	4	12
All regions	27[a]	14	14	55

SOURCE: ILO, GB, *Draft Minutes*, 202nd sess., March 1977.

[a]A vacant seat was reserved for China, which had not joined the ILO.

should have an opportunity at suitable intervals to occupy an ordinary elective seat on the Governing Body."[9] The less developed nations have favored the principle because they believe it would increase their influence.

The Soviet Union has favored regionalization for another reason. As indicated in Table 3., no Communist employer and only one trade union representative served on the Governing Body in 1977. The controversy over the election of communist employers to conference committees has already been discussed in Chapter 2. The same problem applied to the election of union and employer members of the Governing Body. The worker group had conceded a seat to the Soviet Union, but the employer group refused to do so. Soviet representatives were constantly raising complaints: "Why should the representatives of socialist employers be elected by those coming from capitalist countries? There was no technical problem in choosing the ten most industrialized countries of the ILO and likewise there should be no problem in selecting representative Employers on a similar basis."[10]

The distribution of nongovernmental seats is of interest in that Western Europe is heavily represented, as are Canada and the United States. These facts reflect the influence of the International Confederation of Free Trade Unions and the International Organization of Employers within their own groups. The heavy representation of Middle Eastern countries among the employers—specifically Iran, Lebanon, and the Sudan—also stands out. This may reflect the growing importance of international commerce in that part of the world.

The U.S. government was adamantly opposed to any regionalization of Governing Body seats. It argued:

> The imposition of such a formula, of course, would fragment employer and worker representation on the Governing Body and other tripartite decision-making organs of the ILO by altering the basis for determining that representation. No longer would employer and worker representation be determined on the basis of their respective distinct group interests, as they now are by each group through the democratic process of the secret ballot. Instead, employer and worker representation would be determined on the basis of geographical distribution. This, of

course, goes to the heart of tripartism in the ILO. It has been,
and will continue to be, strongly opposed by the United States
Government.[11]

U.S. employer and union representatives were against regionalization for similar reasons. Most Western European representatives tended to follow the lead of the United States, but often
without enthusiasm. The Scandinavian group's stand on this issue has already been mentioned.

In 1976, Italy, on behalf of the Western European countries
and Canada, introduced a resolution in the Working Party on
Structure that would have raised the number of voting Governing Body members to sixty-four. Of the thirty-two members representing governments, twenty would have been nominated by
the most industrialized states *in each continent,* while the other
twelve would have been elected at large. The final allocation,
therefore, would have consisted of seven seats for Africa, nine
for the Americas, seven for Asia, and nine for the European continent. No regionalization was proposed for employer and
worker delegates. Since this proposal did not eliminate the nonelective seats, it was rejected by the Group of 77.[12]

An excellent summary of the Soviet position on ILO structure was presented by one of its representatives at the March
1971 session of the Governing Body. He began by asserting that
the Working Party members "had divided into a group anxious
to modernize an obsolete structure dating back to the Treaty of
Versailles and a rigidly conservative faction which sought to justify its attitude by invoking the sanctity of tripartism." He followed up with these points:

1. Nonelective seats should be abolished.
2. The "veto right" of Article 36 of the Constitution should be
   removed.
3. Election to the Governing Body should be based on a system
   that ensured fair geographical distribution in all groups of the
   Governing Body.
4. Elections of industrial committees should also ensure geographical representation.[13]

Predictably, the United States was squarely opposed to all of these proposals. It was fighting a losing battle on geographical representation, however, as it was on the other issues. Out of deference to the United States, the Western European nations held the line by threatening to veto constitutional changes. How much longer they would have done so had the United States remained a member is problematical, for once the United States departed, major changes came under immediate and serious discussion.

Authority of the Governing Body

Another set of structural/operational issues revolved around the power of the Governing Body vis-à-vis that of the conference. The principal matters involved were the appointment of the director-general and the determination of the conference agenda.

The constitution provides that the director-general must be appointed by the Governing Body, which is also given final authority to settle the conference agenda. The director-general runs the daily business of the Office and wields great influence in policy discussions within the organization. Most of the initiatives for new programs come from his office, and while he is subject to the general policies adopted by the Governing Body, he usually has a major impact on the formulation of these policies.

The director-general of the ILO has always come from an industrialized Western nation. The first was Albert Thomas of France, who served from 1919 to 1932. He was succeeded by Harold Butler of the United Kingdom, who held the post for the next six years. John Winant, an American, held the position only three years, resigning in 1941 to become U.S. ambassador to Britain. Edward Phelan of Ireland served until 1948, and he was succeeded by David A. Morse, the second American to serve. Morse remained on the job until 1970, thus completing the longest term of office of any ILO director-general. Wilfred Jenks, an Englishman, replaced Morse, and after his death in 1974, Francis Blanchard of France took over.

Thus, during the first sixty years of the ILO's existence, its top post has been held by nationals of only four countries. And for nearly one-third of that period, an American citizen has held the office, despite the fact that the United States did not even belong to the ILO until after it had been in existence for fifteen years. Clearly, the United States has had little cause for complaint. Other countries have, however. The Governing Body's power of election was ultimately looked upon as a way to perpetuate the grip of a few countries on the office of director-general. A demand arose, therefore, that full authority to appoint him be shifted to the conference.

The United States was willing to accept a compromise in 1973 by which the conference would be notified in advance of any impending vacancy in the director-general's post and invited to endorse the appointment after it had been made by the Governing Body. What "endorse" meant was unclear, but it did not seem to imply any right of veto by the conference.[14] The non-Western nations refused to accept this formula. The matter was brought into sharp focus in the 1974 election of a director-general to succeed Wilfred Jenks. Albert Tevoedjré, an African, ran against Francis Blanchard, and although Blanchard won, the African challenge was a straw in the wind.

A questionnaire addressed to member states that same year showed clearly that the Communist and less developed countries were strongly in favor of granting the conference final authority over the election of the director-general, while the Western nations preferred the status quo.[15] When the debate continued in 1975, the U.S. labor and employer members of the Governing Body added their strong opposition to any change. They maintained that the director-general was more a manager than a politician, and that the conference was not in constant touch with him, making it logical for his appointment to be in the hands of the executive body of the ILO, which met more frequently.[16] Shortly after the withdrawal of the United States, Francis Blanchard was reelected director-general almost unanimously by the Governing Body, amid predictions that he would be the last to be elected in that manner.

Clearly, this issue became a matter of power, not of principle.

If the authority were shifted, the Group of 77 and the Communists could, by cooperating at the conference, choose the director-general. Their influence in the Governing Body was not so great, however. The United States argued consistently that the countries which were financing the ILO should have more influence in selecting the man who would supervise its spending. The one country–one vote system was not considered a formula designed to assure careful handling of funds.

The second issue, which involved the Governing Body's authority to fix the agenda of the conference, did not arouse as much concern. Although the conference has the constitutional authority to change the agenda by a two-thirds vote, this has almost never been done. A suggestion was made in 1976 that delegates to the conference be given an opportunity to express their views on items scheduled for inclusion in future agendas by the Governing Body, as well as to propose new items. This proposal was not accepted.[17] The United States, opposing any change, feared that if the conference were permitted to determine its own agenda, extraneous political issues would override the more sober business normally specified by the Governing Body, a prospective danger made more real by the continuous wrangling over resolutions.

Operation of the Conference

Several other issues involving the day-to-day running of the annual conference have also stirred controversy. The most important of these is the control over conference debate, including the resolutions to be considered.

The ILO conference is governed by an elaborate set of rules called the standing orders. Among the most important of these has been Article 17, which covers the introduction of resolutions. (Attempts to modify this in the interest of greater relevancy of debate are discussed in Chapter 7.) A resolution that involves a matter not listed on the conference agenda cannot be considered unless it is deposited with the director-general at least fifteen days before the opening of the conference session. The conference president can, however, with the approval of the three vice-presidents, permit introduction of a resolution on the ground of urgency. The Resolutions Committee, using a system of preferential balloting, selects five resolutions for consideration by the conference.

A closely related matter had to do with permissible limits of debate. During the 1960s, U.S. involvement in Vietnam was repeatedly attacked in the conference. Portugal, Greece, and other countries that happened to be out of favor with the Left were also frequent targets. These speeches were not related to the ILO's purposes or its agenda, and they often transcended the bounds of parliamentary decorum. The U.S. government maintained a policy of refraining from counterattacks on issues not relevant to the ILO mandate; it also tried to have ruled out of order statements that were not germane to the issues under debate.[18]

A report to the 1969 conference by a working party on structure attempted to establish some guidelines for the scope of debate. Among its recommendations were the following:

1. All debates should abide by parliamentary language and avoid references to extraneous matters. Slanders directed against heads of state or insults to fellow delegates should be stopped immediately.
2. Freedom of speech is essential, and no one should be immune from criticism. Freedom of speech includes freedom to reply.
3. There is a distinction between the purposes and responsibilities of the ILO and the broader political responsibilities of the United Nations. This distinction should be reflected in the limits to debate.
4. Differences of opinion arose within the Working Party on how these principles were to be applied in practice. The majority took the position that, while current political events might be cited if they were closely connected with ILO responsibilities, "it is out of order for delegates to discuss the merits of political disputes between member States . . . otherwise than in relation to the fulfillment of specific obligations under International Labor Conventions."[19]

The Soviet Union took the view that "any attempt to place restrictions—other than the obligation to refrain from the use of nonparliamentary or insulting language—on freedom of discussion would be extremely dangerous and would prove fruitless."[20] This prediction proved accurate, for the conference failed to take any action. At the 1970 conference, the Bulgarian minister of labor recommended: "This Conference should condemn the aggression of the United States against the peoples of Viet-Nam, Cambodia, Laos, and the whole of Indo-China. It should also insist on the termination of Israel's aggression against the Arab countries, and the liquidation of its results."[21] The Polish workers' delegate asserted that "the ILO cannot be indifferent to the pursuit by the United States of the war in Viet-Nam." It went on to attack Israel, South Africa, and Portugal.[22] The Byelorussian employer delegate demanded "an immediate end to imperialist aggression in Indochina and the Middle East . . . on behalf of the Byelorussian managers."[23] The delegate of the Mongolian government joined in the condemnation,[24] as did virtually all the other delegates from Communist countries.

The U.S. government representative responded sharply by attacking the Soviet Union for its refusal to help bring about a settlement of the war in Vietnam.[25] This marked a distinct change in American policy, toward a tougher line in ILO debate.[26] Points of order were raised against political attacks, and an immediate right of reply was sought. After the end of the war in Vietnam, charges against the United States continued over the issue of Puerto Rican independence and America's alleged complicity in the overthrow of the Allende regime in Chile. In each case, U.S. delegates arose to challenge the statements and to protest their irrelevancy. Political invective continued, but at least the U.S. government delegates were now able to vent their frustrations. It soon became clear that the only solution to this problem was a strong conference president, someone who was willing to use his gavel when speakers went too far afield.

Another matter concerned the less developed nations, which periodically requested an amendment to the ILO constitution that would enable those countries that could not afford to finance full tripartite delegations to have their expenses paid by the organization. A working party was set up by the Governing Body in 1971 to deal with the problem, but it was unable to reach an agreement.[27] The employers' group introduced a resolution at the 1973 conference requesting the Governing Body to insure the effective participation of tripartite delegations by underwriting full or partial ILO payment of travel and subsistence costs. That resolution also failed to be adopted.[28] Although considerable support for the idea was expressed at various sessions of the Working Party on Structure,[29] no action was taken by the time the United States withdrew: the countries that bore the greatest burden of the ILO budget were not prepared to take on even more financial responsibility for this purpose.

Operation of the Office

U.S. delegates have occasionally objected to the way in which the International Labor Office was being administered. During the tenure of David Morse as director-general, these complaints were soft-pedaled; with his retirement in 1970, they became more severe.

Staffing

One complaint of long standing stated that the number of U.S. nationals on the ILO staff was low compared to the U.S. budgetary contribution. Of all internationally recruited officials on the staff as of December 31, 1971, some 9.9 percent were American, compared with 11.7 percent British and 10.1 percent French. In addition, of 194 professionals not subject to geographical distribution requirements, only 15 were American; of 1,376 nonprofessionals, 20 were American; and of 894 persons financed by the United Nations Development Program and other technical assistance donors, 77 were American.[30]

Yet the ILO was not unique in this respect. In 1976, U.S. nationals made up 11 percent of the ILO's professional staff, compared with 11 percent for the World Health Organization, 9 percent for the Food and Agricultural Organization, and 14 percent for the Educational, Scientific, and Cultural Organization.[31] In all these agencies, the United States provided at least 25 percent of the total budget. Among the major factors cited as contributing to this state of affairs are the following:

(a) *Relatively low ILO salaries.* U.S. officials have often complained about low ILO salaries.[32] Nevertheless, the comptroller general noted in 1970 that a large number of Americans were applying for ILO employment. Moreover, a law enacted in 1969 allowed federal employees to join international organizations for a maximum of five years and provided for reimbursement of any salary loss they might incur during that period.[33]

Even if salary had been a factor prior to 1970, it was certainly not so in the years following. In 1976, some seventy-five ILO officials received remuneration, including post allowances, which, on an after-tax basis, exceeded the salaries of U.S. cabinet members, congressmen, and most federal employees.[34] The ILO's explanation is that living costs are higher in Geneva than in Washington and that these allowances merely equalized incomes. But a recent analysis showed that this disparity in income was generally true for employees of the United Nations, including those personnel who were stationed in New York. "Total U.N. salaries now substantially exceed U.S. civil service salaries," it revealed, and "the difference in salary levels between U.N. and U.S. employees is most extreme in the highest level jobs."[35]

(b) *Slow recruitment procedures.* In the view of the Labor Department, many good U.S. candidates were lost to the ILO because of its slow and cumbersome recruiting procedure. The personnel office in Geneva has been the source of a large number of complaints from many ILO members, and there is no reason to believe that U.S. applicants have been singled out for this treatment.

(c) *Need for foreign language competence.* The relatively poor preparation of most Americans in French and Spanish has been cited by the ILO as a problem. Yet this disadvantage may be offset by Western Europeans' lack of fluent English.

(d) *Lack of interviews.* It has been alleged that while European applicants are brought to Geneva for interviews, U.S. applicants have not been given the same privilege because of the expense involved. Moreover, the ILO Office in Washington lacked recruitment officers with the technical skills necessary to evaluate applicants. Beginning in 1970, however, after a recruitment officer was assigned to Washington, matters seem to have improved.[36]

The flurry of activity surrounding the withholding of U.S. funds in 1970 did not seem to alter the proportion of Americans on the ILO staff significantly. This may have been caused partly by ILO financial difficulties and partly by similar pressures exerted by the less developed countries and the Soviet Union directed against European hegemony in the ILO Office. According to the U.S. Senate's Committee on Government Operations, another factor may have been operative:

> In the view of some [U.S. officials] it is more important to concentrate on placing Americans in the most influential positions than on the sheer number of positions at all levels filled by Americans. It is argued that placement of officials at lower levels may be used as a reason to deny the United States appointment of its nationals in higher level jobs. Fears were also expressed that too large a contingent of U.S. nationals, or too much U.S. pressure on personnel matters, would generate resentment and prove counterproductive.[37]

When David Morse resigned as director-general of the ILO, the United States, in keeping with its strategy of going for the top jobs, managed to place John McDonald, a State Department officer, in the post of deputy director-general in charge of administration.

An inhibiting factor in the hiring of Americans may have been U.S. reluctance to insist upon geography and budget share rather than competence as the main qualifications for the distribution of appointments. For citizens of less developed countries, an ILO job means a great leap forward in living standards; thus, ILO nominations usually reflect an important source of political patronage. Although the United States had not substantially increased its ILO representation by 1977, this was not a major factor behind the withdrawal.

A recent U.S. Senate committee report has pointed out what must be done to overcome the failure of international organizations to hire more U.S. personnel:

The reluctance of many organizations to hire U.S. nationals in greater numbers, and the reluctance of many Americans to work for many organizations, makes it imperative that the U.S. Government engage in an extensive, affirmative recruitment program that can locate the relatively few Americans who are genuinely interested in working for the organizations, and who are fully qualified for the job. Only the most systematic and coordinated recruitment effort will succeed. [38]

Soviet Personnel Practices

Some Soviet practices with respect to their nationals in the ILO, as well as concessions made to them by the ILO on other matters, have acted as an irritant to the United States. The Soviet Union, which is the second largest contributor to the ILO budget, was also underrepresented in the Secretariat and constantly demanded additional posts. In 1971, its nationals occupied only 3.8 percent of ILO posts, compared with almost three times that many for France and Britain. David Morse, prior to his resignation, had agreed to increase the number of Soviets on the staff from 30 to 45 by January 1, 1971. [39]

In part, the problem has been of the Soviets' own making. While most other countries allow their nationals to become permanent international civil servants, the Soviets rotate their nationals every three or four years. The result is that by the time an official has become habituated to his work and the problems of living in Geneva, and has become of some use to the Office, he is called home. Moreover, Soviet nationals are kept in close touch with their government; in Geneva, they meet weekly at the Soviet Mission. [40]

The manner in which Soviet officials were recruited also contributed to staff politicization and lack of competence within the ILO. George Meany, who complained about this practice, described it as follows:

> To give you an indication of the double standard, under the ILO procedure, when any national member of the ILO feels that he should have representation on the staff by putting employees in, the rule has always been that they submit a list of candidates for any particular spot with their qualifications. Then they are looked over and the ILO Office makes the decision. The Rus-

sians never have accepted that. They have the special privilege of submitting one candidate for any position to which they aspire, and there is no right of the Office to question the capability of that particular candidate.[41]

Francis Blanchard, the present director-general, claims that he now requires the Soviets to provide several candidates from among whom the ILO may make a selection. If so, he is ahead of the United Nations, whose Staff Association continues to complain that the Soviet Union does its own screening of job applicants and rotates its nationals every few years, thus denigrating the concept of an international civil service.[42]

Research

The ILO's research product has often been criticized by the Governing Body as being too academic and not immediately applicable to the needs of the member states. Yet by the standards of any American university or most U.S. government agencies, the ILO's publications fall under the category of applied research. The Governing Body strictures have often reflected a failure to understand the necessity of going beyond elementary manuals and handbooks as a preliminary to the formulation of policy and the choice of methods of operation. To say that the research output of the ILO is of uniformly high quality would be an overstatement, but the Office has established a reputation for the production of useful material, at least when it does not stray beyond the limits of its competence.

In one serious respect, however, the ILO has failed to maintain objectivity in its publications. George Meany called attention to this by referring to an article entitled "Lenin and Social Progress" in the April 1970 issue of the *International Labour Review*, the journal of the ILO: "The article pleads for revolution in the developing countries and holds up the Soviet form of revolution as a model and the best road to social progress, and it portrays Lenin as the great benefactor of mankind . . . . this indicates the official attitude of the ILO Office in which they extol the virtues of a dictator, of a man who destroyed the Russian trade union movement."[43] The article in question is perhaps the most egregious example of the ILO's willingness to open its major publication, which is circulated throughout the world in three languages, to material that is little more than propaganda. It is not the only one, however. Two or three articles devoted to the Soviet Union appear annually in the *International Labour Review*. Apart from those articles devoted to purely technical subjects, they conform to the following specifications: (1) they are written by Soviet nationals; (2) they rely entirely on Soviet sources and never cite the voluminous body of foreign material available about the Soviet Union; (3) they extol the virtues of the Soviet system, containing only as much criticism as allowed in the official Soviet press; and (4) they are purely descriptive, non-analytical articles having little scholarly merit. They are, in fact, the kind of mass-produced summaries one regularly finds in Soviet publications devoted to labor affairs; as such, they stand in sharp contrast to the usual standards set by the editors of the *International Labour Review*.[44]

Those who seek a realistic picture of Soviet labor conditions should not rely on ILO publications. The organization has published books and articles dealing with unemployment and other labor market flaws in Western nations, but it maintains complete silence about similar phenomena in the Soviet Union. The only plausible explanation for this double standard is that the Office has yielded to political pressure in formulating its program of research and publications, thereby casting a cloud of doubt over its entire program. Similar problems may exist with other countries, but the Soviet case is certainly the most glaring.

The Distribution of Honors

"The single greatest Russian threat or problem in the ILO is probably related to the distribution of honors. By this is meant the election of representatives of all three parts, government, employers, and workers to positions of influence, whether that be as Officer of its committees, as members of the GB, as leaders or members of GB committees, Industrial Committees, specialist panels, etc."[45] The fear expressed in the above quotation is, of course, that these positions will be used to undermine the credibility of democratic society. Actually, the Soviet Union does not appear to have been very successful in gaining influential positions within the ILO. Efforts to elect a Soviet delegate to the chairmanship of the Governing Body were defeated on four occasions between 1971 and 1977. This post, which is second in importance to that of the director-general, was held by nationals of the following countries during that period: Nigeria, Canada, Mexico, Australia, and West Germany. The prestigious but much less important position of president of the annual conference was held in that same period by nationals of France, the Netherlands, Zaire, Peru, the Philippines, Ireland, and Ghana.[46] Communist delegates have been elected as conference vice-presidents and as members of the Governing Body (the Soviet Union is entitled to a nonelective government seat). The composition of the Governing Body suggests, however, that the Communist states were not successful in increasing their share of the "honors," at least prior to the U.S. withdrawal.

The strong position taken by the United States on this issue was undoubtedly a major factor in keeping the Soviets out. At an informal meeting of Western members of the Governing Body in November 1975, Roberto Ago, the Italian government delegate and one of the most influential members of the body, stated that in his opinion the election of an Eastern European as chairman of the Governing Body would not sound the death knell of the ILO, although he realized that it would increase the chances of American withdrawal. The American government member made it clear, on the other hand, that "the election of an Eastern European to a high ILO post such as Chairman of the Governing Body or president of the annual Conference would be taken by U.S. 'domestic interests' as a dramatic and symbolic blow against tripartism and would turn them against participation in the ILO."[47]

Among the other issues that contributed to American unhappiness with the ILO were personnel decisions, budgetary problems, and opposition to specific policies, all of which will be dealt with in Chapter 4. The political, structural, and operational problems that have been considered here, however, were the ones perceived by the U.S. participants as the most important. In view of the considerable differences in viewpoint in both do-

mestic and foreign policy among the three U.S. partners in the
ILO, it is significant that there was a large measure of agreement
among them on the matters that have been discussed. If anything, the trade unions and the employers tended to be closer
together on fundamental issues than either was with the government, which was often reduced to the position of counseling caution. This will become clearer in the following chapter, in which
the history of the final decision to withdraw is detailed.

Chapter 4

The U.S. Decision to Withdraw

The United States did not act in haste in leaving the ILO. There were clear signs over a period of seven years that withdrawal was a possibility. Yet contradictory signals were being sent out by those who were involved in the decisionmaking process. The responsibility for handling ILO affairs within the federal bureaucracy was split among three departments—Labor, State, and Commerce—and each of these held a different view.

The adjustment of foreign policy formulation to take into account domestic interests is always a complicated process. In the usual case, while the executive branch of the government must heed the views of domestic pressure groups, it is mainly through the Congress that these are expressed. In the case of the ILO, however, not only was Congress brought into the picture, but two powerful interest groups—organized labor and management—had to be directly involved in decisionmaking. Both of them could and did exert pressure through Congress, and also by threatening to withhold their participation in the ILO, they made it difficult for the government to proceed against their wishes. This was particularly true of labor, since most people tend to identify the ILO as being within the legitimate scope of trade union interests.[1]

To further complicate matters, the Departments of Labor and Commerce tend to follow the lead of their traditional constituents, whereas the State Department is more concerned with general foreign policy objectives. In the end, it was the president who made the final decision to withdraw, and he had to take into account not only the advice he received from members of his cabinet but also the possibilities open to the government in the face of the positions of its tripartite partners.

Federal government departments had tried many times to define the proper role of the United States in the ILO, but without much success. The comptroller general's office reviewed these efforts in 1970 and offered the following conclusions:

1. An attempt made in 1956 by State, Labor, and Commerce to define U.S. objectives in the ILO resulted in a statement so broad that it was "practically useless" as a guide. The same held true of a policy statement issued by the secretary of state on May 7, 1965. A Labor Department task force, set up between 1965 and 1967 to consider the administration of U.S. participation in the ILO, did not produce anything; indeed, the State Department officials responsible for ILO affairs were not even aware of the existence of this task force. And the Department of Commerce played little part in any of these efforts.

2. There was a lack of coordination and consultation between employer and worker delegates and the U.S. government.

3. The report quoted a U.S. labor attaché in Geneva as writing that "our domestic and international policies have been vigorously and continually attacked, with almost no organized defense or effective responses. One might say that silence has been our main policy vis-à-vis our totalitarian opponents in the ILO. . . . The U.S. Government has exercised no real initiative on its own behalf in recent years. In fact, the position of the United States Government delegations to most ILO meetings seems to have almost invariably supported the position of the Office itself with little critical approach to the Office programs or with new or different proposals of their own."

The comptroller general recommended that State, Labor, and Commerce develop and implement a firm policy and workable plan to achieve U.S. objectives in the ILO.[2]

One reason for the failure to develop a vigorous and independent U.S. policy may have been the fact that throughout this period the position of ILO director-general was occupied by David Morse, a forceful and persuasive American with considerable political support at home. As long as he remained in office, the feeling persisted that American interests were being well cared for. Occasional differences arose, as in the U.S. refusal to support an ILO training center in Turin which Morse had endorsed. But few government officials appreciated Morse's position, the fact that he had to satisfy many different constituencies, or that pressures were placed on him to act in ways not always consonant with American policy objectives. This problem was made even more serious by the ineffectiveness of U.S. government representation in the Governing Body.[3]

The Jenks Succession

A decade of relative calm came to an abrupt end when David Morse announced his resignation in February 1970, effective May 31. His retirement was completely unexpected, since his term of office had two more years to go. A vigorous campaign to succeed him was waged by two candidates who had long held top posts in the ILO directorate—Wilfred Jenks of Britain and Francis Blanchard of France. One of the main issues of the campaign was the candidates' position on a demand made by the Soviet Union for representation in the directorate in the post of assistant director-general. This post is a political one, with no tests of qualification required. The high salary and customarily long tenure attached to the position make it a desirable political plum. Moreover, as the second largest contributor to the ILO, the Soviet Union had a strong claim to it.

Morse had been under Soviet pressure for many years to take such action, but the counterpressure exerted by the AFL-CIO, which adamantly opposed a top ILO job for a Soviet, prevented Morse from taking what to most of the nations seemed a logical action. In 1967, he warned American government officials that the time was fast approaching when the ILO would have to appoint a Soviet assistant director-general and that in his opinion they were entitled to the post.[4] He managed to hold the line until 1970, but the Soviet pressure could no longer be resisted. In January 1970, Morse told the officers of the Governing Body that the nomination of a Soviet official had to be considered seriously, that the Soviet government had put forth a candidate, and that several additional names were to be submitted at his request.[5] The Soviet ambassador in Geneva called upon Morse in April 1970 and urged him to act upon the candidate originally put forward, but Morse took the position that since he had resigned his successor would have to make a determination of the issue.[6] In sum, Morse had engaged in extensive discussion with the Soviets, but he had never given them a final commitment on a specific individual.

It was generally believed that Blanchard would accede to the Soviet demand, since, among other things, he was receiving their support. The United States decided to back Jenks, and an American official went to talk with him in Caracas, where he was attending an ILO regional meeting, to present U.S. views about what the next director-general should do:

> Among the points that I made, one had to do with our opposition as a government and the opposition of our worker and employer delegations to the appointment of a Russian to the top directorate of ILO. . . . I told him it would cause great difficulties for the U.S. Government if this appointment were made, precisely because our employer and worker groups in this country were sensitive on this point and rightfully so. Mr. Jenks made no commitment to anything I had to say because he took the quite proper position that as an international civil servant he could not do so and he was making no commitments to anyone as a candidate for Director-General.[7]

Jenks was elected by a vote of 25 to 23. Not only did the United States provide him with 3 votes, but it electioneered for him with other nations. Without American support, Jenks could not have won, and he certainly would not have had U.S. support if he had indicated that he was looking favorably on the Soviet appointment. Yet a month after assuming office, he told the

American representative, "quite casually," that he was appointing a Soviet as assistant director-general.[8]

Jenks had spent his entire working life as an ILO official; and as second in command to Morse in ILO officialdom, he had a great deal of experience in the organization's politics. To be sure, he had never made any commitment to the United States on the policies he intended to follow, but he must have been fully aware that the Soviet appointment was a key issue in the election campaign. Whatever his motives, Jenks's action was interpreted by all Americans concerned as an acceptance of U.S. support under false pretenses, and the reaction was immediate and sharp. The chairman of the House of Representatives subcommittee in charge of the budget for international organizations called a hearing "because of the concern of the head of the AFL-CIO, Mr. George Meany, at what might take place insofar as installing a Russian national in a No. 2 position in this International Labor Organization."[9]

At the hearing, Meany reviewed American labor's outstanding grievances against the ILO and argued that the Soviet appointment "is about the last straw because whatever assignment this man gets departmental-wise in the ILO he will have hundreds of employees under his supervision. . . . he will use that position to make each and every employee a Communist agent whether he wants to be or not. They do not fool around. They don't acquire power that they put on the back burner. They use it."[10] Meany was seconded by the U.S. employer delegate, who asked the committee to hold up the ILO appropriation. The only dissenting note came from the assistant secretary of state for international organizations, who urged caution and expressed concern that the withholding of funds "might also serve to wreck the Organization." When he added that the United States should seek support for its position from Western Europe and Japan, Meany remarked, "You will not find it there," and Meany's remark was seconded by Edward Neilan, the U.S. employer representative. This shared perception by U.S. labor and management concerning Europe's unwillingness to face up to the Soviet Union makes for an interesting commentary.

By then, the ILO appropriation had already been approved

by the U.S. House of Representatives. Rep. John Rooney, chairman of the subcommittee, notified his opposite in the Senate, however, that if the ILO appropriation were omitted from the Senate bill, the House would concur in the conference committee. That is precisely what happened. As Rooney put it, "Mr. Jenks needs to be rocked. I know of only one way to rock him, cut off his water." [11]

At the next two meetings of the ILO Governing Body, in November 1970 and March 1971, full-scale debates on the U.S. action were held. The Communists launched an immediate attack, accusing the United States of an "inadmissible attempt to exert pressure on the Organization in order to perpetuate and strengthen discrimination against the socialist countries," [12] a charge that could hardly be denied. Other members, in particular the Canadian and Australian employer members, defended the United States. The U.S. government members also took the occasion to note that for a considerable number of years the Soviet Union had not paid its own arrears to the United Nations. [13]

One consequence of the congressional decision to withhold funds from the ILO was the preparation of the first comprehensive review of U.S. participation in the organization since the 1957 Johnson Committee report. Although labeled an interagency report, it was prepared primarily by the Labor Department. Among the report's many observations and recommendations, the most important, in terms of U.S. participation in the ILO, were the following:

1. U.S. withdrawal would allow the Soviet Union to become the dominant member of the ILO; it could then exploit the organization's resources in order to enlarge its own influence. The United States would be better served by staying in the ILO and fighting for its position.
2. Withdrawal from the ILO would cause the United States to be attacked for abandoning an organization that helped working people all over the world; it would also be accused of cold war politics.
3. A more constructive policy would be to pay the arrears,

specify objectives, and see whether or not they were achieved within a reasonable trial period.

4. The ILO had been serving U.S. interests, and efforts should be made to find out whether this could be done to an even greater degree.
5. The United States was urged to ratify ILO Convention No. 87, dealing with freedoms of association, then press complaints against the Communist countries for violating its provisions. [14]

The report noted that the ILO was almost completely unknown to the American people and had little support in Congress. Its funds had been appropriated year after year because of AFL-CIO interest, and the report warned that if the AFL-CIO were to oppose membership, it would be very difficult to get funds from Congress. This was the crucial point: the AFL-CIO had virtual control over ILO appropriations because the organization had no other important constituency in the United States. Apart from a few scholars who had spent sabbatical years in Geneva, a few members of Congress who attended the annual conference, several businessmen for whom the ILO was a hobby, and a handful of federal bureaucrats (probably no more than half a dozen) who were handling ILO affairs, few in the United States knew or cared about the ILO. The only group that had firsthand experience were those employers and trade unionists who had attended ILO industrial committee meetings, but their support was never effectively marshaled.

The report also noted that the U.S. Chamber of Commerce, with the probable urging of foreign employer groups, had favored continued affiliation with the ILO. It had developed a thoughtful program to make U.S. participation more effective. The Chamber also expressed its intent to double the number of its advisers to the employer delegate at the next annual ILO conference, and it agreed to support U.S. government efforts to augment governmental staff resources.

The main effort within the government to restore full ILO participation came from the State Department. An assistant secretary of state told the House Subcommittee on Appropriations in 1972 that the ILO had made progress in meeting U.S. complaints, and he cited the following events:

1. In 1970, the Governing Body did not add any Communist members to committees to which they had not been elected by workers and employers, as had been done in previous years.
2. The 1971 conference passed a resolution calling for the strengthening of tripartism.
3. In 1971, for the first time in nine years, the Soviet Union's failure to comply with the convention on freedom of association was discussed.
4. Czechoslovakia was cited in 1971 for similar shortcomings.
5. In 1971, an employer was elected conference president for the first time.[15]

Since the State Department had opposed any halt in U.S. payments to the ILO, the reaction of the AFL-CIO to these events was more significant. A review of the 1971 and 1972 conferences by a member of the U.S. labor delegation echoed several of these points, and he added a few more:

1. There was less political vituperation. The conference presidents in both years firmly established the principle that the conference was not to be used for political purposes, and deprived offending speakers of the floor.
2. The AFL-CIO conference delegate was elected vice-president of the worker group over a Chilean candidate who was supported by the Communist bloc.
3. The ICFTU and other democratic groups had begun to realize that they would have to organize themselves to fight the Communist threat to the ILO.[16]

Thus, in the eyes of all three parties, the withholding of U.S. funds had the desired effect. The Western Europeans had aligned themselves more firmly with the United States, orderly procedures had been reestablished, and the "double standard" seemed to be on the way out. The United States paid its arrears, and the ILO was once again solvent.[17]

The Renewal of Friction

The 1973 conference was also satisfactory from the AFL-CIO standpoint. A labor leader from Zaire who was considered friendly to the United States was elected conference president; an anti-Israeli resolution was staved off; a critical conference report on Communist labor legislation was submitted; and some effective work was done by various technical committees.[18] But some clouds had begun to gather, this time in the Governing Body. The Western European government members, with the support of Eastern Europe, nominated Ivan Goroshkin, the Soviet government member, to the chairmanship of the Governing Body, the second most important post in the ILO. This was a cardinal sin as far as the AFL-CIO was concerned, but it was defended by a European as follows:

> The nomination was in conformity with the Governing Body's unwritten rules of equity, which, alongside its written code or procedure, determined the relationships which should exist among its members. In the many years of the USSR's membership of the Governing Body the chair had never been occupied by a representative of an East European country. It was therefore the European Government members' unanimous view that a chairman should come from Eastern Europe.[19]

The United States responded by securing the last-minute nomination of Arturo Muños-Ledo, a Mexican. A European spokesman labeled this development "highly regrettable." The Mexican won the ensuing election by a vote of 26 to 20, in all probability because he received the votes of most labor and employer members. This provoked an outburst from the defeated candidate, Goroshkin, who refused to congratulate the winner. Other Communist speakers joined the fray, accusing the ILO staff, among other things, of maneuvering against the Soviet Union.[20]

The election of a Soviet delegate as Governing Body chairman, with Western European backing, might have led to an even earlier withdrawal by the United States. As it was, the strong support accorded Goroshkin by Western Europe was interpreted by the United States as a weakening of Western resolve to prevent Soviet domination of the ILO. The Europeans may have calculated that the recent payment of U.S. arrears might make it more difficult for the United States to use the power of the purse again soon. Thus, this would be an opportune time to satisfy the legitimate aspirations of the Soviet Union.

The 1974 conference marked a continuation in the trend toward worsening relations between the AFL-CIO and ILO. The adoption of an anti-Israeli resolution was a major factor, but there were others as well. In the view of AFL-CIO representatives, the majority of the conference had fallen under the influence of the Communist states. The ICFTU and the Communist World Federation of Trade Unions had agreed that the latter would have a vice-chairmanship and an additional member of the Workers' Bureau (the executive committee of the workers' delegation to the conference) as well as a vice-chairmanship of most of the technical committees. "In spite of official pronouncements to the contrary," an article in the AFL-CIO newsletter reported, "the International Confederation of Free Trade Unions is moving ever closer to tight cooperation and consultation with the Communist World Federation of Trade Unions in the ILO."[21] Matters were not helped by an all-out personal attack on George Meany by the Soviet government delegate:

> Yesterday we heard Mr. Seidman, an envoy of the reactionary leadership of the AFL-CIO, headed by the well-known George Meany, who pathologically hates and fears socialism. We know that neither Mr. Seidman nor his chief reflects the views and convictions of the American workers and are merely mouthpieces for major American capitalism and monopoly, carrying out an anti–working class policy and deceiving the American workers. They are guilty of provocations on the international level.[22]

This outburst should have triggered increased activity in Washington, but not much happened. Clearly, a new crisis in U.S.–ILO relationships was at hand; yet little in the way of top-level attention was being devoted to it. This was not a case of benign neglect, but simply of neglect.

The year 1975 was ushered in by a new blast at the ILO in an authoritative AFL-CIO publication. The article began with a complaint that U.S. government decisions on the ILO were made at too low a level; and it praised the ILO work in setting international labor standards, mentioning in particular its human rights machinery. The ILO's World Employment Program, which was then reaching its peak, was termed "a modest but useful effort to give advice and assistance to a limited number of developing countries on how they can expand employment opportunities." But, the article continued, a political shadow hung over the ILO, and it cited several familiar AFL-CIO complaints. The author concluded: "I cannot imagine that the AFL-CIO would continue to support or even to participate in the ILO under such circumstances. And I doubt that the U.S. Congress would continue to finance 25 percent of the ILO's budget. Indeed, it seems quite possible to me that a takeover of the ILO by the Communists and their allies could well be followed by U.S. withdrawal from the organization."[23]

As already noted, the admission of the Palestine Liberation Organization to observer status at the 1975 conference, resulting in a walk-out by the U.S. trade union delegation, brought matters to a head. The U.S. secretary of labor, who had been scheduled to address the conference on the same morning that the motion on the PLO was to be discussed, canceled his visit to Geneva on the ground that the conference action "had further politicized the ILO."

Consequently, the House of Representatives cut the proposed U.S. contribution to the ILO for the next fiscal year from the State Department budget. On July 23, 1975, George Meany went before the House International Affairs Committee to request that all U.N. Development Program funds that provided support for ILO technical assistance activities be deleted from the 1976 AID appropriation; but an amendment to this effect was defeated.

On July 30, 1975, the AFL-CIO executive council called upon the U.S. government to give the two-year notice of withdrawal required by the ILO constitution, and it urged Congress to withhold all ILO funds until such notice had been given. Lane Kirkland, then secretary-treasurer of the AFL-CIO and its chief spokesman on ILO affairs, wrote: "Unless the democratic members of the ILO make a serious joint effort to reverse its political degeneration, the Organization will become just another organ of antidemocratic ideological warfare. . . . The once proud and unique organization for the defense of working men and women throughout the world will have become just another meaningless bureaucracy in the U.N.'s family of bureaucracies."[24]

The advisory council on the ILO of the U.S. Chamber of Commerce felt that a letter of withdrawal should not be sent until a study of U.S. interests in the organization had been made. However, Charles Smith, the U.S. employer delegate to the ILO, was personally in favor of withdrawal.

The government's response was to initiate still another study of U.S. participation in the ILO. Although this report was never published, it merits some comment because it depicts the views held by the three departments responsible for handling ILO affairs (Labor, State, and Commerce). The original draft was made by the Labor Department, with the other two departments providing comments. The report begins with a review of the U.S. government's goals within the ILO:

1. To help less developed countries advance in social and economic directions compatible with U.S. ideals.
2. To serve as a multilateral technical assistance agency, with an American presence, in the field of human resources development.
3. To promote free labor movements in pluralistic societies.
4. To advocate the American economic, social and political system, and to stress the advantages of a pluralistic society as opposed to communism and other totalitarian systems.
5. To protect and promote U.S. trade and investment interests through international labor standards that reduce competitive advantages of others.[25]

In responding to these propositions, the State Department, in a memorandum of July 28, 1975, signed by the assistant secretary for international organization affairs, made the point, first, that the United States had never used the ILO to help attain its foreign policy objectives, and pointed to lack of sufficient staff as well as the fact that U.S. participation was generally limited to a few weeks of "politicking" at the annual conference, where immediate political questions were paramount. The memorandum continued:

> In any event, the potential for influencing other governments through our contacts with the ILO is marginal. Our main target groups at the ILO would be mainly LDC ministry of labor and trade union officials. LDC ministers of labor are not powerful men in their own countries. Rarely do they have the power to shape their national institutions. That power lies with the people who control the national budget or the political structure—the president or the ministers of treasury, defense, interior, or public works.
>
> LDC trade unionists are generally even less influential than ministers of labor. In most LDC's the trade unions have been brought under government control. Governments decide who will represent the workers at the ILO, and they insure that these representatives accurately reflect government views. . . . No matter how persuasive American spokesmen might be at the ILO, LDC trade unionists will not change things when they get home.[26]

These paragraphs illustrate a view prevalent in the State Department that many both inside and outside the government have long felt concerned about. There is some truth in these assertions, but there are many exceptions to the broad generalizations. It is far from true, for instance, that labor ministers always have little power. In some countries—Mexico is a good example—the labor ministry has been a stepping-stone to the presidency. It is not at all unusual for labor ministers to have important policymaking roles, particularly since LDCs have begun to recognize employment generation as a central problem. As for the trade unions, the degree of attention paid to them by international Communist bodies suggests that they can play crucial roles in both the political and economic life of less developed nations, particularly during periods of political turmoil. For example, the ability of Communist parties to build a power base in the trade union movements of Spain and Portugal, where the unions of a decade ago would have pretty well conformed to the State Department's description, suggests that unions are often of much greater significance than the State Department acknowledges. This long-standing myopia on the part of American foreign policy makers has not helped the United States in its quest to spread democratic institutions.

The State Department memorandum also pointed out that Soviet membership in the ILO had helped win international acceptance for Soviet trade unionism. Thus, "by withdrawing from the ILO, we would make it clear to the world that we do not admit that the Soviet Union has a valid trade union system." To the argument that participation in ILO work demonstrated U.S. concern for the welfare of the less developed nations, the department replied that the U.S. position on many ILO issues, including budget increases, had created conflict, not cooperation.

The department stressed that in order to retain the support of American labor it was often necessary to oppose our Western allies in the ILO. Western Europe appeared willing to allow the Communist states to secure positions of importance or honor; U.S. withdrawal would not only reduce the area of disagreement, but it might induce our allies to do more in their own defense, rather than rely so heavily on the United States. As for international labor standards, State argued that no evidence supported the claim that they had increased foreign labor costs to such an extent as to contribute to the protection of American markets.

The Department of Commerce, in its reply to the Labor Department's statement of governmental interests in the ILO, stressed several other objectives: assisting private enterprises in LDCs; promoting the adoption of standards relating to health and safety at the workplace, thereby preserving American trade competitiveness; supporting international efforts to improve the working conditions of foreign maritime workers, thus helping the American merchant marine; and cooperating with the comparative research being undertaken by the ILO.

The second part of the Labor Department draft concerned U.S. worker and employer interests in the ILO. The American trade unions were said to be mainly interested in "the promotion of free trade unions and the implementation of the basic human rights Conventions on Freedom of Association, Forced Labor, and the Right to Organize and Bargain Collectively." Employer interests, on the other hand, were more restricted: "In promoting international fair labor standards set by the ILO, in advancing LDC's along pluralistic lines, and in advancing American rather than totalitarian labor relations. . . . Employer interest at the moment is focussed most directly on the ILO's work on multinational corporations."

The Labor Department report included a checklist of trends in ILO affairs following the 1970 financial crisis:

1. Political attacks on U.S. and other Western powers—a *plus* because the level of attacks was no greater in the ILO than in other international bodies.
2. Lack of adherence to parliamentary procedure—a *minus*: "The ILO is slipping back into parliamentary anarchy. . . . We are moving to a point of making important procedural decisions on the basis of what the Communist/LDC alliance wants rather than what the book says."
3. The preservation of tripartism—*no change*.
4. Chairmanship of the Governing Body remaining in Western hands—a *plus*, but with an uncertain outlook.
5. Decline of double standard in application of conventions—a *modest plus*.
6. Budget growth—a *minus*. Referring to the increase of the ILO budget—from $69,674,000 during 1972–73 to $143,982,000 in 1976–77—the report noted: "What we are buying for our budget inflation is a new building and a continually rising salary scale."
7. Diversions of the conference from its technical work into politics—a *minus*, citing Israel, Chile, the PLO.
8. Industrial committee operations—a *plus*.
9. Little new employment of Americans—a *minus*: "We are still underrepresented at professional levels with only some 10–11 percent of total strength."
10. Managerial improvement—a *slight plus*. Program analy-

sis had improved, but the conduct of conferences and
other meetings had not.

This weighing of U.S. progress in the ILO was followed by a
list of steps that could be taken to improve the situation and
perhaps insure continued U.S. participation in the organization.

1. Elevate the level of attention by the U.S. government
   directed toward ILO affairs.
2. Improve the government, Chamber of Commerce, and
   AFL–CIO staffs dealing with the ILO. As the report
   pointed out, the Labor Department had only enough
   staff to handle routine matters relating to the ILO; the
   State Department did not have a full-time professional;
   and the AFL–CIO and Chamber of Commerce people
   involved in ILO work were operating on a part-time
   basis.
3. Coordinate positions among government, labor, and employer delegates earlier and more effectively.
4. Seek ratification by the United States of Convention No.
   87, on freedom of association. This would make it easier
   for the United States to raise complaints against other
   member states, the Communist states in particular.
5. Improve efforts to end the double standard in the Conference Committee on Application of Conventions by encouraging trade unions to file complaints.
6. Press resolutions against forced labor.
7. Secure a better exposition of the American system of industrial relations through ILO machinery.
8. Make program proposals for strengthening ILO substantive work, particularly in the area of the working environment.
9. Secure an increase of American representation on the
   ILO staff both qualitatively and quantitatively.
10. Improve U.S. effectiveness in evaluating ILO programs,
    bringing employers and workers into the process.

This list was followed by an evaluation of the possible impact
of U.S. withdrawal upon the U.N. system and the ILO. The

State Department had advanced two hypotheses: first, that withdrawal would create animosity against the United States for damaging a valuable international agency, causing the United States to suffer a loss of prestige and goodwill, and second, that withdrawal would shock members of the U.N. family into believing that the United States was prepared to take drastic action in defense of its interests. In its memorandum, the department endorsed the second: "The Department of State believes that the second hypothesis is more likely to prove correct, and finds the probability of administering a beneficial shock of value to the rest of the UN system a reason for supporting withdrawal from the ILO." As for the effect of U.S. withdrawal on the ILO itself, some observers, according to State, believed that the ILO would collapse, while others felt that it had enough financial flexibility to survive. The report added: "If enough other important contributors were to follow us out, the ILO might, indeed, collapse. But if so many countries were to decide that they had no further interest in the ILO, wouldn't that be the voice of the truth? And shouldn't it be heeded?"

The Labor Department report concluded with the following recommendations:

1. That a notice of intent to withdraw be issued.
2. That if the Department of State and the president were opposed to an aggressive U.S. effort in the ILO on East-West issues that were important to the maintenance of its tripartite principles and human rights objectives, the United States should cease participation immediately.
3. That, in the absence of the above, the current level of participation should be maintained until a full study of the problem had been completed.
4. That action should be taken to restore appropriations for ILO dues as soon as notification of intent to withdraw was issued.

The State Department, in its response, cautioned that withdrawal might impair U.S. efforts to bring about peace in the Middle East: "Should we signify our intent to withdraw in a way that would link our action to the ILO's granting the PLO observer status, our withdrawal could be regarded as an unfriendly act by the very Arab states whose cooperation we will need in achieving our Middle East foreign policy objectives." The department insisted that the letter of withdrawal should include no mention of the PLO; the timing of the notice was equally important.

Why did the State Department take such a hard line in 1975, especially in view of its much more cautious approach in 1970 and 1977? A clue may be found in the concluding paragraph of its memorandum:

> We must consider the peculiar unpopularity of the ILO with Congress. From the very first moment of our ILO membership, there has been substantial Congressional opposition to the ILO. On four separate occasions, this opposition has resulted in a Congressional withholding of funds for the payment of our ILO assessments. The ILO has been one of the more unpopular international organizations with Congress. Withdrawal would remove this source of friction.

Divergent views surfaced within the State Department itself. The International Organization staff at State was strongly opposed to U.S. withdrawal, whereas Secretary of State Kissinger supported the move and so informed the president. The timing of the letter of intent was delayed repeatedly so as not to interfere with diplomatic efforts going on in the Middle East. Eventually it was sent.

The Notice of Intent to Withdraw

The letter of intent included a commitment to establish a cabinet-level committee to consider how the United States could work within the ILO to help bring about changes that would permit the United States to remain a member. This step was taken at the initiative of the then Secretary of Labor, John T. Dunlop, who was the only cabinet member since Frances Perkins, Franklin Roosevelt's labor secretary, to have a personal knowledge of the ILO's structure and activities. It was planned that a number of working parties would be set up to establish precise guidelines for U.S. policy initiatives and to study the problems of ILO–U.S. relationships in depth. This intent was frustrated by Dunlop's resignation in the spring of 1976, and although the cabinet committee held a few meetings, little was accomplished. A working group, which included lower-level representatives of the three departments and private groups, was established, but it met only a few times.[27] The national election campaign and the change in the federal administration undoubtedly contributed to inactivity.

Many feared that U.S. withdrawal would be regarded by other countries as nothing more than a diplomatic move aimed at achieving a few specific objectives. To prevent this reaction, President Ford sent a special representative to the major industrial nations in January 1976 to warn them that the U.S. position should be taken seriously. The belief persisted, nonetheless, that in the end the United States would not withdraw.

The Labor Department prepared another memorandum in May 1976 that merely reiterated earlier objectives: to strengthen ties with other Western members of the ILO, to establish new relationships with developing countries, and to seek ways to benefit more directly from U.S. participation in the ILO.[28] A second paper of August 1976 set forth as objectives "to improve the effectiveness of U.S. participation in the ILO through efforts designed to (1) better prepare members of U.S. delegations, and (2) exert greater influence over the technical content of ILO programs to make them more effective and, in particular, more responsive to U.S. needs."[29] Effective implementation of these objectives, however, was frustrated by the fear that enhanced U.S. activity might detract from the credibility of the U.S. threat to withdraw. Thus, although technical comments on the ILO budget proposal for 1978–79 were prepared in greater detail than at any time in the past, they were never used.

The Labor Department hired additional staff to work on the ILO in the fall of 1976, and the State Department increased its quota from one to two officers. But the State Department posts were filled by foreign service officers subject to rotation. One of the major reasons for lack of State Department expertise on the ILO was the absence of permanent commitment. The Chamber of Commerce staff member who handled ILO affairs observed that during the seven years he had done so, there had been six different assistant secretaries of state charged with responsibility for the ILO.[30] As for Commerce, its participation was characterized as "essentially a one-person operation."[31]

In the spring of 1976, the secretary of labor appointed a retired foreign service officer as a special assistant to coordinate ILO affairs. But his work was kept quite separate from the Bureau of International Labor Affairs, where the responsibility for ILO operations resided. This splitting of responsibility within the Labor Department undoubtedly contributed to the failure of governmental initiatives.

The special assistant made a series of trips to some thirty-one less developed countries in late 1976 and early 1977 to explain the U.S. position and elicit their support. On the two issues that were critical to the United States at the 1977 ILO conference, the government delegates of these thirty-one countries could have cast a maximum of 124 votes (2 delegates × 31 countries × 2 record votes). The actual voting tally was as follows:

Votes for the U.S. position	7
Votes against the U.S. position	74
Absences and abstentions	43
Total	124

In a report delivered to the Senate Committee on Governmental Affairs in May 1977, a month before the ILO conference that was to prove decisive, the comptroller general of the United States summarized U.S. governmental formulation of objectives subsequent to issuance of the letter of intent to withdraw in November 1975 as follows:

> Except possibly for objectives associated with U.S. withdrawal, agencies have developed their objectives according to their own interests. The Department of State has short-term political objectives tied to the question of withdrawal from ILO. The Department of Labor developed objectives within the Department for U.S. participation in ILO. We were advised that Commerce's statement of objectives was the work of one staff member and was only approved by the Bureau of Domestic Com-

merce. There has been little consultation among the agencies, the U.S. mission [in Geneva], or with employer and worker groups. Neither employer nor employee representatives have been informed what U.S. agencies' objectives were beyond the political aims.[32]

While the report pointed to some increase in U.S. activity in the ILO after 1975, it concluded:

Past U.S. participation in ILO has suffered from the lack of sustained interest and effort on the part of all the agencies involved. Improvements have been temporary. If the United States remains in the ILO, a high-level concern within the Departments of State, Labor, and Commerce must continue in order to maintain our commitment. We believe that such a commitment has not yet been made and that the improvements we observed in U.S. participation may quickly evaporate if and when circumstances return to normal.[33]

When the letter of intent to withdraw was issued in November 1975, both labor and management strongly endorsed it. George Meany stated that the organization's members must now decide "whether the ILO will resume its proper role as a practical instrument for the improvement of conditions of life and labor for working people, or will continue to degenerate as an arena for empty rhetorical and ideological warfare."[34] Charles H. Smith, Jr., chairman of the executive committee of the U.S. Chamber of Commerce and employer delegate to the ILO, outlined the major sources of employer dissatisfaction with the ILO: the erosion of tripartism, triple representation for the Soviet Union (Byelorussia and the Ukraine in addition to the Soviet Union), voting power with no relation to financial responsibility, politicization, and the failure of the ILO to secure implementation of ratified conventions. He urged that the two-year period of notice be used to bring about internal reforms in the ILO, so that the United States might be encouraged to remain a member.[35]

A few months later, the AFL-CIO executive council committed their organization to full cooperation with all democratic groups within the ILO so as to effect the changes desired by American labor. "No honorable means will be left untried to re-

verse the course charted by those nations seeking the enslave-
ment of workers and the destruction of their human rights."[36]

A report on the 1976 ILO conference by the AFL-CIO secretary-treasurer was headed "Mixed Results." On the positive
side, it noted the cohesion that existed within the democratic
countries and the refusal by many of the less developed countries
to follow the dictates of that group's radical members. The negative factors cited were the disorderly procedure of the World
Employment Conference and the persistent attempts to do away
with the special list of countries charged with violation of ILO
conventions. Nonetheless, the report asserted that the future of
the ILO seemed more promising than it had a year earlier.[37]

This note of optimism continued right up to the 1977 conference and was sustained by several events. One was the vote of
the Governing Body in March 1977 authorizing the director-general to drop a special inquiry of Israel and allow the charges to
follow their normal constitutional course. At the same meeting,
the Governing Body agreed to recommend a change in the
standing orders of the conference that would make it more difficult to introduce political resolutions. Hopes for a solution were
dashed, however, by the U.S. defeats at the 1977 conference on
issues that have already been discussed. By the end of June 1977
little doubt remained that the United States would make good
its threat.

At a cabinet-level committee meeting on August 16, 1977,
the positions of labor and management were clear, and they were
supported by the secretaries of labor and commerce. But the
Department of State, now under the Vance leadership, asked for
postponement until October to examine possible alternatives to
withdrawal, and this was agreed to.

Since so little public knowledge existed about the ILO, public opinion could hardly be brought to bear upon the issue of
withdrawal. The *Washington Post* argued that "it is hard to make
a persuasive case that the organization is so important to American diplomacy that Americans should overlook the damage to
credibility and the invitation to anti-Americanism that could result from slinking away, unrequited, from the Ford and Carter
Administrations' two-year warning to pull out."[38] The *Wall Street*

Journal termed the postponement of a final decision a "failure of nerve." Its lead editorial of September 26, 1977, stated that there was not much reason "to go back on our decision and let other people think our intentions aren't to be taken seriously. The harm that impression would do to American interests and principles might well outweigh any good we could accomplish inside the ILO." Only the *New York Times* urged restraint, noting that the objectives of the 1975 letter had been achieved and that "the I.L.O. is clearly worth preserving and only American membership will keep it so."[39]

One of the most forceful statements in favor of withdrawal during this final period of decision was delivered by the U.S. employer delegate. He had been connected with ILO work since 1953 and had participated in twelve conferences. In a speech to the International Industrial Conference in September, he stated that all U.S. delegates to the 1976 and 1977 conferences had agreed that no tangible progress had been made toward meeting the conditions set forth in the 1975 Kissinger letter; in fact, he said, a good case could be made that the situation had deteriorated. In his opinion, "the Director-General [of the ILO] and his Cabinet have within the appropriate limits for international civil servants lent full support to the improvements called for by the U.S." He then explained the adverse votes at the 1977 conference:

> [For the Communists] due process and a reduction in political issues are not supportive of world revolution. The Arab Bloc had a quite different reason: in my opinion, they view due process as an obstacle to the use of the ILO as a battlefield in their conflict with Israel. The African states that voted to kill the proposed amendment to the Standing Orders were in my opinion probably guided by one of two possible reasons: a call for group solidarity by the North African Arab states of the Organization of African Unity and/or to demonstrate their intent to have a large role in the Organization, particularly in the Governing Body. . . . The real problem is the fundamental voting structure of the Organization—a voting structure that bears little resemblance to the real world—a voting structure that encourages irresponsible actions—a voting procedure based on the simple formula, one country–one vote. . . . The relationship between

authority and responsibility is completely unrealistic, and to my mind represents the primary reason why the ILO has lost during the last decade most of its usefulness and its prestige.[40]

In their attempt to keep the United States from withdrawing, ILO and State Department strategy was to bring a maximum amount of foreign pressure to bear upon the three parties involved in the decision. Pope Paul VI made official representations to President Carter, as well as a personal appeal to George Meany against U.S. withdrawal.[41] At the August 1977 meeting of the General Council of the International Organization of Employers, employer representatives from India, France, Japan, Australia, Germany, Canada, and Mexico, among others, reminded the U.S. Chamber of Commerce of the importance of maintaining U.S. membership in the ILO. Prime Minister Leo Tindemans of Belgium, on behalf of the Council of the European Community, addressed a letter to President Carter, dated September 9, in which he conceded that the 1977 conference had been disappointing. He urged the president, nevertheless, to revoke the notice of intent to withdraw, or at least to extend the formal notice to a new period. Even in this last-ditch appeal, the nine countries of the Common Market were very cautious in their commitments of support for the U.S. position:

> Working together with the United States in the Organization and seeking the support and goodwill of the many member states who share our objectives, we consider that there would be a reasonable prospect of making progress in the right direction and of preserving the integrity of the Organization. This would of course require flexibility on the part of all involved in the negotiations which lie ahead. We believe it will be possible to secure a strengthening of the defense of the process through amendment of Article 17 of the Standing Orders. The necessary restructuring of the Organization, including, for instance, changes in voting procedures, will require the most careful consideration. But if the discussions are approached in a spirit of mutual understanding, the essential requirements of the membership of the Organization, including the preservation both of the principles of tripartism and of the partnership between the industrial and developing countries, can be satisfied.

This letter, which was released to the press on September 21, well before the date of the final cabinet decision, was exhibit no. 1 for those in the State Department who were attempting to delay the U.S. withdrawal. But it promised too little, and it was too late. It was anything but a ringing declaration of support for the principles espoused by the United States, and there was not even a hint that other countries might follow the U.S. lead toward withdrawal if due process, antipoliticization, and so forth, could not be achieved. If anything, it served to reinforce the view held by American labor that the countries of Western Europe could not be relied upon to oppose the Communist and Arab blocs.

The AFL-CIO answer to this entreaty was later presented in an article written by a Danish journalist entitled "Why Did the USA Leave the ILO?" He pointed out that, while Denmark, a small country, might have to yield to outside pressures, the United States "cannot permit the Communist world or the developing countries to lead it down the garden path, as they have tried in the ILO." If the United States were to remain in the ILO, he added, it would have to share responsibility for a political procedure in direct contravention of human rights; it was high time, moreover, for the United States to disassociate itself from the Soviet Union's efforts to entrap Western trade unions. He concluded: "The ILO is no longer . . . a forum for the promotion of human rights. Therefore, Denmark should really follow the example of the USA and temporarily say goodbye to the ILO. This might contribute to speeding the day when the ILO majority again reverts to a course in conformity with the ILO's original aims."[42]

At a cabinet-level committee meeting held on October 12, 1977, Labor, Commerce, the AFL-CIO, and the Chamber of Commerce all voted for withdrawal, while State and the National Security Council both supported a one-year extension of the letter of intent. It was agreed that the Labor Department would prepare the case for withdrawal and the State Department would handle the extension proposal, both to be submitted to President Carter. The case for withdrawal prevailed. On November 1, 1977, the president announced that since the corrective measures requested by the United States in its original letter of intent to withdraw had not been made, U.S. membership in the ILO would be terminated. He added: "The U.S. remains ready to return whenever the ILO is again true to its proper principles and procedures."

The assistant secretary of state for international organizations wrote later that "the President pondered this problem up until almost the final hour and then decided the United States should let its letter of withdrawal take effect."[43] While this may have been the perception of the State Department, it would be more accurate to say that the adverse votes cast at the 1977 ILO conference had made U.S. withdrawal inevitable. Both the AFL-CIO and the Chamber of Commerce were determined to stand against any further participation. The government had the option of sending only governmental delegates to ILO meetings, but that would have been inconsistent with the U.S. emphasis on the importance of tripartism. It could have selected delegates from among other groups, such as the United Automobile Workers, which is not affiliated with the AFL-CIO and which was opposed to withdrawal. But such a move would have risked an open break with the labor movement, an impolitic route for a new Democratic administration to take. Finally, there was a strong possibility that, no matter what the administration decided to do, Congress would have refused once again to appropriate ILO funds.

Several other basic factors contributed to the decision to leave the ILO:

1. While the various interest groups in the United States had long-standing grievances against ILO procedures and practices, it required some immediate challenges to focus these grievances and lead to action. For the labor movement, the catalytic agents appear to have been, first, the issue of Israel and the PLO, and second, the growing acceptance of Soviet trade unions in and out of the ILO. For employers, the issue that appears to have been uppermost was increased pressure for upgrading the role of Communist employers in the various organs of the ILO. None of

these had much to do with the day-to-day work of the ILO, but all were in the spotlight at the annual conference.

2. The federal administration nominally made the decisions, but in fact it had little control over the final outcome. The Labor Department tended to back the AFL-CIO, while the Commerce Department, to the extent that it played any role at all, followed the line of the U.S. Chamber of Commerce. The State Department alone among the responsible governmental agencies had an independent policy, but it was unable to effectuate it. Broad foreign policy considerations may have dictated staying with the ILO, an international body that had been in existence for almost sixty years and which was presumably dedicated to human rights and the improvement of the lot of the poor. To sell this policy to the American people and to Congress, however, would have required a great deal more effort than the State Department made, particularly since it had to overcome the opposition of powerful interest groups with more parochial concerns and with effective lobbies.

3. Whatever continuity of government concern with the ILO existed was provided by the Labor Department, but this was on a routine, bureaucratic level. Over the years, reviewing bodies—the Johnson Committee, the comptroller general—urged the various federal administrations to develop objectives for U.S. participation in the ILO, to coordinate these objectives with the other interest groups, and to maintain a high level of interest in ILO activities, but the conclusion reached in 1977 was that "past U.S. participation in ILO was one of crisis management alternated with periods of neglect. As each crisis with ILO subsides, U.S. attention also subsides."[44]

4. The reason for the failure of successive administrations to accept this advice, particularly after 1970, may have been that it was misguided. It would not have been difficult to develop a comprehensive statement of objectives, to provide some monitoring of ILO technical activities, to make careful plans for U.S. participation at every level of the ILO. A few additional staff members at Labor and State would have sufficed. But the American officials most closely involved were aware that the conditions

that were crucial to continued U.S. participation, such as the blocking of the appointment of a Soviet assistant director-general, were being determined outside the government. It is unlikely that the United States would have left the ILO if the State Department had been in control. UNESCO has given the United States as much provocation as ILO, and in fact, Congress has on occasion cut off U.S. dues to that organization, but there has never been any serious move toward withdrawal. Other international bodies, such as UNIDO, enjoy much less prestige in the United States than does the ILO; yet there have not been similar problems with it.

5. In the final analysis, it was the American labor movement that gained the power to determine the nature of U.S. relationships with the ILO. It was not only a matter of the unique tripartite structure of the ILO, since employers have a much weaker voice. Yet tripartism was certainly a factor, since it is unlikely that the labor movement could take the United States out of any other international body. The reasons for the transfer of this part of foreign policy decisionmaking to a private organization are complex, but if an attempt were made to summarize them, one would have to say that there is a belief on the part of the informed public, and particularly of the Congress, that the ILO falls within the orbit of organized labor's main interests; that its appropriate goals coincide with those of the labor movement; and that if the spokesmen for labor declare that it is acting against their interests, logic dictates nonmembership.

Little has been said thus far about two of the ILO's major activities: providing technical assistance to less developed countries and setting international labor standards. The reason for this neglect is that these activities were not among the decisive factors leading to U.S. withdrawal—a remarkable fact considering that the performance of an organization is the usual criterion for such decisions.

The United States has been fairly consistent in expressing its support for the technical activities of the ILO. The problem is that these activities were subordinated to politics, particularly at the annual conference. If the ILO had stayed within its sphere of competence, no major difficulties need have arisen. All three American parties—government, labor, and management—have paid scant attention to ILO technical programs. Therefore, they have been unable to evaluate them and determine whether, in fact, the ILO has done a good job.

If public opinion in the United States is to play any role in the pattern of future U.S.–ILO relationships, the public needs more information on what the ILO has done in the sphere of influence over which it has jurisdiction. The following two chapters constitute an effort to provide both information and an evaluation. It is not the first such attempt—other studies will be summarized—but a book dealing with the ILO that failed to provide an analysis of the activities for which most of its resources go would be inadequate. Moreover, since all the political and structural changes the United States wishes made in the ILO are hardly likely to materialize, knowledge of what the ILO has actually achieved may prove to be decisive in the determination of whether the United States should maintain permanent membership. The question is one of costs versus benefits. Thus far, we have concentrated on the costs. Now we come to the benefits.

Chapter 5

The ILO's Technical
Cooperation Program

Until the mid-1950s, the ILO was concerned primarily with the promulgation and policing of international labor standards. As the number of new nations grew, so did the need for technical assistance, or technical cooperation, as it is now called. This aspect of the ILO program gained in relative importance, and is now a major activity.

Technical cooperation played no part in the U.S. break with the ILO. Those groups in the United States concerned with ILO policy had very little interest in the technical cooperation program. In fact, in 1977, the U.S. comptroller general submitted the following report: "In 1970, we recommended that the United States obtain better information from ILO and evaluate the Organization's programs. The United States is still not effectively evaluating ILO programs to ascertain that U.S. monetary contributions to ILO have been used to accomplish intended objectives. Further, ILO officials view the Organization's own evaluation efforts as inadequate."[1] Likewise, the Chamber of Commerce staff member responsible for ILO affairs told the author in 1977 that there was no hard evidence concerning the ILO's accomplishments in the less developed countries. The representative of the AFL-CIO was somewhat more concrete. In his opinion, ILO technical assistance had been spotty. Industrial training had not been linked closely enough to economic planning, and he felt that there was need for a genuine evaluation of the effectiveness of ILO technical assistance.

But while the technical cooperation function of the ILO has not been an important element in past ILO-U.S. relationships, it is significant for potential future relationships. Generally speaking, the kind of work that the ILO does in less developed countries is consistent with U.S. foreign policy objectives in that its purpose is to improve the social and economic conditions of wage earners in the less developed countries. If ILO projects are in fact being carried out efficiently and effectively, it would be logical for the United States to cooperate with the organization. If the United States can do a better job on a bilateral basis, this argument for working together with the ILO carries less weight.

Unfortunately, the science of evaluating development projects is still in its infancy, whether in regard to the ILO or to other international organizations and to U.S. bilateral programs.[2] The director-general of the ILO conceded the deficiencies of ILO evaluation procedures in the following statement to the 1977 conference:

> Their primary shortcoming is the basically unstructured nature of the evaluation process and the diversity of the personnel conducting them. To some evaluators, the mark of success is the timely delivery of inputs, to others the production of outputs, and, more rarely, the achievement of the stated immediate objective. Another major shortcoming of the present evaluation practice is that it does not automatically provide for the results of evaluation to be fed into the design of new projects and into the planning of technical co-operation programs.
>
> Today, one cannot point with confidence to the difference that many ILO technical co-operation projects have made in the lives of the intended beneficiaries. It has not been established that one approach has been more effective than another in reducing poverty, providing quality training, improving conditions of work or increasing employmentability. Lack of a solid information base about the performance of past and present projects limits the ILO's ability to map out sound future projects

reflecting the lessons learned and the experience gained.[3]

The willingness to make so candid an admission does credit to the ILO; few top international administrators have been prepared to write so frankly. Moreover, there is reason to believe that the ILO in fact has not done all that badly in its evaluation efforts.[4]

There are a number of reasons for weaknesses in the evaluation system. Apart from the formidable problems involved in measuring the impact of individual projects on development, most of the people engaged in project administration and execution have a vested interest in reporting success. Experts sent to the field are generally concerned with reappointment to new projects when their current ones are completed, and report of failure is not a good recommendation for renewal of tenure. Moreover, the experts tend to be enthusiastic about the work in which they are engaged, and can hardly be expected to be objective.

The administrators at headquarters are more interested in maximizing the quantity rather than the quality of projects. This is due in part to the usual bureaucratic desire for aggrandizement, but there is a practical reason as well: the ILO, and other executing agencies, currently levy a 14 percent overhead charge on project costs, which helps maintain supervisory staff. Particularly since 1970, the ILO has faced periodic financial crises caused not only by the temporary loss of the U.S. contribution, but also by the devaluation of the U.S. dollar against the Swiss franc, since country assessments and payments are made in dollars.[5]

The staff of the U.N. Development Program (UNDP), which is supposed to coordinate and monitor the projects it finances, has its own bureaucratic interests, which may also be antithetical to objective evaluation.[6] The same holds true for the various governmental agencies that administer assistance in the recipient countries.

ILO Evaluation Procedures

There are various levels of evaluation used by the ILO. First, at the conclusion of every project, and sometimes on an interim basis, a report is prepared by the project administrator, addressed to the host government, in which the project results are set forth. A report on the establishment of a national vocational training program in Jamaica, completed in 1975, is typical.[7] It describes in some detail the nature of the new vocational training institute, the staffing of industrial training centers, the promotion of in-plant training, the organization of an apprenticeship program, the setting of testing and certification standards, and the execution of vocational rehabilitation work. The project was supported by a UNDP contribution of $1,314,000, with the Jamaican government supplying additional funds in the form of cash, land, buildings, equipment and supplies, and local personnel.

The conclusions are self-congratulatory: "The substantial achievements described in this report fully justify the contributions made by the Government and the UNDP towards the development of a national vocational training program in Jamaica. . . . The Institute is now regarded as a model of its kind in the Caribbean and with its ample capacity could fulfill a wider role in helping to meet the training needs of other countries in the region."[8] A few deficiencies were noted. The water supply and telephone service were inadequate, for example, as was the supply of materials. There had been delays in an overseas fellowship program; the project's facilities were underutilized because of inadequate publicity; and more expert assistance was required to complete the training of the national staff. But all this was considered minor compared to the project's overall accomplishments.

The Jamaican project may very well have been successful, but this report, even though it includes a list of the training courses given and the number of trainees, is hardly an objective evaluation. The fact that the "expensive facilities" of the Vocational Training Development Institute had been "only partially utilized" and the recommendation that "the program be thoroughly and continuously publicized" suggest that the project may have been too ambitious in view of Jamaica's limited needs for skilled manpower. Fourteen experts from a number of countries, mostly Germany, Britain, and the United States, were associated with the project, some for long periods. The German project manager, for example, spent more than five years in Jamaica; and terms of two to five years were the mode.

A second example of such project reports involved the establishment of a productivity center in Cyprus. Again, this was a fairly typical ILO project. Facilities for both management and worker vocational training were created. The UNDP contribution during the life of the project (about ten years) amounted to $2,011,000, with the government of Cyprus contributing the equivalent of $1,341,000.[9] The summary of achievements in this case was less favorable than for the Jamaican project. While the Cyprian center was "firmly established and generally recognized as the most competent management development and vocational training body in the country," it was not yet financially self-sustaining. Its professional staff was too small, its premises needed basic improvements, it was not doing enough management consulting, and its training program "has not been at all times demonstrably attuned to needs."[10] All told, each of some thirty-six international experts spent more than a year in Cyprus.

A good deal could have been learned by careful analysis of these and other reports. Simply on the basis of the documents on file, the Jamaican project seemed to have been more successful than the one in Cyprus. Despite the large sums of money spent in both instances, no evidence exists that anyone in the United States, which paid about 25 percent of the total bill through its UNDP contribution, was engaged in an evaluation. The reports were placed in the ILO files, and no one was the wiser, except perhaps the administrators in Geneva.

A second level of ILO program review is provided in the form of annual reports by the Office to the Governing Body Committee on Operational Programs. The minutes of this committee indicate that the Governing Body has been seeking more and better information on the technical cooperation programs. Requests for additional data were often submitted, particularly by U.S. representatives on the committee. In 1971, for example, the U.S. labor representative called upon the Office to provide more detailed project descriptions and results. He pointed out that existing Office reports contained "regrettable gaps, espe-

cially in the section on evaluation."[11] Two years later, the U.S.
government delegate suggested that "machinery for evaluation
should be set up which would make it possible to avoid the difficulties already encountered in unsuccessful projects and to
draw lessons from successful ones."[12] In 1975, the U.S. government representative urged "an objective assessment of the ILO's
operational programs and a clear distinction between its successes and its failures. The difficulties were not new and were all
quite familiar, whether they arose on the side of the recipient
government or on that of the executing agency. Instead of merely
sifting through information derived from evaluation exercises,
the time had come to make a synthesis of such information and
draw conclusions."[13] And in 1976, he deplored an Office proposal
to suspend, for reasons of economy, a proposed technical cooperation management information system.[14] Unfortunately, none
of these interventions was followed up by the United States in
an effective way.

Given the persistent requests for additional data from the
United States and others, it does not appear that the Governing
Body was involved in any searching evaluation process. The Office reports to the committee improved from an analytical point
of view,[15] but no government seemed willing to devote the time
and resources necessary to make the review procedures more
useful or revealing.

A third type of project evaluation is tripartite in the ILO
sense—that is, labor and management representatives are involved in the review process. In 1973, the Governing Body decided to nominate tripartite teams to evaluate ILO programs on
a countrywide basis. The first of these teams spent a week in
Colombia, and the second visited Ghana, both in the fall of 1976.
The reports of these two teams, both of which are discussed later
in this chapter, include some interesting observations on specific
programs, but as the Colombia team noted, "the limited time at
the mission's disposal made it impossible for the evaluation team
to reach definitive value judgments on many of the matters
which came up for its attention. Rather it only allowed the team
to form useful impressions of them."[16] The Ghana team concluded in a similar vein: "The time allotted for the evaluation

exercise was too short to allow an in-depth study of all ILO technical cooperation projects. More time should be allotted for future exercises of this nature."[17]

A fourth type of evaluation, also tripartite but in a different sense, involves mid-term reports required by the UNDP; these are prepared on the basis of reviews carried out by the UNDP, the executing international agency, and the host country. The Program Office of the ILO characterized these documents as follows:

> These reports . . . are of a largely monitoring nature. Evaluation is made for purposes internal to the project and little attempt is made to assess project impact or to compare that impact to other possible courses of action. The accomplishment of objectives is often assessed in incomplete terms. These reports serve the specific purpose of identifying corrective action for projects in the course of implementation. The tendency of the reports is to restate or readjust objectives in the light of the current situation and recommend a modification in the mix of inputs. These are of course useful and essential things to do. However, the very existence of the project is seldom questioned, the underlying preoccupation of the evaluators being usually to save the initial investment. There is no common methodology (or even a common terminology) among the different evaluation reports and the quality of the evaluation depends heavily on the analytical capabilities of the persons undertaking it.[18]

One of the problems facing those who prepare these reports, a problem shared by evaluators at other levels, is that the project document itself often does not specify the objectives precisely enough to provide a clear definition of the various steps to be implemented. Deadlines are often not included, particularly for government inputs. There are emergency controls if something obvious goes wrong, but projects normally contain no funding for overall review after they are completed.

Finally, the regional advisory committees of the ILO in Asia, Africa, and Latin America have regularly included a review of ILO activities in their regions. But since these committees meet only at three- to four-year intervals, their reports are very general.

To sum up this brief review of ILO evaluation procedures, it simply is not possible, on the basis of existing materials, to reach any definitive conclusions on the relative merits of ILO projects. Apart from one fairly ambitious evaluation effort commissioned by the ILO, the Kilby Study, discussed below, most of the relevant reports are impressionistic. It is possible, however, to draw some tentative conclusions about the value of ILO technical cooperation projects for less developed countries as seen though the eyes of the various groups involved in them.

The ILO Programs

ILO technical cooperation programs are divided into eight categories for budgetary purposes. The amounts allocated to the various programs, along with the sources of the funds, are shown in Table 4. These figures were projected for the biennium 1978–79, and they represented ILO intentions just prior to the U.S. withdrawal. The amounts derived from the regular ILO budget have since been revised because of the ILO's financial difficulties, but the funds supplied by the UNDP and other extra-assessment sources were presumably unaffected.

As the figures in Table 4 indicate, the bulk of ILO technical cooperation is financed outside the regular budget. In 1978–79, about 60 percent was scheduled to come from the UNDP. Another 30 percent derived from so-called trust funds, which consisted of money supplied by member nations engaged in joint projects with the ILO (multi-bilateral programs), and from joint programs with other international organizations, such as UNICEF and the United Nations Environment Program (UNEP).

The actual expenditures for technical cooperation were $17,878,000 in 1967. Even allowing for inflation, the projected total of almost $50 million a year for 1978 and 1979 represented an increase in the availability of real resources. Another interesting trend is the growth of multi-bilateral projects, and the resulting growth of support from trust funds. In 1967, only 9.3 percent of total funds came from such sources, compared with the anticipated 30 percent in 1978–79. The UNDP share fell from 78.6 percent in 1967 to 60 percent as projected for

TABLE 4. Estimated Costs of ILO Technical Cooperation Projects in 1978–79
(In Constant Thousands of 1976–77 U.S. Dollars)

Program	Funding source			Total costs
	Regular budget	UNDP	Trust funds	
International labor standards	105	0	0	105
Employment and development	2,625	9,900	12,000	24,525
Training	1,575	36,500	7,500	45,575
Industrial relations and labor administration	3,045	3,750	1,650	8,445
Working conditions and environment	1,365	2,000	500	3,865
Sectoral activities	525	3,500	5,700	9,725
Social security	525	1,500	400	2,425
Statistics	735	300	350	1,385
All programs	10,500	57,450	28,100	96,050

SOURCE: ILO, *Director-General's Programme and Budget Proposals for 1978–79* (Geneva, 1976), p. viii.

1978–79, even though the absolute contribution rose from $14,047,000 in 1967 to about $29 million in 1978–79.[19]

In terms of resource allocation, the largest individual program involved training, and it consisted of two major activities: vocational training, which received two-thirds of the funds, and management development, which received the balance. Historically, vocational training has been the principal activity of the ILO in developing countries, and this activity continues to be featured, although the management development program has been gaining.

The second largest program, employment and development, is the so-called World Employment Program, discussed below. It consists of a heterogeneous group of activities: employment planning strategies, income distribution, poverty reduction, manpower policies, technological choice, international trade and migration, and population policy. All relatively new and uncharted, these activities are more difficult to assess than the traditional ones.

Sectoral programs are those that apply to special economic groups: individual industries, salaried employees, maritime workers, and multinational enterprises.

The bread and butter of the ILO consists of activities that fall in the general area of industrial relations. These include labor legislation, collective bargaining, employment service administration, the labor inspectorate, assistance to workers' and employers' organizations. Since the UNDP allows its assistance to go only to governments, much of the direct help given to labor and management must be funded out of the regular budget (see Table 4.).

Finally, projects that involve assistance to countries for the improvement of their statistical systems and the development of their social security programs have proved important in gaining goodwill for the ILO, even though they may not involve large amounts of financing. These projects are usually specific in their purpose, and the recruitment of experts, which is often not an easy task for poorly defined programs, is not difficult. The ILO social security department in Geneva enjoys a high reputation throughout the world, and the statistical department has had

many years of experience in its program to standardize labor statistics.

The ILO has not always been its own master in determining
which of these programs is given priority. Much depends on
what the UNDP is willing to finance, what individual member
nations are prepared to support, aside from their regular dues
payments, and what the recipient countries want. While labor
and management representatives in the ILO Governing Body
continually press for an expansion of industrial relations work,
most of the less developed countries show little interest in
strengthening labor unions and employer associations or in setting up collective-bargaining systems. The opposite side of the
coin has been the temptation, to which the ILO has occasionally
yielded, of engaging in certain activities primarily because outside funds are available. According to a Mexican employer member of the Governing Body,

> the ILO was organizing plenty of committees, symposia, work-
> shops and seminars, sometimes financed by bodies with obscure
> initials, but it was not always clear what need they met and what
> had been the criteria for their choice. Why, for instance, should
> the ILO deal with questions of family planning, however inter-
> esting that subject might be, or with matters of housing, except
> in relation to workers' housing? . . . Even if financed by extra-
> budgetary funds, all such meetings placed demands on ILO staff
> who might otherwise be assigned to more useful jobs. . . . The
> fact that the funds came from outside was not sufficient reason
> for [the ILO] to join in just any kind of activity.[20]

Surprisingly, the United States never objected to the practice
whereby an individual country, by means of a relatively small
extra-budgetary contribution, could push the ILO in directions
that were sometimes not germane to its mission. If a particular
country or private organization feels that the ILO deserves more
support, a general-purpose grant is in order. Or if aid-giving
agencies in the industrial nations believe that critical gaps are
hindering growth in the less developed countries, they have the
option of providing bilateral assistance on their own. The Netherlands, among other countries, has adopted a system of support
for ILO technical assistance that might well be regarded as

within proper bounds. Young Dutchmen are assigned for one or two years to the ILO, or to some other international agency, as "associate" experts. They can be used in any capacity the ILO deems appropriate, and their salaries are reimbursed by their government. These associate experts are highly regarded by international officials, and they have performed well. Their services represent general-purpose grants in kind.

ILO projects, like those of other international agencies, are characterized by high labor costs. In 1976, for example, 76 percent of total ILO expenditures for technical cooperation was allocated to expert services, leaving only 7.7 percent for study grants, 11.1 percent for equipment, and 5.2 percent for miscellaneous items.[21] In 1978, the annual cost of an ILO expert was about $50,000, the amount varying with local living costs.[22] A widespread view in less developed countries holds that U.N. agency experts' earnings are too high, particularly when compared with local earnings.[23] When experts are drawn from the less developed countries themselves, as is increasingly the practice, their earnings are many times greater than what they could expect in their own countries. Since it is impractical to pay experts of equal ability salaries that vary with the levels in their own countries, these costs can only be reduced by revising the entire scale.

In conclusion, mention should be made of regional units created by the ILO to coordinate country programs and to provide occasional advice. These include,

For employment:
  Jobs and Skills Program for Africa (JASPA)
  Regional Employment Program for Latin America (PREALC)
  Asian Regional Team for Employment Promotion (ARTEP)
For labor administration:
  African Regional Labor Administration Center for French-
    Speaking Africa (CRADAT). This has now become an independent body.
  African Regional Labor Administration Center for English-
    Speaking Africa (ARLAC)
  Inter-American Labor Administration Center (CIAT)

Asian Regional Project for Strengthening Labor and Manpower Administration (ARPLA)

For training:

Inter-American Vocational Training Research and Documentation Program for Latin America (CINTERFOR)

Asian Regional Skill Development Program (ARSDEP)

ILO Self-Evaluation of Program Results

Recent efforts by the ILO Office to evaluate its own programs have taken two main forms: annual reports to the Governing Body, which are more analytical than before, and a one-time, indepth review of all Office programs, including technical cooperation.

The first of the "analytical" reports, in 1974, pointed out that ILO activities were highly concentrated on vocational training, an area that might not be adapted to needs in coming years. The proportion of "socially oriented" projects, those designed to relieve poverty and bring about improved social conditions, remained low. The main cause of delay in project execution, the report suggested, was the difficulty of recruiting experts.[24] Certain skills, such as accounting and language, are in short supply. For example, French-speaking experts who are not of French nationality are needed in Africa. People with excellent qualifications on paper are often not able to adapt to field conditions. One common complaint heard in less developed countries is that the knowledge possessed by these experts is too theoretical and does not apply to the crude working conditions often found in these areas.

The report for the years 1975–76 highlighted a financial crisis of the UNDP which began in November 1975. It was caused by mismanagement of funds, including the accumulation of large amounts of nonconvertible currency, and delays in the payment of contributions. As a result, the ILO was forced to cut its field staff by 30 percent during 1976 and 1977; this was so traumatic that the report failed to mention other implementation problems, apart from the fact that the quota of "social" projects remained low.[25]

The in-depth reviews are somewhat more informative. Their

conclusions regarding four ILO programs may be summarized as follows:

1. *Management Development.* The purpose of the management development program was to help raise productivity by improving the competency of management. Productivity missions to developing countries began as early as 1952. The program kept expanding until 1972, when it began to decline, partly because of growing competition from the United Nations Industrial Development Organization (UNIDO).

Until 1960, projects were mainly small; but thereafter, emphasis was placed on the establishment of management development and productivity institutes, with individual project costs rising as high as $5 million. Some seventy countries were given assistance, and many training fellowships were granted, though the in-depth report noted that the training was often not of sufficient length to permit acquisition of adequate knowledge. Most training courses offered were of short duration, with emphasis on financial, production, and marketing management.

A large number of training manuals were prepared and sold. For example, an introduction to work study sold 177,000 copies, and a manual on how to read a balance sheet, 78,000 copies.[26]

The report on this program is written in very general terms, and is devoid of any real content. It leaves unanswered the basic question of how best to provide managerial talent for the less developed countries. The assumptions made are that what the ILO has been doing is correct, and that more of the same is called for. The Office missed an opportunity to use its years of experience with these programs to tackle basic questions of management training in the new nations. Efficient small entrepreneurs have emerged in the more successful less developed countries without the benefit of five-day courses and elementary manuals. Modern Western management techniques would seem to be more appropriate for large enterprises, which in less developed countries are likely to be either government enterprises or affiliates of multinational firms, while ordinary business school training might be more suitable for the more typical small enterprises.

As the ILO program was originally conceived, the emphasis was placed on raising labor productivity; hence the term "productivity center" for the institutions that were established. But there was a tendency for the programs to collapse as soon as the experts left, so that emphasis switched to courses of short duration, rarely lasting beyond a few months. The productivity centers began to be involved in consulting work, and it was hoped that they would eventually become self-sustaining. Students were occasionally given internships with large Western management consulting firms.

The financial problems of the 1970s forced some rethinking. Instead of formal courses, emphasis was placed on conferences and research and on small enterprises. With very little research on the content or methodology of management training having been done, the ILO has simply been passing on Western doctrine.

Data on the nationality of ILO experts are available only for the totality of its programs, but they do suggest that for management development, as well as for other programs, experts have not been drawn primarily from the countries that were most successful in achieving economic growth. The following data show the nationality of ILO experts in post on December 31, 1975:[27]

Country	Percent of total experts
United Kingdom	16.5
France	14.2
Sweden	6.9
United States	6.3
Belgium	4.7
India	4.3
Netherlands	4.2
Germany	3.9
Japan	0.3
Other	38.7
	100.0

Britain, the largest supplier of ILO experts, is not renowned for pioneering work in management training. The United States, Germany, and Japan, countries in which a good deal of attention has been devoted to management organization and training, contributed only a bit over 10 percent of all ILO experts. This figure is probably higher for management development programs; the ILO would undoubtedly ascribe the fact that six European countries, three of them small, supplied half its experts to language difficulties and to the availability of recruits. Nevertheless, this nationality bias has served to deprive the less developed nations of much recent thinking on entrepreneurial development, unless they enlisted the services of private consulting firms.

2. *Rural Development.* Rural development is not ordinarily associated with the ILO, which in the past had largely restricted its jurisdiction to the industrial sector. However, the growth of its technical assistance component brought the ILO into contact with rural problems, and in recent years, its rural program has reached respectable proportions. In the biennium 1974–75, almost $19 million was expended for operational activities in rural areas. The type of activity undertaken is indicated by the following figures, for the period 1970–75:[28]

Activity	Percent of total rural development expenditures
Training of rural workers or instructors	26.1
Development of rural cooperatives	28.3
Advisory institutions for nonagricultural activities in rural areas	24.4
Advisory services for rural development projects	13.6
Helping solve rural poverty	3.3
Other	4.3

The ILO's first major involvement in the rural sector was the Andean Indian project, initiated in 1954. Its purpose was to integrate the indigenous population of the Andes into the modern economies of their countries in order to improve their living standards.[29] The program was launched and carried out with much fanfare, but it gradually petered out, and its results are buried in the ILO files. There is no evidence that the large sums expended on the project over a period of fifteen years contributed to any significant improvement in Indian living standards.

Another expensive program was initiated in 1969 to help retain the farming population in western Nigeria through the creation of small-scale manufacturing.[30] Apparently, this project also failed to attain its objectives, although the reluctance of the ILO to record its failures makes conclusive evidence hard to come by.[31]

The ILO rural development program received an unexpected setback in 1975, when a U.N. coordinating committee found that it was deficient in several respects:

1. It lacked focus. The committee recommended that the program concentrate on improving the lot of the poorest sectors of rural populations.
2. The ILO had tried to cover too much ground. The committee "expressed concern about the apparently limited impact which the rural development activities of the Office have had in the last decades in comparison to the immense needs; this apprehension pertained to all program components."
3. Many committee members felt that the ILO had been involved too heavily in research and surveys at the expense of action.[32]

The committee added that rural development was a difficult field because there was a lack of basic operating concepts. Conventional approaches had proven inappropriate, and the political, economic, and social institutions that are needed to bring about rural progress are often nonexistent.

The subsequent ILO in-depth review met this criticism by admitting past errors and embraced the new orthodoxy of concentrating on the poor peasants. It confessed to having assisted rural cooperatives in which medium- and large-scale farmers were sometimes the most active members. The review continued: "Also, the most vigorous small-scale entrepreneurs have utilized the services of small-scale industry institutes more frequently than their poorer colleagues. The sons and daughters of village headmen have sometimes been the first to profit from craft training facilities."[33]

The ILO had fallen into error, the U.N. report stated, because it had been following the goal of economic growth, according to which "the overriding concern is with the growth of production, which is expected to come largely from relatively modern sectors of agricultural and industrial activity." Having purged itself by a *mea culpa* exercise, the ILO promised that its rural development program would be devoted in the future to the improvement of land tenancy, ownership, and distribution; the organization of poor rural workers; improvement of the lot of rural women; and "collection and analysis of information needed for assessing the nature, extent, and causes of poverty and underemployment." It agreed to drop integrated rural development projects, those involving new agricultural settlements and farm technology, and ambitious packaged programs designed to take account of all the socioeconomic factors that influence rural development. Fortunately or unfortunately, sister U.N. agencies were prepared to fill the gap left by the ILO.

The response of the Governing Body to the Office report was predictable. The workers' group found it deficient because it failed to place major emphasis on the organization of farm trade unions, and relied too much on what could be accomplished through rural cooperatives, which "too frequently . . . are controlled by the privileged or the semi-privileged sector of rural society and are frequently used to further exploit the lower income group in the rural sector." On the other hand, the employers' group felt that the report was overly concerned with organizing the rural poor. "The only thing common to the poor in rural areas is poverty, and any organizations which made poverty the sole qualification for membership would inextricably become entangled in politics. . . . If they are to develop, organizations should make the sharing of interests, and obviously not that of poverty, the qualification for membership."[34]

The fact remains that, without government intervention, it is very difficult to achieve organization in developing countries. What the ILO will do in its future rural development program remains to be seen. Its past activities do not appear to have made any significant contribution to development.

3. *Social Security*. Between 1950 and 1970, about 350 ILO experts in social security were involved in technical assistance. Virtually every developing country received advice from the ILO on problems relating to the institution of social security systems. The ILO in-depth review of this area pointed out that while the projects were typically low in cost, their yield in terms of social progress was potentially high. For example, the cost of preparing proposals for the introduction of a comprehensive social security system in a medium-sized country, including the actuarial work, was only $20,000 to $35,000.

There were a number of reasons for the acknowledged failures. Some experts lacked the adaptability or imagination to apply their skills to the problems of developing nations. Countries sometimes made unrealistic requests, and there was an occasional "lack of initiative and understanding from national counterparts, lack of determination of the recipient country to carry out reforms and improvements, political instability which makes ineffective or impossible the implementation of ILO recommendations."[35]

The ILO claims credit for dispelling the widespread view that less developed countries cannot afford social security and welfare programs. This is a well-merited claim, since conventional wisdom dictates that social measures must be accorded a low priority relative to investment in productive resources. In fact, appropriate social security plans can lead to higher productivity by improving the health and efficiency of workers. They can also make an important contribution to political stability, without which no economic development program is likely to succeed. Long before the current preoccupation with poverty, ILO social security projects were tackling income redistribution in a scientific and orderly manner, to the great advantage of low-income people.

This being said, it must be added that the Office in-depth review was rightly criticized by the Governing Body for its failure to suggest criteria that could be used to evaluate this program. The Canadian government representative stated that "the advice given to a member state through a technical cooperation project might or might not be fully accepted and applied, but the degree of acceptance and implementation of this advice nevertheless gave some objective indication of its value; it was thus useful to know, in addition to the number of significant suggestions made, the percentage of suggestions accepted and implemented."[36] The Office acknowledged the need for evaluation along the following lines: (*a*) the degree of acceptance accorded the ILO by recipient countries; (*b*) the degree of actual implementation of advice; (*c*) a demonstration that action taken by a government, following ILO advice, constituted an improvement.[37] There is no evidence that this form of evaluation was ever put into practice.

4. *Workers' Education.* Although workers' education is not a large program in terms of expenditures, it is an important one. Its focus is on those educational activities intended to strengthen trade unions and to improve the capacity and performance of workers' representatives. The in-depth report on this program acknowledges that in developing countries, strong and responsible organizations of the rural poor have yet to emerge. The same might be said of the industrial sector: strong trade unions, independent of government and employers, are not to be found in a majority of less developed countries, although it would be incorrect to say that they are nonexistent.

It is not a function of the ILO to organize trade unions. Once unions are in existence, however, the ILO can help by training their officials, helping to establish research and library services, and operating courses for union members so that they can participate more fully in union affairs. Unlike other technical assistance programs, workers' education is funded largely from the regular ILO budget.

The in-depth review acknowledges that no systematic effort had been made to develop indicators by which to measure project effectiveness. The difficulty of measurement is compounded by the fact that unions in less developed countries often have a fleeting existence. An organization in which the ILO has invested considerable time and money is often simply abolished or allowed to die following a change in the local political regime.[38]

The reaction of the members of the Governing Body who

commented on this report was generally laudatory, except for employer reservations about the organization of rural workers. The prevalent view in the ILO appears to be that workers' education is justified per se, whatever its results. Without effective trade unions there cannot be genuine tripartism; and most Western nations, and U.S. labor in particular, regard independent unionism as a necessary condition for the preservation of political democracy in an industrial society. Nevertheless, it would have been useful if the ILO had attempted to distill out of its experience a judgment on which substantive and methodological aspects of its work were the most successful. This may be too much to expect, however, for such an evaluation would necessarily entail classifying country projects by some index of prevailing political democracy, an impossible task for an international organization. Courses and seminars appropriate to one country might not be tolerated in another. Subjects that might be usefully taught to officers of independent unions may be a waste of time when union officials are in fact government agents. But there can be no doubt that from an American point of view, worker education is one of the ILO's most significant areas of technical assistance, particularly if the task is done effectively.

Tripartite Evaluations

The idea of tripartite, on-the-spot investigations of technical assistance was approved by the Governing Body in 1973, but the first mission did not go into the field until 1975. The program then proceeded slowly, and by the time of U.S. withdrawal, only two such investigations had taken place, in Ghana and in Colombia.

The mission to Ghana was composed of Governing Body members representing the Mexican government, the Ghanaian employers, and the Nigerian workers. It seems odd that a group charged with providing an objective evaluation should include a national of one of the countries involved. At any rate, the investigation was carried out in Ghana during the week of November 21–27, 1975.

Only three specific projects were covered. A management development project, according to the mission, had been completed successfully, and its training program had been turned over to Ghanaian nationals. The mission further concluded that government and UNDP investment in the establishment of a national vocational training institute had proved extremely worthwhile. A project aimed at the improvement of manpower planning, the group reported, had also achieved its objectives.

The UNDP cost of these three projects was about $2.5 million. Although some data were added to the report to document the output of management and blue-collar trainees, plus the data from several manpower studies that had been completed, no attempt was made to determine whether or not the results justified the cost. The principal recommendations of the mission concerned the need for (1) more consultation with employer and worker organizations; (2) improvement in ILO procedures for recruiting experts and purchasing equipment; (3) better orientation of experts who are called in from advanced countries and a greater proportion of these experts being selected from developing countries; and (4) more attention to rural areas.[39]

Even considering the minimal investment of three manweeks, this report was not one to inspire confidence. Yet the only American representative on the Governing Body who expressed concern was the U.S. worker delegate, and he merely stressed the need for more tripartite participation in project administration. His reference to the report as a "model of honesty and frankness" is difficult to understand, since it was bland, noncommittal, and minimally informative.[40] This first exercise in tripartite evaluation can hardly be termed a success.

The report of the Colombian mission was much more interesting and informative. The members of the team consisted of Governing Body representatives of the German government, the Argentine employers, and the Venezuelan trade unions. While no quantitative evaluation was undertaken, the comments of the Colombian officials interviewed were recorded in some detail. The net result of ILO activities, to quote the minister of labor and social security, was that the "ILO's past and present technical cooperation activities could not be described as entirely satisfactory or unsatisfactory."[41]

A project designed to improve and expand the social security system was reported not to have taken into account the realities of Colombia, since the expert recommendations merely envisioned the transplantation of foreign systems. "In general, the project's objectives could be considered as having been fulfilled in their theoretical aspects, but in its implementation the Government had had no machinery capable of suggesting specific solutions to meet the country's needs."[42] In the execution of this project, as well as of others under the jurisdiction of the Ministry of Labor, there had been long delays between request and performance, with the result that needs had changed and the projects had to be redesigned. Blame for the delays was shared by the government bureaucracy and the ILO.

A project involving the national apprenticeship service had not achieved its objectives because private firms had shown little inclination to develop vocational training programs. The ILO had attempted to develop a questionnaire preparatory to the promotion of small-scale industry in rural areas, but the questionnaire was not appropriate to the needs of the country and it had to be redrafted by the apprenticeship service itself.

A workers' education project analysis was summed up as follows: "On arrival of the expert the Government decided to abandon the idea of setting up a large center and instead to develop a program to inform non-unionized rural workers of their rights. . . . The expert's work had given poor results because of a lack of knowledge of national conditions. Employment of national experts should therefore be contemplated."[43]

On the plus side, a project relating to labor migration was completed without difficulty. A CIAT course in labor statistics for trade unionists, PREALC cooperation in the development of an employment project, and CINTERFOR's activities in providing advice on vocational training all received high grades. Also acknowledged was the ILO role in the establishment of the apprenticeship service.

The Union of Colombian Workers, which was unhappy about the direction taken by the workers' education project, charged that the ILO was not respecting its own philosophy of tripartism. Another labor federation agreed that ILO experts had virtually no contact with the trade union movement. These complaints illustrate the difficulty often faced by the ILO in handling workers' education and other projects with political overtones: all too often the organization must follow the lead of the government or else abandon the project. The Colombian National Association of Industrialists declared that its relations with ILO experts had been nonexistent and that it had not been involved in either the formulation or the implementation of technical assistance work.

The mission acknowledged that the week it had spent in Colombia was not long enough for it to reach any definitive value judgments. The impressions it had gained, however, proved useful, for the group had succeeded in pinpointing some real problems. Among its recommendations was that for future guidance, those technical cooperation models that had achieved favorable cost-benefit ratios ought to be identified.

The Colombian evaluation was one of the few occasions before 1977 when a realistic appraisal of an ILO country assistance program was presented to the Governing Body. The fact that the report was received with almost no discussion typifies the degree of supervision which that body exercised over ILO technical assistance activities. This experience does suggest, however, that the tripartite evaluation device may prove useful, especially if the team members are given more time for their work and have access to professional advice while in the field.

The Kilby Study

In 1976, the ILO invited Peter Kilby, an American economist with considerable experience in economic development work, to supervise the preparation of case histories of ten ILO projects within a formal cost-benefit framework. This was the first attempt by the ILO at a comprehensive, quantitative review of its technical assistance programs. The projects all fell within the jurisdiction of the ILO branch dealing with technology and employment. In three of the cases, measurement of benefits did not prove feasible, although case histories were compiled. The final result was a report that generalized the experience gained from this area of ILO activity.[44]

Despite difficult problems of measurement, the authors of the report were able to produce a document that for the first time provided guidelines for judging the success or failure of specific ILO projects. If an exercise like this had been tried a decade earlier, a great deal of effort and money might have been saved.

The projects studied and the results of the evaluation are shown in Table 5. In only four of the ten cases shown did benefits exceed costs. For the remaining projects, benefits were very low in relation to costs. The findings were summarized as follows: "The most striking aspect of these calculations is the generally low benefit/cost ratios. This is so despite the fact that many of our procedures are biased in the opposite direction. . . . More data and greater rigor would most probably have resulted in even lower ratios."

A summary of the details of some of the individual project studies will be found in Appendix A. Some of the more interesting observations that emerged from them were the following:

1. Two of the successful projects "had experts possessed of truly outstanding energy, adaptability, and imagination." The experts in these cases enjoyed considerable autonomy and freedom from local bureaucratic meddling. There was also a timely provision of input.

2. "The projects that arouse most enthusiasm among officials in both the donor and the host countries seem to be those calling for simultaneous action on several fronts." The successful projects were those that helped remove a bottleneck by supplying one or two missing ingredients. Large-scale projects involving many experts do not work well.

3. There is a tendency to seek to create employment by training the unemployed. It is more effective to improve the skills of craftsmen who are underemployed. "Although less dramatic than working directly with the unemployed, the indirect method is far more sure; as technical cooperation with producers in an existing industry reduces costs or introduces new products, output expands and the number of unemployed diminishes."

The reaction of ILO officialdom to this study was one of cau-

TABLE 5. Evaluation of ILO Employment Creation Projects

Project	Industry	Duration	Project cost (thousand U.S.$)			ILO experts		Ratio of benefits to costs
			UNDP	Counterpart	Total	Posts	Man-months	
A	Woolen carpets	1967–76	246	285	531	3	164	-2.12
B	Woolen carpets	1964–70	120	1,305	1,425	1	72	0.15
C	Woolen carpets	1972–76	210	76	286	1	53	5.29
D	Artistic handicrafts	1973–76	1,215	625	1,840	10	308	0.04
E	Artistic handicrafts	1973–76	1,032	767	1,799	15	297	0.35
F	Ceramics	1972–76	146	75	221	1	42	1.28
G	Wood carving	1960–74	144	48	192	1	47	1.57
H	Leather tanning	1959–71	220	0	220	1	128	
	(1) Tanners							3.56
	(2) Preservers							0.26
	(3) Technicians							0.49

SOURCE: Peter Kilby and Paul Bangasser, Jr., "Assessing Technical Cooperation," *International Labour Review*, May–June, 1978, pp. 344, 350.

NOTE: The source identifies the countries in which the projects were executed by letter only. However, they have been identified by an ILO official as follows: A—Mauritania, B—Syria, C—Madagascar; D—Netherland Antilles, E—Eastern Caribbean, F—Netherland Antilles, G—West Irian, H—Afghanistan.

tion. The final version of the summary paper published in the *International Labour Review* was carefully edited to remove whatever might give offense to local or international officials. Yet this is precisely the kind of evaluation that the ILO and other international agencies should have been doing all along. If they had, the effectiveness of technical assistance would probably have been much greater, since people everywhere are usually willing to learn from their mistakes.

A word of caution: the Kilby Study was commissioned by the ILO itself and was not the result of outside pressures. It was confined to a narrow range of ILO activities in a new and difficult field—employment creation—and as such, it does not necessarily characterize other types of technical assistance. Had there been half a dozen more studies like this one, it would be possible to comment on the efficacy of ILO assistance with much greater authority.

The ILO and the United Nations Development Program

The effectiveness of technical assistance under UNDP administration remains unexplored territory. A brief description of the system is necessary for an appreciation of the constraints under which the ILO operates, for the UNDP has a great deal of authority, not only in choice of project, but also in execution.

The present UNDP machinery was established in 1966 in an effort to rationalize the distribution of multilateral aid. Financial resources are made available by annual voluntary donations from member countries. The major contributors for 1977 are listed in Table 6. Among the large contributors, the Scandinavian countries and the Netherlands also carry on their own bilateral programs. France and Japan prefer the bilateral route.

Communist participation in the financing of the UNDP is token. Moreover, the Communist states tend to make their contributions in nonconvertible currencies that can be used only in their own countries. Communist experts who are sent out on UNDP projects receive their maintenance payments in convertible funds so that other countries must bear the burden. It is also difficult to procure equipment with the blocked currency. There are long delays in delivery from the Soviet Union, for example,

TABLE 6.   Pledges to the United Nations Development Program by Selected
Countries, 1977
(In Thousands of U.S. Dollars)

	Amount	Percentage of total
United States	100,000	19.1
Sweden	57,562	11.0
The Netherlands	56,747	10.8
Denmark	45,294	8.7
Germany	39,206	7.5
United Kingdom	34,421	6.6
Canada	32,381	6.2
Norway	28,298	5.4
Japan	22,000	4.2
France	10,000	1.9
U.S.S.R.	4,332	0.8
Other Eastern European Communist countries	3,085	0.6
Total of all pledges for the year	523,136	

Source: UNDP, *Annual Report of the Administration for 1977*, Statistical Annex, Table 15.

because of the low priorities Russia assigns to such orders. Spare
parts are also a problem. Courses of study given in Russia are
expensive, and the international agencies often have little control over their content.

Available funds are allocated to each recipient country according to a formula based in principle on that country's population and its per capita GNP. Thus, the largest recipient in the
planning period 1977–81 is India, with 5 percent of the total,
followed by Indonesia and Bangladesh. The Communist countries of Eastern Europe are receiving 1.5 percent among them,
which means their receipts will exceed their contributions.[45]
Once a country has received its allocation, disposition of the
funds is determined by its own officials, subject to the concurrence of the UNDP resident representative. Usually, a department in the office of the prime minister coordinates assistance
requests from the various ministries.

This system of block grants to countries, which began in

1969, has developed some serious faults. Each country tends to regard such grants as its own money, to be spent as it likes. The UNDP has lost leverage for that reason, and it may have difficulty requiring adequate counterpart assistance. The ability of the resident representative becomes an important variable, for he is expected to develop a coordinated plan of priorities. Since he is generally a professional administrator without any technical knowledge of economic development, however, he tends to be an arbiter instead of an initiator.

In actual practice, each national ministry, aided and abetted by the international agency with which it is working, tries to get as large a share of the total aid amount as possible. The resulting allocation of funds may reflect political power rather than developmental needs. The ILO works primarily with labor ministries, which sometimes rank low in the political influence scale. This helps explain the moderate share of UNDP funds that the organization normally receives. (See Table 7.)

The success indicator for an international agency administrator at the regional or country level is the portion of the UNDP budget he secures for his agency. Large allocations mean more jobs and more overhead money. In the determination of the project requests to be submitted, there is a good deal of negotiation between the ministry and the international agency. The latter may try to convince the ministry that particular areas are in need

TABLE 7.   Expenditure of UNDP Funds by Selected Executing Agencies, 1977

	Percentage of total
United Nations	15.4
Food and Agricultural Organization	26.5
Industrial Development Organization	10.2
Educational, Social, and Cultural Organization	9.0
International Labor Organization	7.8
World Health Organization	4.5

SOURCE: UNDP, *Annual Report of the Administration for 1977*, p. 11.

of development, and it may succeed in doing so. However, neither the ILO nor any other international agency is in a position to resist ministry requests, even if they do not make sense from a technical point of view. If the minister of labor, or the president (or the president's wife, as in the case of one of the projects discussed in the preceding section), wants a project, the ILO will normally acquiesce. To refuse to do so is to risk its future share of the aid market. The result is that "in practice project selection tends to be heavily influenced by considerations which are extraneous to a rational screening process. Two such considerations that frequently bear on the decision are the immediate sociopolitical events that lead up to the project request and the personal background of the U.N. advisers assisting in project identification and project formulation."[46]

Projects often take on a political character. They may arise out of the need to soothe certain social groups after political disturbances. They may support the desire of the government in power to bring about changes in political and social structure. In the latter case, which is not at all unusual, a change in government leads to the demise of the project or to its transformation into something quite different from what was originally intended. In any event, the purpose of the technical assistance program—to promote development—is frustrated.

The international agencies have had reservations about the UNDP system. Some would have preferred to receive funds directly from the UNDP, funds which they could then allocate among countries on the basis of perceived needs. The UNDP resident representative is often referred to as a czar by agency field personnel, who feel that they are not consulted sufficiently in the allocative process. Some of these resentments surfaced when the UNDP experienced its liquidity crisis in 1975–76, as evidenced by the following quotation from an ILO annual report on technical assistance, which is worth quoting at length:

> In recent years the specialized agencies have detected with some concern a certain tendency in the UNDP to limit their participation and contribution to the program. The ILO has found increasing difficulty in participating in the country programming procedures and in regional programming. The resi-

dent representatives have sometimes interpreted their role of coordination as entitling them to almost exclusive control over relations with government authorities in charge of program planning. Even in consultations between the UNDP secretariat and agency headquarters the agencies' views have not always exerted the influence one might expect them to have in a system which constantly pays lip service to the idea of association of all the partners. . . .

At the request of their governing bodies some agencies, such as the WHO and the FAO, have already taken steps to increase their autonomy in preparing and executing technical cooperation programs. Some ILO member states seem to be fully aware of the seriousness of the problem. They are worried that under the present UNDP programming system fairly low priority is being given to social objectives, labor problems, tripartite participation in the development campaign and aid to the poor.[47]

The last paragraph in this quotation reflects a long-standing ILO complaint: that the UNDP is reluctant to finance "social" projects of the ILO type and that the present allocative system affords no opportunity for labor and management participation in formulating and executing projects. U.S. representatives on the ILO Governing Body have repeatedly expressed concern about the lack of any tripartite consultation; on the other hand, there is no evidence that they attempted to move the UNDP in that direction, despite the great influence the United States has always had within the UNDP.

Another difficulty with the UNDP system is the intense rivalry it creates among U.N. agencies. The ILO's main competitor is the U.N.'s Industrial Development Organization, whose charter cuts across the traditional ILO jurisdiction. When the United Nations created UNIDO in 1965, it was obvious that this overlap would cause problems. Long and arduous negotiations took place in search of some clarification of spheres of activity. A memorandum establishing general guidelines was initialed by the two organizations in 1968, but still there is conflict, particularly in the area of management development.[48] It is difficult for the ILO to turn down a project request when it knows that UNIDO, UNESCO, or FAO are prepared to step into the breach.

In particular, if the UNDP favors a project, it is almost a certainty that the ILO will accede to a country request even against the advice of its own technicians. A specialized agency like the ILO should refuse to become involved in technical assistance when it considers such a move unjustified, but the present system of allocating aid funds works against such objective evaluation.

There are arguments to be made in favor of centralizing multilateral assistance funding, but as has already been noted, there has been no serious study external to the U.N. system of current UNDP organization and practices. The UNDP has not been noted for its ability to manage its own internal affairs, and there is a real question whether it should have as much power as it presently enjoys.[49] The main point here is that the blame for poorly conceived projects should not be laid solely at the door of the ILO. The UNDP and its major contributor, the United States, are also at fault.

Country Visits

In the spring of 1978, I visited six less developed countries in order to have a firsthand look at some ILO technical assistance projects. The countries were those in which the organization had conducted a large number of projects; more important, they were areas in which the political and social conditions were considered favorable for technical assistance. No international project can withstand cataclysmic political events.

Each visit lasted about a week; none would have been possible without the full cooperation of the ILO, which scheduled interviews and made other arrangements. This may have biased the resultant evaluations in a direction favorable to the ILO, but a random selection of countries would have led to a much less productive expenditure of time. The impression I gained was that the great majority of ILO officials in the field were candid in responding to questions and that they welcomed the opportunity to discuss their work with an interested observer from outside the system.

It is proper to ask how much can be learned about a complicated set of problems in the course of a week. My perception is that while it would have been desirable to have had longer study terms, even a brief visit can yield a realistic picture of technical assistance problems. Documents are indispensable, but complete reliance on them is not likely to provide sound results.

Two countries were chosen from each of the less developed continents. Some of their economic characteristics are summarized in Table 8. Large countries were avoided because the effects of foreign aid are more difficult to discern, and information centers are diffuse. The countries are intermediate in terms of per capita income; they are by no means the poorest of the less developed countries, where successful aid administration is a more difficult matter. All but Peru had fairly satisfactory rates of economic growth for the period shown, 1965–73. They have had more political stability than the generality of less developed countries. This is a good group from the point of view of ability to absorb technical assistance successfully.

The details of the country visits are contained in Appendix B. It is not easy to summarize them, for the evidence is often conflicting. The information secured is far from complete, and opinions expressed in interviews may have been idiosyncratic. Nevertheless, a few broad regularities do appear to emerge from interviews and documents. They are subject to challenge, and indeed, some of them were questioned on a subsequent visit to ILO headquarters in Geneva, but they strike me as consistent with currently available materials.

1. In its traditional fields of vocational training for industry, social security, and occupational safety and health, ILO projects receive universal approbation. Almost without exception, the projects achieved the objectives that had been set for them. The ILO has clearly had the expertise and experience to do a good job in these areas.

2. Moving away from these activities, however, the record becomes weaker. The ILO has undertaken management development work for many years, but apart from the intrinsic difficulty of providing such training, the quality of ILO expertise appears less than satisfactory. Perhaps the ILO is simply not equipped to provide training in marketing, accounting, produc-

TABLE 8. Economic Characteristics of Six Less Developed Countries Visited in 1978

| | GNP per capita, 1973 | | Labor force, 1970 (thousands) | Average annual growth of GDP per capita, 1965–73 | |
	U.S. $	Rank[a]		%	Rank[b]
Costa Rica	710	61	540	3.1	64
Ivory Coast	380	87	2,600	3.9	49
Kenya	170	110	5,100	3.6	55
Malaysia	570	68	2,900	3.0	68
Peru	620	65	4,300	1.7	95
Thailand	270	102	16,700	4.2	42

SOURCE: World Bank, *World Tables, 1976.*

[a]Of 145 countries.

[b]Of 141 countries.

tion, and the like. The ILO's special competence lies in personnel work, for which there is not a great demand, particularly in large-scale industry, where managers have access to business schools and private management consulting firms. As for small entrepreneurs, the area in which the ILO proposes to concentrate,[50] it is not at all clear what sort of useful training can be given them. Chinese entrepreneurs in Malaysia or Indian entrepreneurs in Kenya need no assistance from the ILO or anyone else. The promotion of small businesses often arises in the context of government efforts to dislodge minority groups, and these efforts have not been conspicuously successful. In general, the purposes of management training programs have been vague, their objectives difficult to define, and the lines of action unclear.

3. Some of the same strictures apply to rural projects. The ILO has been successful in narrowly defined efforts to improve the quality of administrators of rural cooperatives, but more ambitious attempts to create employment through rural development schemes have not proved their worth. The root of the problem appears to be that no international agency, including the ILO, possesses the knowledge to do much more than improve yields through better agricultural technology—which is the FAO's responsibility. Models of rural organization do not appear to be exportable because of different physical, political, and cultural differences among countries. The case for continued ILO activity in rural development is questionable.

4. A "political" project is undoubtedly the quickest road to failure. This should come as no surprise to ILO officials. In the case of the Peruvian SINAMOS project,[51] for example, they expressed strong initial doubts but were unable to resist pressures from the government. If, because of the present system of allocating aid through UNDP, one cannot refuse a project on the ground that it is not technically justified, then the system itself is in need of overhauling.

5. Paradoxically, one finds that even in countries where major ILO projects have failed, the overall reputation of the ILO is good. This favorable image may be due to decades of successful assistance work in traditional areas or to a general belief that the ILO is dedicated to the interests of the less affluent social

groups. Employer antipathy to much of the ILO activity may reflect the latter. Trade unions seem to be solidly behind the ILO. This fund of goodwill is the ILO's greatest asset.

The World Employment Program

During the 1960s, it was becoming increasingly clear that a combination of slow economic growth and rapid growth of the working-age population was producing an employment crisis in almost all the less developed countries. Their cities were being invaded by large numbers of people who were unable to make a living in rural areas. The result was spreading urban slums, which brought in their wake rising crime rates and the threat of civil disorder.

The ILO response was the creation in 1969 of the World Employment Program "to make productive employment for large numbers of people a major goal of national and international policies for development."[52] Launched with a great deal of fanfare, the program from the outset had little conception of how new jobs were going to be found. Regional machinery was to be established, and it was proposed that countries be urged to adopt "measures for rural development, for the reduction or reversal of the rural exodus, for the application of more labor-intensive techniques, shift work in industry, and so on."[53] All of these things would have to be done by national governments, of course, but the ILO was to provide the requisite knowledge and act as a catalyst.

The United States had a favorable initial reaction to the program. President Nixon sent a message through his secretary of labor promising support for the program, "which continues to offer practical solutions to the problems of unemployment to enable all men to share more fully in the fruits of a rapidly expanding world economy."[54] George Meany, who attended the 1969 ILO conference where the World Employment Program was launched, referred to the "forward-looking spirit" that had led to its formulation, and he endorsed its goal "of enhancing the opportunities of workers in all nations to secure full, freely-chosen and productive employment."[55] Charles Smith, who spoke on behalf of the U.S. employers, was apparently one of the few at the conference who had carefully gone over the proposed program. Although he endorsed it, he made a number of cautionary observations, including the necessity of generating large amounts of capital investment in order to provide productive employment, and the need to restrict population growth.[56] A dramatic climax occurred when Pope Paul VI addressed the ILO conference in person, praising the ILO for its efforts to help unemployed young people. "Who has not sensed," he asked, "in the rich countries, their anxiety at the invasion of technocracy, their rejection of a society which has not succeeded in integrating them into itself; and, in poor countries their lament that, for lack of sufficient training and fitting means, they cannot make their generous contribution to the tasks which call for it? In the present changing world, their protest resounds like a cry of suffering and an appeal for justice."[57]

The easiest part of the program to implement was the setting up of a bureaucracy. Regional employment teams were established in Africa, Asia, and Latin America, and a new department was created in Geneva to oversee the program. It then became necessary to develop a research plan in order to develop a fund of information out of which advice could be generated. It was also decided that some direct assistance would be provided from Geneva in the form of comprehensive employment strategy missions.

Looking first at the last-named instrument of activity, the idea of sending employment missions originated in the need to determine more precisely the dimensions of the unemployment problem and to find out what countries were doing about it. By 1970, no government leader of a less developed country could have been unaware that he had a major problem on his hands, and some countries had already begun to seek ways of alleviating unemployment. It was originally envisioned that small teams of experts would be sent out to a few selected countries, where they would spend a minimum of six months studying the situation in cooperation with local officials. It was hoped that after information had been accumulated by a sufficient number of these missions, some lines of action could be developed that might lend themselves to general application.

Things did not turn out that way. The public relations potential of the employment mission device was quickly recognized, and it became the most visible part of the World Employment Program. The first mission, to Colombia, had a staff of twenty-seven professionals representing twelve different organizations, including FAO, UNESCO, WHO, UNIDO, and the World Bank. The mission stayed in Colombia for five weeks, although some of its members were there for only a few days. It then returned to Geneva and turned out a report of almost 500 pages in two weeks.[58]

The success of this mission, whose report was eventually presented to the president of Colombia with maximum ceremony, provided a model for similar visits to other countries. Massive reports were prepared for Kenya, Sri Lanka, and the Philippines, and smaller ones for Iran, the Dominican Republic, and the Sudan. Advice was offered on a wide range of subjects: agricultural policy, including land reform; the pattern of industrial development; foreign trade; fiscal and monetary policy; construction and housing; the appropriate role of foreign capital; education and training; wage and price policy; and the distribution of income. It was the theory of these reports that appropriate action along the recommended lines would lead to increased employment.

No real effort has been made to determine whether the recommendations that emerged from these so-called action-oriented studies had any effect upon the course of economic events in the host countries. In Kenya, the only such country I visited, officers of the Ministry of Finance and Planning suggested that the World Employment Program study had a favorable impact on development theory, and they were hopeful that the national plan for 1979–83 would incorporate some of its recommendations. The study's major contribution was in identifying the key area of difficulty as the so-called traditional sector, where most of the working poor were concentrated, whereas Kenya had been concentrating on the modern sector. By 1978 it had not yet been possible to carry out most of the recommendations, partly because of opposition from employers and large landowners.[59] A progress report prepared by an economist from the Institute of

Development Studies at Sussex University, which had provided
the leadership for the Kenya mission, reached the following conclusions:

> While it is true that many of the ILO report's recommendations
> have been implemented, implementation has been distinctly
> patchy. Some of the measures taken are perhaps surprising in
> the extent to which they confront vested interests . . . but on
> the whole measures implying structural upheaval, such as land
> ceilings and redistribution, land tax and a freeze on the incomes
> of the higher paid, have been avoided. Given the *totality* of the
> recommended strategy . . . this partial implementation would
> have been ineffective even if economic recession had not in-
> tervened.[60]

If the comprehensive employment strategy missions are to
be judged in terms of their impact on employment, it would be
difficult to rate them as successful. There seems to have been no
reduction in unemployment of any consequence in Colombia,
Kenya, or Sri Lanka, where the governments have had from six
to eight years to follow the ILO blueprints. Factors were at
work, particularly the world economic recession of 1974–76, that
would have made success doubtful regardless of the appropriate-
ness of the recommendations.

Even if the economic environment had been more favorable,
however, it is unlikely that the reports would have had any great
impact. Perhaps their basic fault was lack of modesty. It was presumptuous of the ILO to assume that it could send thirty people
to a country with which most were unfamiliar for a period of a
month and expect them to produce a developmental model that
suited the environment of the country concerned. It was equally
presumptuous to think that one brief visit could generate policies
that had not already occurred to the national experts of those
countries. It is sometimes said that the main achievement of international missions like these is to advance policies on behalf of
certain groups in the community who are themselves unable to
promote them for political or other reasons. In other words, international advocacy somehow makes these policies more respectable. If so, such missions are fraught with political risk and
may prove unproductive in the long run.

No attempt has been made at seriously evaluating the achievements of the regional employment teams. They do not appear to have had any major impact on employment policy in the six less developed countries that I visited.

As for research, the World Employment Program has turned out a vast amount of material, and it is still being produced at such a rate that any attempt at a comprehensive evaluation would be a labor of Sisyphus. A bibliography prepared in 1976 listed 456 items, including books, articles, and reports, published under the program.[61] The cost involved was around $11 million, of which about one-third came from the ILO and two-thirds from outside sources.

An evaluation study commissioned in 1976 by the World Employment Program itself gave the research program mixed reviews. It was praised for having led to a better understanding of the employment problem; for clarifying the feasibility of labor-intensive technology; for emphasizing the critical importance of land and educational reforms; for improving understanding of the "educated unemployed" problem; and for promoting greater insights into the role of the traditional, or informal, sector. On the debit side, it was noted that in the area of labor-intensive technology, "not much has been achieved with regard to the identification and specification of policy measures." As for income distribution and employment, the evaluation found that "it does not appear that the studies of this project have been of much operational usefulness to decision-makers up to now." The World Employment Program was advised to "de-emphasize and, in general, shy away from ideological approaches to the development process, be they from the right or from the left. Not only are these positions bound to be controversial with at least some segments of ILO's diversified clientele, but perhaps more importantly, are often based on very shaky, unconfirmed and untested bodies of theories." A large computer model of development strategy financed by the ILO was termed simplistic, and "any policy inferences which can be drawn from such simulation can almost be dismissed as somewhat irresponsible."[62]

A World Bank observer at a conference called to discuss this evaluation report thought that it was not sufficiently critical. He also noted that heads of other ILO departments appeared at the conference to attack the World Employment Program and its research program. The World Employment Program had become somewhat unpopular within the ILO because of its failure to coordinate its work with that of other branches.

None of these activities—employment missions, regional teams, research—appears to have generated any interest on the part of the U.S. government, labor, and management officials who were managing American participation in the ILO until the results surfaced at the 1976 conference. Some of the studies and recommendations had ideological biases that should have raised the hackles of all three groups; this was true particularly of a general antipathy to multinational corporations. It would appear that no attempt was made to monitor the work of the World Employment Program in the United States, either because not enough personnel were assigned to the task or because the whole enterprise was considered to be unimportant. There was very little knowledge of the program even in American academic circles. A few books, mainly those written on commission, received favorable notice,[63] but most of the shorter publications appeared in the *International Labour Review*, which does not have a large readership in the United States.

The climax of the World Employment Program came in 1976, when the ILO mounted the World Employment Conference. Similar conferences had been held, or were being planned, by other international agencies on population, food, and industrialization, and apparently, the ILO did not want to be left out. When the idea of a conference was first discussed by the Governing Body, representatives of Western governments and employers (including those of the United States) expressed doubts about its potential value relative to its cost. Some of the topics suggested for the conference, such as income distribution and the international division of labor, were considered outside the competence of the ILO.

The workers' group nevertheless pressed for the conference, and the Governing Body authorized it. At its next session, however, questions were once again raised in the Governing Body concerning the scope of the proposed agenda. The U.S. government representative objected to the implication that the conference was expected to recommend changes in patterns of world production and trade or that it was committing the ILO to support the New International Economic Order.[64] A revised agenda was then submitted that met with the Governing Body's approval. The U.S. representative still had reservations about the scope of the proposed conference. He was also concerned about the tendency, implied in the agenda, to rely upon international action to solve local problems: "In general it seemed better to concentrate on national employment policy than to try to draw up universally applicable codes, since measures taken by individual countries usually produced quicker results than did multilateral efforts."[65]

A draft document designed to serve as the basis for conference discussion was drawn up by the Office. It was discussed in August 1975 by an advisory panel of consultants, who criticized it for its reliance on a new development strategy that stressed redistribution of assets rather than growth, not to mention its antipathy toward multinational corporations. A subtle shift of emphasis away from employment and toward the fulfillment of unspecified "basic needs" was also noted.[66] The reservations expressed by the advisory panel were disregarded, but the Governing Body, which had not been sent the draft, reacted strongly a few months later, after several members had received copies. The Swedish employer representative called it "extremely bad and lacking in the ILO's usual objectivity," and he expressed the fear that the conference was "on its way towards becoming politically infected and a failure, but above all a disaster for the ILO as a whole." The U.S. government representative called its approach "grandiose." The U.S. worker representative hoped that the ILO would produce a "realistic and practical document rather than a statement of pious principles that would never be carried out."[67]

U.S. officials had an opportunity to consider the draft document in detail at a meeting called by the Department of Labor, at which the director of the ILO employment department, who was in charge of the conference preparations, was present. The AFL-CIO failed to send a representative, but the Chamber of

Commerce people who were involved with ILO affairs, including the U.S. employer delegate, attended. The meeting was a
heated affair, with the U.S. participants denouncing the draft on
many counts, and the ILO official defending it just as strongly.
Among the objections of the U.S. representatives were the following:

1. The World Employment Conference was being asked to
   make declarations on a broad range of trade and fiscal policies that were beyond its competence.
2. The proposed standing orders of the conference invited
   polemical speeches.
3. The conference could not properly consider the macro-
   economic policies necessary to improve the incomes of
   poverty groups.
4. The "basic needs" development strategy that was being
   advocated was not defined.
5. The draft advocated a controlled economy on the basis of
   strong government intervention.
6. It was not clear how a redistribution of productive assets
   would raise productivity and ultimately benefit the poor.
7. The draft was highly critical of multinational corporations,
   in complete disregard of the findings of half a dozen studies that had recently been completed by other divisions of
   the ILO itself.
8. There was Marxist language in the draft that had no place
   in such a document.[68]

The U.S. attitude toward the preparatory work for the conference was summarized in a letter from the U.S. government
representative to the ILO official who had been present at the
meeting. After stating that the conference, as planned, might
exacerbate relationships between the United States and the
ILO, the letter made the following suggestions:

1. The conference should be technical in nature and "not become embroiled in free-wheeling debates on sweeping

political and economic issues going far beyond the mandate and competence of the ILO."

2. The conference should not attempt to pioneer a new development strategy and to restructure the world. Its goals should be more modest.
3. The conference should focus on the ILO's potential contributions toward the creation of more job opportunities. It should also analyze the successes and failures of the World Employment Program, particularly in rural areas.
4. Human rights should be given greater emphasis.[69]

The U.S. employer representative, C. H. Smith, Jr., sent a similar letter to the ILO official, pointing out that the draft downgraded capital investment as a means of creating jobs. The letter concluded: "I urge that you and your associates give very serious consideration to these points, as well as the scores of other points that were presented verbally to you at our meeting yesterday. Failure to give proper consideration to these points could very well result in the World Employment Conference becoming known in a few years as the 'World Conference to Discourage Employment.'"[70] At the same time, he sent a letter to the director-general of the ILO expressing shock at the ILO representative's reply to the question of why the draft document had paid no attention to the ILO's own studies of multinationals. Smith warned that if this attitude were to prevail, there would be no doubt about the U.S. decision to withdraw. He urged the director-general to make "individual department heads understand that they cannot cavalierly reject the results of ILO studies and substitute other information and studies that fit into their own philosophical viewpoint more appropriately."[71]

It was unfortunate that this was the first real look the United States had at the World Employment Program. It was also unfortunate that the ILO permitted its staff to steer the World Employment Conference in a direction so antithetical to American views. This was bound further to tarnish the image of the ILO in the United States. Moreover, not only was the proposed conference document politically biased, but it was technically poor as well. The top leadership of the ILO was clearly at fault for permitting a small group of its employees to undermine what might have been a useful conference under different circumstances.

The final conference document, while considerably modified because of the criticisms, still showed signs of its original provenance. Some of the emotive terminology was removed, and the section on multinationals was brought into conformance with the ILO's previous findings. But the emphasis remained on the fulfillment of "basic needs" rather than on employment or economic growth. These basic needs were never defined; in fact, the World Employment Program had not made any significant attempts to assess the various aspects of poverty and how they could be alleviated. Without even examining a number of successful case histories of post–World War II development, the ILO had stated: "In the great majority of developing countries . . . reliance on growth alone is likely to postpone the meeting of basic needs until well in the next century." The magic remedy, according to the ILO report, was "redistribution":

> The magnitude of the redistribution that is required will depend mainly on the rate of growth that can be achieved and on the distribution of income at the outset. The redistribution may be obtained entirely through redistribution from growth, through an initial redistribution of productive resources, or through a combination of the two. The appropriate combination will depend partly on the magnitude of the required redistribution, partly on the degree to which the fiscal and administrative system can be relied upon to redistribute from growth, and partly on political choice. In many cases, *at least some initial redistribution of productive resources, particularly land, is likely to be found necessary,* even in order to provide the basis for future redistribution from growth. However, the redistribution of land by agrarian reform may lead either to public ownership or to continued private ownership.[72]

A number of problems arise from this line of argument, and they spring primarily from a lack of careful analysis. The first has to do with the definition of "growth." Annual gross domestic product growth rates of 3 percent are not likely to relieve poverty to any great extent, but the 7 to 10 percent rates achieved by some countries are another matter. There should have been a more precise specification of what was meant by such broad statements as "economic growth by itself may not solve or even alleviate the problem."

Second, the estimates of the number of people living in poverty and the changes in the number over time are of dubious quality. One has only to recall the great difficulty of measuring the extent of poverty in the United States to realize that this is a virtually insoluble problem for most less developed nations.

Third, there is the concept of redistribution. Among the policies suggested as redistributive are land reform, involving either parceling land into small holdings or establishing farm collectives; nationalization of nonagricultural assets; public investment in infrastructure; credit and services for the rural poor; manipulation of relative prices; provision of free education and health services; an increase in wages; abolition of piece rates and other incentive payments; participation of the poor in decisionmaking; and subsidized food and transportation. Other possibilities might include highly progressive taxes, government allocation of all housing, equalization of urban and rural incomes, restriction of the production of consumer goods to those required by the poor, or simply the abolishment of all private property. The ILO did not make clear which of the many redistributive policies were compatible with the level of economic growth required to reduce poverty. Countries were simply advised that "although there will usually be some common elements, the components of the packages suitable for different countries will obviously vary in accordance with their economic and social conditions, as well as political choice."[73]

The one theme that runs through all of the distributional literature is land reform. But again, this is no answer, for there are many models to choose from: Communist China, Taiwan, Peru, Cuba, India, to name a few. Which one is likely to be the most effective in reducing poverty? The ILO seemed to assume, moreover, that fundamental transformations in the structure of production and in social relationships can be achieved at little or no cost. This position is hardly tenable where major changes in property relationships are envisioned.

The issue was not whether the goal of eradicating poverty

was an appropriate one. No one would argue about that. The question is, How can poverty best be alleviated in the shortest possible time? Most experts agree that static redistribution will have little effect. The disagreement concerns the dynamic path one must take to that goal. Many well-intentioned experiments have ended up badly for the poor; these experiments, along with the successful cases, must be analyzed and studied carefully. It is not by chance that the dominant objective function among contemporary governments is economic growth, for there is hard empirical evidence attesting to its efficacy as a means of solving economic problems. There may be better solutions, but exhortation based upon unsubstantiated theory is an invitation to disaster.

The ILO proposed that governments dedicate themselves to the elimination of poverty within a generation (the year 2000 was implied as the target date) and offered its services to help countries define basic needs and determine appropriate strategies. What was envisioned, among other things, was a worldwide program of household surveys under ILO leadership. The World Employment Conference limited the role of the ILO, however, to cooperation with other U.N. agencies and national governments to consider the "feasibility of initiating a worldwide program of household surveys to map the nature, extent, and cause of poverty." It was also to assist countries in setting up the necessary statistical and monitoring services. This contraction of the planned ILO role was due largely to U.S. pressure.

I was asked by the U.S. Department of Labor to prepare a technical paper presenting the U.S. position on the ILO's basic needs approach. Shortly before the conference was to begin, the Department of State objected to the paper, presumably out of fear of offending the less developed countries. The Labor Department was obliged to withdraw it, but I was encouraged, as a member of the U.S. delegation to the conference, to distribute it at the conference for discussion, which I did.

The statistical basis for my conclusions have been published elsewhere.[74] I found that rapid, sustained growth has had positive effects on the living standards of all economic groups in those countries that experienced it. Growth has not "failed";

there has simply not been enough of it in the great majority of less developed nations. It is not helpful to call for "massive, wide-ranging attacks" on the maldistribution of income without any evidence that such policies have ever worked.[75]

The World Employment Conference itself was utterly devoid of any technical content. The ILO had persuaded governments to send cabinet members to head their delegations, and they made speeches extolling the virtues of their national policies. There was neither the time nor the inclination to exchange views on what was presumably the central issue: how to increase productive employment. Nor was there any review of the World Employment Program, what it had accomplished, where it had gone wrong.

From the U.S. point of view, the conference did not go smoothly. Shortly after it opened, word got out that the authors of the original conference document were circulating a proposed set of final conclusions. The director-general repudiated this paper as contrary to his explicit instructions; nevertheless, parts of the draft appeared in recommendations advanced by the Group of 77 (the caucus of the less developed countries). In a second incident, a U.S. trade union representative was insulted in an open meeting by the director of the World Employment Program, and this led to a demand by the entire U.S. delegation for the director's removal.

The day before the conference was to end, a small working party, including the chief U.S. government representative, put together a report that appeared to have a chance of acceptance. There was a last-minute attempt by militants in the Group of 77 to disrupt the plenary session, where final approval was to be given, but when the chairmen of the worker and employer groups announced that any attempt to amend the report would lead to adjournment without recommendations, the compromise draft was maintained.[76]

The final report adopted by the conference was acceptable to the U.S. government because it "was more realistic in its objectives than the Office proposals and tended to confine the Office to its traditional area of competence."[77] It stipulated basic needs as a priority objective of development and defined those needs

as adequate food, shelter, clothing, and essential community services. The objectionable phrase—"initial redistribution of assets,
especially land"—remained, although it was softened by the requirement of "adequate and timely compensation."[78] No one
raised the question of how asset redistribution was to be
achieved if the former owners were compensated adequately.
Full employment was to be attained by the year 2000. Rural development was to be given priority. Included in the basic needs
strategy was the effective mass participation of rural populations
in the political process. Women, the youth, and the aged—all
were to be helped.

Although the New International Economic Order was endorsed, a number of the Western industrialized countries, including the United States, placed on record their reservation
that the entire section on international economic cooperation lay
outside the ILO's competence. Recommendations were made on
migratory labor and technology. The ILO proposed the creation
of a new international technology unit, which was endorsed by
the Group of 77 and opposed by the Western nations (the West
prevailed). Since it was not possible to reach any any agreement
on the proper role of multinational corporations in development,
the final conference report merely summarized the widely divergent views of governments, workers, and employers.[79]

The conference was nonetheless considered a success. The
ILO had launched a new theory of economic development. The
director-general informed the Governing Body at its next meeting that other international agencies had "eagerly" joined the
ILO in long-term actions to combat worldwide poverty and unemployment.[80] It was agreed that the 1979 conference was to be
devoted largely to discussing ILO progress in implementing the
basic needs strategy.

But the less developed countries, who were to be the beneficiaries of this new approach to development, had a change of
heart. A conference of foreign ministers from these countries was
held in Belgrade in September 1978, and the following conclusions were reached:

The question of the "basic needs approach" should be viewed as one of the many priority objectives for rational policy; and not as a substitute for authentic development which by its nature encompasses other priorities too. . . . The Foreign Ministers stated that a "basic needs approach" at an international level would inevitably imply the imposition of global priorities on developing countries, thereby not only distorting the allocation of domestic resources of the latter but also perpetrating their technological dependence on the developed countries. . . . The Foreign Ministers decided that the coordinating countries in the sector of Employment and Development of Human Resources should present the above point of view to the sixty-fifth session of the International Labor Conference, which will be examining this question.[81]

In retrospect, it is interesting that the United States was the only country that objected to the political and economic implications of the "basic needs" approach of the 1976 conference, although, because of State Department fears, even the U.S. opposition was muted. Other developed nations had reservations, but they were not willing to join the United States in criticizing what appeared at the time to be a newly emerging ideological orthodoxy favored by the poor nations.

One thing the World Employment Conference did not accomplish was an improvement in U.S.–ILO relationships. Although all parties concerned breathed a sigh of relief when the conference ended without having caused an open break, the skirmishes that took place in the preparatory stages, and the events at the conference itself, resulted in a hardening of attitudes. The U.S. employers were incensed at attempts to condemn multinational corporations out of hand; and an American union leader at the conference was quoted as saying: "We are not here to do anything. We are here to keep others from doing something harmful to us."[82]

The rejection of the basic needs approach by the less developed countries created a dilemma for the ILO because the 1979 conference was already committed to a discussion of the progress of that program as a major agenda item. Therefore, the strategy adopted in the conference was to claim that the ILO's basic needs approach had been misunderstood:

What explains the distrust of a basic needs approach to development which has been manifested recently, especially in some United Nations and related fora? Some of the objections appear to result from a misconception of the nature of the approach. . . . The basic needs approach is not an alternative to the strategy of growth but represents the introduction of a new variable into the general equation of development. It is not a collection of nonproductive social assistance measures, which some people have called charity, but an instrument of growth, an instrument to create economic infrastructures, and, accordingly, employment.[83]

That this effort was disingenuous is evident from a comparison of the document placed before the 1979 conference with the one prepared in 1976. There is no longer advocacy of a general redistribution of productive assets; even the not very radical issue of land reform is handled gingerly. Economic growth and employment were once more enthroned: "In developing countries, while accelerated growth is the first prerequisite of progress, unemployment and underemployment—including low productivity employment yielding inadequate incomes—are at the heart of the problem of poverty."[84] The pursuit of basic needs, the report stated, is not necessarily an optimum policy, since an excessive proportion of economic resources may be devoted to consumption, "thus drying up the sources of private savings and investment."[85]

The theme was repeated when the 1979 conference considered the Office report. Future objectives were listed in the following order: full employment, accelerated and balanced growth, satisfaction of basic needs, and more socially just patterns of income distribution. It was noted that, "without important improvements in economic growth, the problems relating to unemployment, poverty and satisfaction of basic needs cannot be solved, and, therefore, a basic needs approach requires energetic action to achieve rapid growth and the generation of productive employment."[86] The final resolution included some objectives that were clearly beyond the competence of the ILO: establishment of a New International Economic Order, reorientation of the policies of international financial institutions, and attainment of disarmament. The employer group registered its dissent to all of these.

The history of the World Employment Program illustrates an unfortunate tendency of the ILO—one that it shares with other international agencies—to substitute unattainable schemes for attainable, small-scale results. As it was originally conceived, the purpose of the program was to make a modest contribution to the solution of unemployment, one of the major problems facing the less developed world. Instead, it rapidly became a means of publicizing the ILO through hasty country studies that left little behind. The culmination was a grandiose plan aimed at solving the problem of world poverty with an approach that lacked analytical grounding and that was soon rejected by its intended beneficiaries. Thus, to all intents and purposes, the World Employment Program ended in 1979 with little to show for itself. A good deal of money had been wasted, and the ILO's reputation was tarnished. In the end, American skepticism of the enterprise was justified.

The Turin Center

The Turin Center for Advanced Training began with an offer by the Italian government to provide a site for management and vocational training on the outskirts of Turin and an initial subsidy of $7.5 million over a ten-year period. For a national industrial fair in Turin, Pietro Nervi, the famous Italian architect, had designed a central exhibition hall with separate buildings for each Italian province. For the training center, the central building was to be converted into a classroom and office bloc, and the subsidiary buildings would become dormitories.

Although the director-general had promised to find extrabudgetary funds to finance the center, the Governing Body was cautious before it gave its approval. The United States in particular was cool to the proposition, fearing that it would be called upon to bear a substantial part of the cost of running the center. The U.S. worker representative questioned the proposed emphasis on management training, much of which he felt was outside the competence of the ILO, and on training for the metal trades, which he did not believe could be accomplished effectively through the short courses contemplated.[87] To repeated questions about finances, Director-General Morse replied that "it had always been understood that contributions to the Center would be voluntary and that there would be no charge on the ILO regular budget."[88] On this assurance, establishment of the center was authorized.

The director-general had been overly optimistic, however, and money was slow in coming. The United States refused to make any contribution; Washington feared that the center would be merely a showcase for Italian goods and machinery, and so it questioned the need for such a facility. It became necessary, therefore, to provide special grants from the regular ILO budget.

The original proposal had envisioned a mixture of management and vocational training, but it soon became apparent that bringing workers to Turin from less developed countries for training in manual skills was not economically sound, since such training could be done locally. The curriculum veered sharply toward training in management subjects, although some resources were devoted to training technical and vocational instructors. To prevent labor from becoming too unhappy, a number of fellowships were provided for trade union officials. The initial employer skepticism toward the center soon vanished, but the early enthusiasm of the trade unions waned. The U.S. government continued to oppose subsidies from the regular ILO budget, making this one of those rare occasions when the United States held views in common with the Soviet Union on ILO matters.

As long as David Morse remained director-general, the United States, despite its distrust of the center, was represented on its board of directors by the labor delegate to the Governing Body. But when Morse left the ILO, the U.S. labor delegate left the center's board of directors. The United States continued to take the position that less developed countries wishing to send people to Turin should secure enough financial help from the UNDP to sustain the center.

Despite these vicissitudes, the center survived, helped in part by added Italian subsidies. Employer representatives in the less developed countries whom I visited generally expressed their satisfaction with the usefulness of the instruction at Turin. The center appears to fill a need for a program of studies somewhere in between an advanced type of business training—the kind offered, for example, by the international business schools at Fontainebleau or Lausanne—and what local universities in less developed countries are able to provide.

The consistent U.S. antipathy toward the center is difficult to understand. The program of studies offered there has been consistent with what most U.S. experts would regard as appropriate for the improvement of managerial skills in a free enterprise society. The center has not become involved in political courses. The practical training given to trade unionists was designed to improve the organization and operation of unions in the less developed countries. It may have been difficult to secure U.S. support funds for the center, particularly in the 1970s, but there were other opportunities for cooperation. Once a negative attitude had been established, apparently no one involved in monitoring the ILO ever suggested that a careful reevaluation of the U.S. position ought to be made.

The financial situation at the center became precarious at the end of 1978. Only subsidies by the Italian government and the Turin municipality enabled the facility to remain in operation. Its future remains clouded as of this writing.

Conclusions on ILO Technical Cooperation

When U.S. relationships with the ILO were reviewed by the Department of Labor in 1971, the potential contribution of ILO technical assistance to the promotion of U.S. interests was summarized as follows:

1. Multilateral assistance reduces friction between donors and beneficiaries, making it possible to draw on the expertise of many countries.
2. ILO projects are welcomed in countries from which U.S. bilateral aid may be barred.
3. ILO technical work in vocational training, labor relations, labor administration, and manpower training are recog-

nized as important by the United States and are undertaken in ways consistent with U.S. views.
4. ILO projects offer an extension of U.S. influence because they offer job opportunities to American experts.

The Labor Department also stated that "so far as assistance is concerned, the ILO seems neither better nor worse than the other international organizations. It has engaged in 'selling' projects to potential recipients. It does not monitor its projects closely. Nor does it evaluate results in any systematic way."[89]

How do these views stand up against the foregoing description and evaluation of ILO technical assistance work? Would the United States be better served by channeling aid through the ILO rather than by means of its own bilateral program? These are complicated questions, and they cannot be answered without much more work, and, in particular, without evaluating the U.S. Agency for International Development (AID). However, a few summary observations about the ILO program may serve to highlight the kind of approach that might be in order for policymakers, if they are to chart a fruitful course of relationships not only with the ILO but with other international agencies as well.

1. During a period of about twenty-five years, the ILO has provided valuable and fairly efficient technical assistance to less developed countries in its traditional fields of activity: vocational training, labor administration, social security, and occupational safety and health. The U.S. investment in these projects probably yielded at least as high a return as the United States could have realized from its own bilateral programs.

2. Many of the ILO projects in management development, employment creation, and rural development have been of questionable value. But Congress has directed that future U.S. economic aid be devoted primarily to assisting the rural poor, which would tend to back the ILO approach. Such projects are best characterized as welfare assistance, not investments that are likely to have multiplier effects. As the ILO has discovered, rural development is intrinsically a difficult area in which to operate.

No one has as yet devised a formula for creating productive employment that does not involve cooperating capital.

3. A clear advantage of U.S. AID over ILO is that it would not sponsor projects clearly antithetical to U.S. interests, such as those designed to replace a free enterprise system with some form of collective society. Although AID might well finance "political" projects, they would presumably be in the U.S. interest.

4. An important hindrance to ILO efficiency lies in the constraints imposed by the present UNDP system. The ILO is virtually forced into competitive bidding with other agencies, to the detriment of rational project selection. The Scandinavian countries and the Netherlands, in particular, are conducting ILO-type activities bilaterally. Indeed, recipient nations appear generally to prefer bilateral assistance because of its greater flexibility and absence of red tape.

5. The scope for the ILO's successful and traditional assistance work has narrowed. Most countries that need vocational training centers have not only established them already, but they also have the resources to improve their own labor administrations. No new productivity centers will be created. Does this mean that the ILO must move toward activities in which it has not yet demonstrated an ability to work effectively? Should not the rural sector, for example, be turned over to FAO?

6. The ILO is not unaware of this problem. It is seeking new and more promising areas of work in industry, such as the installation of wage systems, training managers of public enterprises, and the enhancement of job satisfaction and enrichment (a popular theme in Western Europe). Worker participation in management, which has so far not been a successful type of ILO project, is also being explored.

7. There remain a few traditional ILO areas that will be in demand for some time to come, even though they may not lend themselves to large, highly visible projects. These include social security systems, occupational safety and health, and workers' education. These activities do not loom large in terms of the budget categories shown in Table 4, but they do represent the type of project that the United States should be most interested in seeing expanded.

The United States did not leave the ILO because of dissatisfaction with its technical assistance performance. An evaluation of the ILO record should be of greater importance in future decisions. The data that have been presented here are introductory, and more precise evaluation is needed as a guide to future policy. From this review of the existing evidence, it appears that the ILO has performed relatively well in some areas and poorly in others. If the areas of relative failure are where the ILO considers its promise to lie, the advantages of U.S. membership are less obvious—unless, of course, it should turn out that the ILO is right and that successful achievement of project objectives can be demonstrated. The U.S. government, labor, and management officials responsible for ILO affairs should give much more attention than they have in the past to monitoring technical assistance. Part of the problem has been the failure to do so, not only by the United States but by the other major contributors to the UNDP as well.

Chapter 6

The Setting of International Labor Standards

The ILO constitution provides that the conference may at its discretion adopt instruments in the form of conventions or recommendations by a two-thirds majority. Which of these two instruments is more appropriate depends on how precisely the subject matter can be defined and on the amount of past experience. If clear and practical rules can be formulated, a convention will normally be preferred. Recommendations are used "where national experience on a subject is lacking, and standards are exploratory; where an agreed aim may be achieved by a variety of methods and it is accordingly necessary to leave a measure of freedom for national action; where it is felt undesirable to overload a convention with detailed guidelines on the application of the principles contained therein; and where it is desired to set out as a target a standard higher than is susceptible of ratification, in a convention, in the foreseeable future."[1]

When a convention has been adopted, every member state submits it to the competent authorities within eighteen months for possible legislative enactment. If the decision is to ratify, then the member state must take steps to bring national legislation into conformance with the provisions of the convention. In the event of nonratification, the member state is still obligated to report periodically on the degree to which national legislation and practice conform to the subject matter of the convention. Similar obligations pertain to recommendations, except that ratification is not called for.

The discussion here will be limited to conventions; they are more important than recommendations, and ratification confers upon them the status of international treaties which the signatories are pledged to respect. As of January 1, 1979, a total of 151 conventions had been adopted by the ILO conference, on a broad range of subjects.[2] The number of ratifications was over 4,600, an average of 33 per member state. There is great variation, however, in the number of ratifications per state and the frequency with which particular conventions have been ratified. Western Europe has a high level (102 for France, the maximum for any country), while Asian countries are generally at the bottom of the list. The Soviet Union, with 40 ratifications, was well above the average. The human rights conventions stood highest on the list in numerical terms, followed by those relating to minimum wages, labor conditions, and the protection of women and children.

The United States has ratified only seven conventions, the lowest number for any major power, with six of them relating to maritime labor and one to a purely technical subject. The official U.S. position has always been that failure to ratify a greater number of conventions rests on the nature of the American political structure:

> Under the American constitutional system, most ILO Conventions and Recommendations require legislative action by the constituent states as well as by the Federal Government. . . . The U.S. Constitution provides that all powers not specifically delegated to the Federal Government are reserved to the states. With respect to ILO Conventions, the United States could not assume a treaty obligation for a Convention whose partial jurisdiction lies in the states. . . . Further, even with respect to those Conventions and Recommendations which are appropriate for action by the Federal Government alone, the Executive Branch can only bring about ratification through concurrence of

the Legislative Branch, in this case the U.S. Senate. Obtaining such concurrence can be especially difficult in the United States because . . . the nature of the constitutional powers in the United States establishes a wholly independent legislative branch co-equal with the Executive Branch.[3]

This reply fails to set forth the real reasons why ratification of ILO conventions has been difficult to obtain: employer opposition and the historical reluctance of the Senate to ratify any international conventions, including those adopted by the ILO. This is a matter of long standing. The Johnson Committee handled the issue cautiously, urging that the United States press for ILO legislation in the form of recommendations rather than conventions in order to permit the United States to support ILO standards without having to ratify them formally.[4] Employer opposition has been grounded in the fear that ILO conventions might impinge upon U.S. custom and practice, particularly in industrial relations, and could provide trade unions with ammunition for domestic legislative gains. Also involved is a dislike of international intrusion into areas that most American employers consider to be inappropriate for outside bodies. This attitude is reflected in the response of an American employer representative to a suggestion made by a Governing Body committee that the ILO concern itself with problems arising out of worker discontent with inequalities in living standards both among and within countries. Allaying work dissatisfactions, he declared,

is a matter of intelligent personal relationships between employer and worker, both honestly seeking real progress in eliminating the source of the problem. . . . It varies so directly according to the character of the enterprise, the backgrounds of the individuals employed, the nature of the organization's structure and other factors that no ILO instrument can be effective. . . . Inequalities in living standards are basically a national problem. . . . I am strongly of the opinion that the ILO needs to establish its competence to apply its existing instruments before it builds any more paper mountains.[5]

The American labor movement, on the other hand, has supported ILO standard-setting through conventions. A trade union spokesman made the following comment in 1974:

Establishment by the ILO over the years of a body of international labor standards has been the ILO's most remarkable
achievement. The fact that members of three groups, representing very different interests and from very different countries,
were able year after year to draft standards for the welfare and
freedom of workers which were widely acceptable to the ILO's
entire membership was most remarkable, all the more so when
it was borne in mind that, without any coercive powers, the ILO
had been able to develop an effective supervisory machinery
which was unparalleled in any other international organization.[6]

The failure of the American labor movement to secure ratification of more than a handful of conventions (those ratified, mainly
involving maritime workers, were clearly within the jurisdiction
of the federal government) is due to a combination of inadequate
political power and of insufficient self-interest in conventions.
This may be illustrated by the fate of Convention No. 105 on
forced labor, adopted by the ILO conference in 1957 by a vote of
240–0, with only the U.S. employer abstaining. The State Department had previously taken the position that a recommendation rather than a convention was called for, but the U.S. government did vote in favor of the convention. Back home, however,
the Eisenhower administration recommended against ratification, and although the Kennedy administration later urged ratification, the Senate failed to act.[7] U.S. labor voted for the convention at the ILO conference and subsequently supported it in
Washington, but was unable to prevail upon the Senate to act in
the face of employer opposition.

If the AFL-CIO had been prepared to expend some of its
political capital in fighting for ratification of this and other conventions, better results might have been achieved. The fact is,
however, that ILO conventions were never high on American
labor's list of legislative priorities. For one thing, the standards
set in ILO conventions were generally below those already prevailing in the United States. Unlike labor movements in other
countries, American labor could not cite ILO standards as an
argument for improved U.S. labor legislation.

The argument has often been made that American workers
have benefited indirectly from ILO conventions through im-

proved labor standards for foreign workers. These standards presumably lead to higher labor costs and prevent the undercutting of domestic standards through imports produced by cheap labor. In answer to this argument, a U.S. government spokesman at an ILO meeting pointed to "the virtual impossibility of proving with what might be called empirical evidence that Conventions did any good in terms of leading to improved conditions for the workers."[8] This point of view was supported in part by a U.S. labor representative, who asserted that "there were many cases where the provisions of a ratified convention were not applied in law, or where even if legislation was in conformity with ratified conventions, this legislation was not applied in practice. The Organization has tended to confuse the lip-service of ratification with actual implementation."[9]

Under the ILO constitution, only those governments that have ratified a convention may file complaints alleging nonobservance by other ratifying states.[10] This provision has led to embarrassment and diminished effectiveness of the United States in the ILO. As the 1971 Labor Department report pointed out,

> The membership in general finds it difficult to believe that the U.S. is as deeply concerned as it professes, when it has not bothered to ratify the basic ILO conventions in (the human rights) field. Many assume that we are being hypocritical over the issue. . . . The U.S. failure to ratify No. 87 undermines the credibility of its whole approach to the ILO, also impairing those elements that make ILO valuable to U.S. interests. We should make better use of this forum to press issues that reveal the basic contrasts between the monolithic and the democratic systems of society as opposing methods for advancing the conditions and rights of the ordinary citizen. . . . Yet for 21 years we have not ratified the basic ILO convention that concerns these basic rights.[11]

In 1976, when the United States was actively considering its future with the ILO, the Department of Labor stated that, in the opinion of its solicitor, Convention No. 87, on freedom of association, probably could be ratified by the Senate. It further noted that such action would be strongly favored by the AFL-CIO.[12] But there was no support from the State Department; indeed, the blame for U.S. government inaction over the years must be laid squarely at State's door. It is the federal government agency charged with responsibility for presenting treaties to the Senate for ratification, but it has not been prepared to do so in the case of the ILO. Taking a strong position in favor of ratification might have antagonized employers and stirred up a hornet's nest in the Senate.[13]

The Soviets have often seized upon U.S. nonratification to answer U.S. attacks. For example, the Soviet Union has requested that all countries which have not ratified particular conventions, especially those relating to human rights, be excluded from committee deliberations on alleged breaches of those conventions.[14] It also urged outright condemnation of nonratifiers of the human rights conventions, provoking an expression of regret by a U.S. labor representative that the United States had failed to act. But the latter added:

> Reports by countries which had ratified the conventions on freedom of association did not necessarily reflect the true situation. On the other hand, he would welcome an examination of the situation in the United States if other countries would agree to similar investigations. Steps must be taken to empower the Organization to find out and study the real situation in respect of freedom of association in member states and the Organization must not remain oblivious to conditions in certain countries which claimed to be implementing these standards.[15]

The allies of the United States have never criticized it openly for failure to ratify, but there is no doubt that they were unhappy. They were being asked to take the lead in bringing charges against the Soviet Union, since the U.S. government was unable to do so.[16] If the United States had been willing and able consistently to hammer away on human rights issues on its own account, they might have rallied more enthusiastically behind it.

The Compliance Machinery

The ILO machinery for policing the obligations assumed by ratification of its conventions is unique among international organizations. While no member state can be coerced, the ILO can, through publicity and other pressures, secure a measure of compliance.[17]

As already noted, there is an obligation on the part of every member state to bring a convention before its legislative authorities within a specified time after adoption by the ILO conference. After this initial step, each country is supposed to report periodically to the ILO on the steps that it has taken to give effect to the provisions of every convention it has ratified. Originally, this was done every year, but because of the sheer volume of the material required, reports are now due every two years for conventions that are regarded as particularly important, including those on human rights, and every four years for the rest. The material submitted includes not only legislation, but also administrative regulations and relevant court decisions.

Since 1948, member countries have also been obligated to report on how closely their law and practice conform with conventions they have *not* ratified. Each year, the Governing Body selects a limited number of conventions (and recommendations) for this purpose. The reports go initially to the ILO Committee of Experts on the Application of Conventions and Recommendations, which consists of nineteen members appointed by the Governing Body.[18] The committee then prepares an annual summary of the reports. Major or long-standing cases of nonapplication are dealt with as "observations" in committee reports, while other cases are set out in "direct requests," which are not published but to which governments are asked to reply in their next reports.

A few statistics from the 1978 committee report may serve to indicate the magnitude of its work load. Some 1,529 detailed reports were requested from governments during the preceding year, of which 76 percent had been submitted. All but 18 of the 125 governments required to submit reports on ratified conventions had done so, but 23 governments had failed to reply to previous observations and requests for more information.[19]

The Committee of Experts has been no respecter of states. Almost every ILO member has been the subject of an "observation," some of which have not been too flattering. In 1978, for example, Sweden was asked to explain why its longshore union had allegedly been denied the opportunity to negotiate an agreement on behalf of its members. Indonesia was queried about its large-scale detention of political prisoners. Pakistan was asked about an ordinance that permitted compulsory labor. And the Soviet Union was asked to explain certain legislation concerning persons' "leading a parasitic way of life," as well as other laws that restricted the mobility of farm workers.[20]

The Committee of Experts has been remarkably consistent in refusing to bow before political pressures. There has been an occasional dissent by members from Poland and the Soviet Union when it came to observations about the U.S.S.R.—the 1978 committee included nationals of the Soviet Union, Poland, and Yugoslavia—but for the rest, the committee has earned universal respect for its impartiality. A student of its work reached the following conclusion:

> The Committee's persistence in demanding full implementation of ratified Conventions is extraordinary. Year after year, in the case of certain recurring delinquencies, pressure continues to be exerted, with the wording of the "observations" developing more and more pungency. This is accomplished by maintaining a public quasi-judicial stance. The conclusions of the Committee are considered by it as proposals based on law, to be submitted to the Conference and to be acted upon by that body. Nevertheless the pungency of the "observations" is unmistakable as the scale of terms is raised from surprise to amazement, incredulity, disapproval, reprobation, and finally condemnation.[21]

The committee uses the country reports on unratified conventions to prepare general surveys that suggest how obstacles to ratification might be overcome. But no criticism is levied for failure to ratify.

Another procedure under Article 24 of the ILO constitution stipulates that any trade union or employer association may make a "representation" to the Governing Body claiming that a member state has failed to honor its obligations. Such representations are examined by a tripartite committee appointed by the Governing Body. Under Article 26, a country that has ratified a convention may file a "complaint" of nonobservance against another state, and the Governing Body may appoint a commission of inquiry to investigate.

In the past, these procedures have been used infrequently. As of the end of 1976, only eleven representations and six complaints had been filed.[22] In 1977, however, the International Confederation of Free Trade Unions made a politically important representation against Czechoslovakia by claiming employment discrimination in violation of Convention No. 111.

Normally, the Committee of Experts' report is transmitted to the Conference Committee on the Application of Conventions and Recommendations, where governments, workers, and employers have equal voting power. To enable the committee to accomplish its task, only about one-third of the observations made by the Committee of Experts are considered, but these tend to be the most serious cases. After debate, the committee's findings are summarized in a report to the conference. This report includes a "special list" of countries that have failed to live up to their obligations. There are seven criteria under which countries may be placed on the special list. The first six involve failure to (1) report during the past two years, (2) send in a first report after ratification for at least two years, (3) supply required reports on nonratified instruments for five years, (4) provide information on whether conventions or recommendations adopted during the last seven years were submitted to legislatures, (5) supply information in reply to direct requests of the Committee of Experts, and (6) participate in conference committee discussions concerning the country in question.

Criterion 7, which covers the most serious cases, is worded as follows: "The Committee examined the application of certain Conventions in various countries and noted with grave concern that in some of them there was continued failure to implement fully the conventions concerned and that full information should therefore be supplied on the measures taken to ensure such compliance. The Committee draws particular attention in this connection, to the following cases. . . ." From 1972 through 1978, all Criterion 7 cases involved the major human rights conventions. Pressure has also been exerted by the threat made during debate that lack of progress might result in inclusion the following year.

An extension of the special list procedure is the so-called "special paragraph" device. Under its provision, the special list is followed by notices that other serious cases have come to the committee's attention. Seven countries were included in this group in 1977, and nine in 1978. These notices indicate to the offending countries that they may find themselves on the special list should they fail to take appropriate measures.

These various procedures do not always result in compliance. But over the years, they do seem to have a positive effect in most cases.[23]

The committee report then goes to the conference plenary session, where it is usually adopted without dissent. On only two occasions has the conference failed to adopt the report. One occurred in 1974, when the Soviet Union was listed under Criterion 7 for violation of Convention No. 29, on forced labor. The other took place in 1977, when the Israeli issue was paramount. It is in this context that the strong reaction of the U.S. delegation to the 1977 conference must be viewed. The conference's failure to accept the report of the Committee on the Application of Conventions meant that the climax of the tortuous and elaborate ILO compliance procedure had been frustrated for political reasons. The body of world opinion represented by the ILO had failed to condemn those nations that were found, after long and careful investigation, to be in default of their treaty obligations.

In addition to those various procedures, special machinery was established in 1950 to monitor freedom of association, which goes to the very heart of the ILO tripartite philosophy. Complaints may be brought against governments regardless of whether or not they have ratified the relevant conventions, Nos. 87 and 98. Such complaints are referred to a tripartite Committee on Freedom of Association, which is appointed by the Governing Body from among its own members. The committee looks into the facts and makes appropriate recommendations to the offending country. These may include suggestions for changes in legislation or for the release of imprisoned trade union leaders, among other things. Where ratified conventions are involved, the recommendation is brought to the attention of the Committee of Experts, which checks upon the corrective steps. An ILO representative may be sent to the country involved to discuss remedial action, particularly where imprisonment of trade unionists is involved. In the event of persistent noncompliance, the ILO's ultimate weapon is publicity.

Another special avenue for securing remedial action in freedom of association cases is referral of a complaint to a fact-finding and conciliation commission. However, the consent of the government concerned is required unless it has ratified the relevant conventions.

The Governing Body's Committee on Freedom of Association has played a very active role. By the end of 1978, over 900 cases covering a wide variety of complaints had been referred to it:

> The nature of the complaints stretches the meaning of freedom of association very far indeed: we find instances of suppression of unions through murder, arrest, and deportation; strike-breaking; restrictive and discriminatory compulsory registration procedures; rigged elections; suppression of union newspapers; seizure of union halls and union funds; discriminatory subsidization; and the persecution of political leaders who are unionists. Since the line between trade union freedom and the freedom to vote, write, speak, and peaceably assemble is very thin, the work of the committee is fertile ground for inquiring how successfully and how far the international protection of one strategically placed legal right can be pushed.[24]

On the other hand, the fact-finding and conciliation commission device has not fulfilled the hopes of its designers. It was used only on rare occasions, the most important involving Japan and Chile. In each case, on-site visits were part of the inquiry process. The ILO concedes that government reticence to receive fact-finding commissions is the cause of their infrequent use. "Too much weight has no doubt been given to the contentious aspect of the procedure, and governments do not like to be in the position of the accused."[25]

The ILO has established an impressive body of procedures to enforce those obligations that are embodied in its conventions or are implied by the very fact of membership. Nevertheless, there has always been much skepticism in the United States about how effective these procedures are in ensuring that nations translate their legal obligations into reality. This skepticism applies to the conventions that relate to both labor conditions and to human rights.

Evaluations of ILO convention effectiveness have been undertaken by the ILO itself, as well as by independent scholars. In the pages that follow, these are reviewed, and I then attempt to apply quantitative methods to the evaluation process. The human rights conventions are treated separately, since they involve questions of particular importance and complexity.

ILO Evaluation of Convention Effectiveness

Recently, the ILO prepared a comprehensive analysis of the effectiveness of the international standards it has promulgated.[26] Although the report is hardly objective—it starts out with some sweeping, pretentious claims[27]—it is useful as a summary of how the Office views itself.

Country officials have reportedly said that they normally refer to ILO conventions in preparing labor legislation. There is undoubtedly a good deal of truth to this claim, particularly for the less developed countries. Credit was claimed in the report for the spread of paid vacations after the adoption of a convention in 1936. Similar influence has been alleged for instruments dealing with termination of employment, minimum wages, and other working conditions.

The ILO report concedes that in the early years of the organization many countries ratified conventions with little intention of enforcing them. This type of window dressing is said to be a thing of the past, "and it is today an undisputed fact that ratification is a solemn commitment to give full effect to the Convention ratified. The development of the ILO's vigilant supervision machinery has removed any shadow of doubt on this point."[28]

It may be remarked parenthetically that U.S. representatives have not always accepted this position. In 1976 the U.S. worker representative expressed his "great concern at the number of countries which were not implementing the standards they had accepted through ratification."[29] The U.S. Chamber of Commerce, in supporting the issuance of the U.S. letter of intent to withdraw, noted that the ILO had devoted maximum attention to securing ratification of conventions, while giving little attention to the record of implementation. "It is hypocrisy to ignore the demonstrated fact that many member states ratify these instruments without the ability or intent to implement them."[30] This view, whether accurate or not, was an important factor in blunting the impact of pro-ILO arguments raised by those opposed to U.S. withdrawal.

The ILO recognizes that not all social progress can be attributed to convention ratification. Ratification may follow, rather than precede, the achievement of good labor standards. Some conventions have proven inappropriate; others could not be ratified by federal states because of lack of jurisdiction by their federal governments.

Great differences among countries in their economic, social, and legal systems often tend to make it difficult to construct meaningful universal standards. The Governing Body has observed that "care should be taken not to make ILO instruments so flexible that they would lose their dynamic influence as a means for achieving social progress or cease to represent a common standard."[31] This problem of excessive generality can be illustrated by reference to minimum wages, an area in which the ILO claims to have exerted considerable influence.[32]

In October 1967, an expert group met to consider the possibility of adopting a minimum wage convention more appropriate to the conditions of developing countries than earlier instruments on the same subject. In its report, this group recommended that the minimum wage be based on the living standards of peasants in countries where they constituted a substantial part of the labor force. It also warned that minimum wages should be raised gradually or else economic development prospects might be impaired.[33] The group took into account the widely held view that any attempt to fix minimum wages by law was likely to have disruptive economic effects.

After a good deal of tugging and hauling by the Governing Body—the labor representatives found the experts' report antisocial and too theoretical, while the employers felt that it did not emphasize the possible deleterious effects of minimum wage determination sufficiently—the issue was put on the agenda of the 1969 conference. Eventually, Convention No. 131 was adopted in 1970. Among other things, the convention binds signatory states to establish minimum wages for all wage earners "whose terms of employment are such that coverage would be appropriate." In determining the minimum level, consideration was to be given to the needs of workers and their families as well as to economic factors, "including the desirability of attaining and maintaining a high level of employment."[34]

By January 1, 1977, the convention had been ratified by twenty countries, fifteen of which could be characterized as underdeveloped. Among them were countries not known for their advanced social policies, such as Ecuador, Libya, Nepal, Nicaragua, Syria, and Yemen. Any country could easily demonstrate its commitment to the improvement of the social welfare of its workers by ratifying the convention and adopting a minimum wage law that conformed fully to the criteria set forth in the convention but that was at the same time operationally meaningless. The trouble lay in the language of the convention, which was vague enough to encompass any interpretation made by a government. Since most economists agree that imposing a minimum wage above the market rate tends to reduce employment and since every nation wants to attain and maintain a high level of employment, the convention requirements could be met by setting an ineffective minimum without being regarded as in bad faith. Many less developed countries other than those that ratified Convention No. 131 have enacted minimum wage laws, but the levels fixed are often below the going market minimum, usually as a result of failure to adjust the legal minimum upward after periods of inflation.

Some of the ratifying countries, particularly the developed nations, already had minimum wage laws in effect before 1970. If it wanted to make a real case for effectiveness, the ILO would have to show that the rest of the countries had enacted economically meaningful minimum wage legislation subsequent to ratification or that nonratifying countries had adopted such legislation under the influence of the ILO convention. Such evidence

would be extremely difficult to gather because the mere citation
of laws already enacted would be insufficient. Not all ILO conventions are as general as No. 131, but those that are remain
subject to similar limits on their evaluation. In such cases, ILO
claims of effective economic impact must be accepted with a
grain of salt.[35]

The International Confederation of Free Trade Unions appears to have arrived at a similar conclusion. In reviewing ILO
standard-setting, it made the following observation: "The ICFTU
very much regrets the present tendency to adopt instruments
which, instead of setting goals, determine the lowest common
social denominator, and which use too loosely worded formulae.
Once again we would like to repeat that a widely ratified convention does not necessarily have more social impact than one which
is ratified by only a small number of States."[36]

In all fairness, the ILO Governing Body has been cautious in
accepting the claims put forward by the Office. A working party
set up in 1973 to examine the ILO program on conditions of work
stated: "In reviewing progress, the ILO should go beyond the
record of ratifications, which was really a starting point, and seek
to measure the degree of application in practice. This should include not only the examination of reports submitted by governments under articles 22 and 19 of the Constitution but also a
broader assessment of progress within countries towards substantive implementation."[37] The ILO has not yet followed this
good advice.

The Landy and Haas Surveys

A careful study of ILO experience with standard-setting, *The
Effectiveness of International Supervision*, prepared by E. A.
Landy, was published in 1966. Although the author was an ILO
staff member on leave from his post, his study was, in contrast to
some official ILO publications, quite objective.

Landy breaks down the reasons for nonobservance of ratified
conventions into two categories, legal and practical. The legal
difficulties he cites are the following:

1. *Detailed and rigid conventions.* A detailed convention can

be monitored more easily than a general one, but ratification may be held up by the impossibility of compliance with one of the conditions specified. The Scandinavian countries, for example, attribute their failure to ratify some conventions to this factor. A more general convention runs into the problem already noted in the case of the minimum wage, and Landy observes that "flexibility is not an end in itself and that it loses its justification and value when the basic I.L.O. purpose of raising and equalizing social standards is no longer served by it."[38]

2. *Premature ratification*. Landy cites the practice whereby some states ratify conventions before they are prepared to implement them, sometimes including an entire group of conventions en bloc. He says that this was a not uncommon practice in the prewar period. The question can be raised, however, whether many of the less developed nations have not continued this practice right up to the present. To take a convention covering accident protection through guarding machinery (No. 119, 1963), one might question how effectively the labor inspectorate (if there is one) polices the law in the Central African Empire, the Congo, Madagascar, Niger, or Democratic Yemen. Premature ratifications may not be just a bygone matter.

3. *Ratifications that raise unforeseen difficulties*. Landy's principal example is the Soviet Union's ratification of the freedom of association convention, No. 87. He outlines the history of jousting between the Committee of Experts and the Soviet Union on this issue. Quite possibly the Soviet Union would have refrained from ratification if it had foreseen the problems ahead. On the other hand, the yearly opportunity to extol the virtues of Soviet labor law and practice may have been an unforeseen bonus.

4. *Retrogression in the application of a convention*. Political changes in a country may lead to changes in social policy. Ratified conventions may be renounced, although this has seldom been done.[39]

The remaining legal problems cited by Landy are of a purely technical nature, including the federal-state problem, and need not concern us. The practical difficulties he lists are the following:

1. *Economic difficulties*. Less developed countries can rarely afford the social measures that characterize the welfare state in the industrial West. Most of them have refrained from ratifying the social security conventions, although there have been attempts to draft suitable conventions with which they could live.

2. *Administrative difficulties*. U.S. troubles with administration of the occupational safety and health laws provide a good example. Add to this the factor of untrained and often corrupt bureaucracies, a not uncommon feature of government in many parts of the world, and an even more cautious attitude toward the meaning of ratification would seem to be in order.

3. *Political difficulties*. This is particularly germane to the human rights conventions, although securing parliamentary concurrence even for noncontroversial subjects may create political problems.

Landy goes on to discuss the problems of ILO supervision, which include the securing of information, the promotion of appropriate governmental action, and the involvement of labor and management in the enforcement process. He concludes that the ILO supervisory system has not discouraged convention ratification and ends on this optimistic note:

> The mere existence of supervisory arrangements operating automatically . . . tends to increase mutual confidence among parties to a treaty and provides at the same time a ready sounding board for ventilating charges on nonapplication without having to go to the extreme of lodging a formal complaint. . . . Even if the methods used are still imperfect and the results leave much to be desired, mechanisms are emerging through which international organizations can exert some influence on the behavior of States.[40]

The Haas study, *Beyond the Nation-State*, deals to a considerable extent with the human rights conventions, but he has some interesting findings about the extent to which different

types of political systems honor their reporting obligations. Industrialized democracies and the developed totalitarian states respond faithfully, as do developing countries with good administrative systems. Intermittent reporters include most of the
countries of Latin America, as well as others characterized by
unstable governments.[41]

Haas's general conclusions are less optimistic than those of
Landy. Reporting was spotty, and it was difficult to discipline
persistent offenders. Trade union delegates called for more effective supervision, and the tendency was to loosen conventions in
order to accommodate the less developed countries. "It appears,
then, that neither the direct stimulus of worker dissatisfaction
and international competition nor the indirect pressure of hu-
manitarianism has given us a marked and uniform transformation
of the international environment."[42]

On the reporting side, at least, matters seem to have improved substantially since the Landy and Haas studies were
completed. In 1977, for example, 76.4 percent of all reports requested on the application of ratified conventions were received.
A majority of them were late, however, making it difficult for the
Committee of Experts to examine them with sufficient care.
During the decade 1967–77, an average of 14.9 percent of all
reports were received by the due date; 79.8 percent were received in time for the committee sessions; and 86.3 percent arrived in time for the annual conference. Moreover, over the
fifteen-year period in which the committee has been listing possible violations in its reports, some 1,200 cases have arisen in
which the committee was satisfied that measures were being
taken by governments to bring their law and practice into line
with convention requirements.[43] Even though this record does
not provide an evaluation of the real impact of the changes, the
sheer magnitude of the reactions to ILO intervention is impressive.

Quantitative Evaluation: A First Essay
     The ILO and its observers have thus far defined progress in
standard-setting in terms of the number of conventions ratified
and the extent to which national legislation has been brought

into conformance with the specified obligations. To probe more deeply into the actual implementation of legislation and its effect on social and economic conditions has been regarded as a difficult if not hopeless task. To quote the ILO: "The question that may obviously be asked is whether the numerous individual cases in which ratification has an impact have an over-all significance. It is impossible to make a comprehensive survey of the situation covering all countries and all Conventions since this would entail a thoroughgoing investigation of each of thousands of cases."[44] And, to quote the ILO again: "In the nature of the case, precise mathematical measurement is next to impossible. Although . . . some statistics do exist, the bulk of the evidence must be gleaned from such documents as government reports, records of Conference discussions, parliamentary documents and official communications."[45]

However, statistical data that make it possible to look behind the legislation are available in the ILO's own annual statistical yearbooks. Unfortunately, the fact that they have never been regarded as a means of monitoring international labor standards has led to their not being ideally suited to this purpose. Had there been more interaction between the ILO lawyers, who have exclusive jurisdiction over standard-setting, and the organization's statistical branch, it is likely that not only could much more be done with existing data, but that better data would have been available. Member states could have been asked to supply quantitative data as well as legal compendia. Since many of them already compile such data, this would not have been difficult for them to do.

The methodological problems involved in confronting convention ratifications with the available data are not simple. As has already been pointed out, clear-cut cause-and-effect relationships between the adoption of conventions and the subsequent achievement of labor standards can hardly be expected. Improvements in social conditions are the result of a complex of forces difficult to standardize internationally, a technique necessary to sift out the independent contributions of ILO conventions. There is also the problem of the direction of causation: countries that ratify conventions may be mainly those that have already achieved the standards embodied in them, so that ratification may follow social progress rather than precede it. Moreover, no international comparative data are currently available for many substantive areas covered by ILO conventions. The present exercise must therefore be regarded as only a first step in the direction of a new type of evaluative procedure, and as a demonstration of the feasibility of statistical evaluation as a supplement to purely legal monitoring.

The methodology employed here involves a comparison of the statistical records of countries that have ratified specific conventions with those that have not, in order to see whether any difference in achieving the standards embodied in the conventions are discernable. If the achievement of the ratifiers in a particular area—say, hours of work—appeared to be superior to that of the nonratifiers, it would tend to support the argument that the relevant conventions are effective, either because they led to a reduction of working hours or because they were regarded as a kind of international seal of approval by those countries that had attained the standards before ratification. The ILO makes a cogent argument for the latter point of view:

> The ratification of Conventions by States whose law and practice have already reached the standard laid down therein may also have a wider influence. It secures for those States international recognition of the level of their social legislation and serves as a guarantee of fair competition. It gives other States an incentive to attain the same standard because it provides both an example and an assurance of widespread implementation and, through the number of ratifications, emphasizes the fact that Conventions constitute positive rules of international law.[46]

If, on the other hand, there were no apparent differences in the performance of ratifiers and nonratifiers, as evidenced by the data, it would be tempting to conclude that the conventions had not been effective. Unfortunately, this option is precluded by the character of the statistical model employed here; not only are the statistical variables not always ideally suited for the purpose at hand, but many relevant factors, such as economic structure and level of development, have not been taken into account. To achieve conclusive results, it would be necessary to formulate a more elaborate framework for estimation and to find more complete data than those presently available in the international statistical yearbooks, perhaps by going to national statistical abstracts or even more specialized studies.

The present work has been conducted along three lines:

1. An international cross-sectional comparison for specified years
2. An aggregate comparison of change over time between ratifying and nonratifying countries
3. A comparison of change over time for *individual* countries before and after ratification

The period under examination is limited to the years between 1950 (in some cases, 1955) and 1975. The pre–World War II period was so different from the postwar years in terms of the number and character of ILO members and of prevailing social conditions that it did not appear fruitful to extend the analysis back that far. During the five-year period 1945–50, many countries were much more concerned with economic reconstruction than with social progress, and it was not until 1950 that some degree of economic normalcy had been restored in many of the large member nations of the ILO. The 1975 cutoff date was dictated by the availability of data at the time of writing.

Some of the conventions examined here have been in existence for relatively short periods of time, and their effects may not yet have been fully reflected. However, since little is known about the speed of their impact, it seemed better to include them.

The choice of substantive areas of analysis was dictated entirely by data availability. For example, it would have been interesting to test the conventions dealing with toxic substances, paid vacations, the employment of young people, the compensation of women, and various aspects of labor administration, among others, but no sets of relevant data were at hand. The following areas were examined:

1. *Industrial safety.* A straightforward subject from a concep-

tual point of view, industrial safety would seem to be an ideal area for statistical testing. If the relevant conventions do in fact promote the adoption of safety measures, ratifying countries should be expected to have lower occupational accident and disease rates than nonratifiers. Moreover, there should be a change in the trend of accident rates after ratification. The conventions and the year of their adoption by the ILO conference are as follows:

> Safety Provisions (Building), No. 62 (1937)
> Guarding of Machinery, No. 119 (1963)
> Maximum Weights, No. 127 (1967)

Unfortunately, data limitations made any cross-sectional comparisons impossible. There are accident statistics for a good number of countries, but the incidence of accidents is measured against bases that are not directly comparable: man-years of work, the number of wage earners, the number employed, the number of man-hours worked per annum. To compound the problem, some countries report all accidents, others only accidents that are compensated by insurance schemes. The procedure in this seemingly promising area thus had to be restricted to comparisons over time.

2. *Hours of work.* Several conventions of prewar vintage deal with this subject:

> Hours of Work (Industry), No. 1 (1919)
> Forty-Hour Week, No. 47 (1935)

The international statistical yearbooks contain data on hours of work in industry, but they are not completely uniform. Most countries report average weekly hours actually worked, but a few report weekly hours paid for. The difference is due mainly to paid vacations. For a full working year of forty-hour weeks, a two-week paid vacation would mean a difference of about one and a half hours a week between the two measures. Combining the two series thus produces some distortion when comparing absolute numbers of hours worked (the trends over time are not affected), but there appears to be no systematic bias between ratifiers and nonratifiers in this respect.

3. *Social security.* The relevant conventions, all intended to promote the improvement of social security systems, are the following:

Old Age Insurance, No. 35 (1933)
Social Security, Minimum Standards, No. 102 (1952)
Invalidity, Old Age, and Survivors Benefits, No. 128 (1967)

The indicators available relate to government expenditures on social security schemes as a proportion of the gross domestic product. The hypothesis may be advanced that countries ratifying one or more of the listed conventions would be expected to devote a greater proportion of their national product to social security purposes than the nonratifiers. Clearly, there is no one-to-one relationship between the variables, since social security expenditures cover more than old-age pensions. Pensions typically constitute a large proportion of total social security expenditures, however, and may be a good index of the magnitude of other programs.

4. *Minimum wage.* There are no available international comparative statistics on legislated minimum wages. Minimum wage standards have been an important area of ILO activity, so that it was felt desirable to use some proxy variable. Inspection of available manufacturing wage data reveals that for most countries, earnings in the clothing industry are at or near the bottom of the industrial wage structure. The proxy variable selected for testing here is the ratio of earnings in clothing manufacture to average earnings in all manufacturing. The argument in support of this choice is that the imposition of a minimum wage, if it is effective, tends to compress the wage structure, particularly near the bottom. Wage differentials generally tend to decline in the course of economic development, but effective minimum wage laws may hasten the process.

The relevant conventions are

Minimum Wage Fixing Machinery, No. 26 (1928)
Minimum Wage Fixing, No. 131 (1970)

The available data take the form variously of rates or earnings, by the hour, week, month, or year. Since we are using a ratio, however, the data may be combined into a single variable.

Statistical analysis may be a useful device despite its drawbacks. There are problems of interpretation in dealing with almost any set of social science data. The statistics may tell us something; there would be something wrong with the performance of a country whose own statistics contradicted the alleged attainment of the standards to which it is committed. The fact that some nonratifying countries fully meet convention standards does complicate interpretation of the results. But even there, if ratification does have a real impact, it should logically be greater in the ratifying countries than in the nonratifiers that are only indirectly influenced by the conventions. If this were not true, the ILO might just as well promulgate a model labor code and discard its elaborate compliance machinery.

The results of the statistical exercise appear in Tables 9 to 12. The first three tables are cross-sectional; that is, they relate to the relative levels of the statistical variables for ratifying and nonratifying countries for specified years. The averages shown are median, rather than mean, values in order to minimize the effect of extreme values at either end of the distribution. The interquartile range, which is the difference between the third and first quartile values of the distribution, is also shown in order to provide a rough measure of the degree of variance among the countries included in the sets.

Data are also shown for a subset of the wealthiest countries. The level of economic development is relevant for both the ability and the will of states to ratify and implement international labor standards, and one might expect a difference in behavior between the richer and poorer countries. However, the sample of countries for which data are available is dominated by the most highly developed nations in most cases, so that differentiation by income level does not add very much to our knowledge in this exercise. If similar work were to be undertaken in the future, when more data will presumably be available, it would be important to subdivide the country sample into several income-level categories.

The results of the cross-sectional tabulations are shown in Tables 9 to 11. Looking first at hours of work (Table 9), we find that for the years 1960 and 1965, the average number of hours worked per week in the ratifying countries was substantially below those worked in the nonratifiers, and that the difference was somewhat greater in the higher income group. By 1970, however, the difference has virtually disappeared, and by 1975, the nonratifying countries were actually working shorter hours.

These results are not inconsistent with the hypothesis that ratification of the hours-of-work conventions was a meaningful act. There has been a general trend toward a reduction of hours of work all over the world since World War II, and the ratifying countries appear to have made an earlier start. The decline tended to level off as forty hours were approached, so that by 1970, all the higher-income countries, at least, were within a few hours of that target. Why hours of work should not have continued down beyond forty is puzzling, but it is not our problem.

Some of the major industrialized nations have never ratified the hours-of-work conventions, among them Germany, Japan,

TABLE 9. Average Hours of Work in Manufacturing, Selected Countries

Status	All countries			High per capita income countries[a]		
	Number	Median	Interquartile range $(Q_{-3}-Q_{-1})$	Number	Median	Interquartile range $(Q_{-3}-Q_{-1})$
1960						
Ratifying	12	43.5	4.1	9	43.2	3.0
Nonratifying	14	45.8	2.3	10	45.9	4.3
1965						
Ratifying	14	43.6	5.5	11	42.2	3.6
Nonratifying	16	45.0	2.1	11	44.1	4.9
1970						
Ratifying	16	44.1	4.4	13	43.8	4.4
Nonratifying	17	44.7	5.6	11	43.3	6.4
1975						
Ratifying	14	41.5	3.7	12	41.0	3.8
Nonratifying	13	41.2	4.9	11	40.4	4.3

SOURCE: *Yearbook of International Labor Statistics*, various issues.
[a]Per capita income over $1,000 in 1970.

the Netherlands, Sweden, the United Kingdom, and the United States. The inclusion of these countries among the nonratifiers contributed to a lessening of the hours differential, which might otherwise have been greater. Average working hours in 1975 were 40.4 in Germany, 38.8 in Japan, 41.2 in the Netherlands, and 39.4 in the United States, among others. Perhaps the soundest conclusion that can be drawn is one the ILO itself deduced from the data: "While the general influence of the [hours of work] Convention on trends in working hours may have operated in the past, it is difficult to know what precise conclusions should be drawn from current differences between the two categories of countries."[47]

The social security data (Table 10) are more clear-cut. The ratifying countries were consistently spending a substantially greater proportion of their national products on social security than the nonratifiers. This does not necessarily mean that convention ratification was the cause of the higher expenditures, but it does suggest that the results observed for the ratifying coun-

TABLE 10.   Social Security Expenditures as a Percentage of the Gross Domestic Product, Selected Countries

Status	All countries			High per capita income countries[a]		
	Number	Median	Interquartile range $(Q_{-3}-Q_{-1})$	Number	Median	Interquartile range $(Q_{-3}-Q_{-1})$
1960						
Ratifying[b]	12	11.9	4.9	12	11.9	4.9
Nonratifying	19	6.0	6.9	13	8.8	4.9
1965						
Ratifying[b]	15	12.8	4.6	14	13.1	5.2
Nonratifying	23	3.4	8.5	12	9.5	6.2
1970						
Ratifying[b]	14	13.6	6.9	12	15.1	6.4
Ratifying[c]	3	18.8	3.7	3	18.8	3.7
Nonratifying	34	3.2	5.3	13	9.4	7.4

SOURCE: ILO, *The Cost of Social Security,* various issues.
[a]Per capita income over $1,000 in 1970
[b]Ratified Conventions 35 or 102.
[c]Ratified Conventions 35 or 102 plus 38.

tries were consistent with the obligations undertaken when they adopted the ILO standards.

The test for effectiveness of the minimum wage conventions was not as successful (Table 11), but this may be due to the variable used as a proxy for the absent minimum wage data. The measure of variance (the interquartile range) for earlier years indicates that for some countries in the sample, earnings in the clothing industry actually exceeded those for all manufacturing, particularly in the ratifying group of countries. In these earlier years, however, the lower end of the wage structure was more compressed in the ratifying countries, and the presence of a minimum wage law may have contributed to this result. A not implausible hypothesis is that the impact of minimum wage legislation may have become eroded over time through failure of

TABLE 11. Ratio of Earnings in Clothing Manufacturing to Average Earnings in Manufacturing, Selected Countries

(Percent)

	All countries			High per capita income countries[a]		
Status	Number	Median	Interquartile range $(Q_{-3}-Q_{-1})$	Number	Median	Interquartile range $(Q_{-3}-Q_{-1})$
1960						
Ratifying	21	92.0	29.0	14	92.5	23.5
Nonratifying	16	79.5	25.0	9	74.0	21.0
1965						
Ratifying	19	83.0	20.0	14	91.0	26.0
Nonratifying	13	75.0	21.5	11	75.0	23.0
1970						
Ratifying	28	78.0	22.0	17	78.0	23.0
Nonratifying	14	77.0	18.0	10	75.0	21.0
1975						
Ratifying[b]	17	78.0	14.5	13	78.0	10.5
Ratifying[c]	6	79.5	34.0	5	77.0	34.0
Nonratifying	7	76.0	17.0	7	76.0	17.0

SOURCE: *Yearbook of International Labor Statistics*, various issues.
[a]Per capita income over $1,000 in 1970.
[b]Ratified Convention 26.
[c]Ratified Conventions 26 and 131.

legislatures to keep the levels up to date. In any event, by 1970 the difference between the wage ratios of ratifying and nonratifying countries had just about disappeared.

A second statistical approach was made by examining the behavior of individual countries over time. This was done by fitting linear functions to the various series for the period 1950 to 1975, or for as great a portion of the period as the data permitted. When a country ratified a convention during the period, separate trend lines were fitted for the years before and after ratification. Table 12 shows the aggregated slope coefficients for the several variables, calculated separately for ratifying and nonratifying

TABLE 12.   Median Coefficients of Fitted Linear Trend Slopes, All Countries

	Number of countries	Median	First quartile	Third quartile
Hours of work				
Ratifying countries	16	− .014	− .010	− .024
Nonratifying countries	21	− .076	+ .145	− .309
Social security				
Ratifying countries	18	+ .270	+ .159	+ .356
Nonratifying countries	36	+ .108	+ .026	+ .214
Earnings ratios				
Ratifying countries[a]	8	− .007	+ .010	− .026
Ratifying countries[b]	33	− .010	− .002	− .016
Nonratifying countries	17	− .004	+ .008	+ .005
Accidents in manufacturing				
Ratifying countries	13	− .005	+ .002	− .011
Nonratifying countries	40	− .004	− .001	− .010
Accidents in construction				
Ratifying countries	10	− .014	− .010	− .024
Nonratifying countries	27	− .014	+ .003	− .035

NOTE: The aggregate coefficients were obtained by calculating the slopes separately for each country and then securing the median of the country coefficients. It would have been preferable to fit a trend line to pooled country data, but substantial differences in absolute values of the variables among countries rendered this impractical; when this was done, most of the slope coefficients were not significantly different from zero. To reduce the effect of extreme values, the median rather than the mean was used. The first and third quartiles are also shown to provide information about the degree of dispersion.
[a]Countries ratified Conventions 26 and 131.
[b]Countries ratified only Convention 26.

countries. As a partial check on their reliability, the pattern of *t*-statistic values for the fitted individual country trend lines are shown in Table 13. (Slope coefficients and *t*-values for individual countries are available from the author on request.)

For hours of work, the results are consistent with the previous data. The reduction in hours of work for the period covered was greater for nonratifying than for ratifying countries. The *t*-values suggest that the slope coefficients for the nonratifying countries were more significant, if anything, than for the ratifying countries. In both sets, about the same proportion of cases had the wrong sign: that is, hours were increasing rather than decreasing.

The social security data clearly conform to the hypothesis that the proportion of GNP devoted by ratifying countries to social security expenditures should rise more rapidly over time than that for nonratifying countries. The average slope coefficient is higher for ratifiers than for the nonratifiers, and almost all the slope coefficients for the former are significant. Moreover, for a number of the nonratifying countries, there was a significant downward trend in relative social security expenditures over the period.

The results of the test for effectiveness of the minimum wage conventions suggest that there was a fairly significant *downward* trend in the ratio of earnings in clothing manufacture to all manufacturing among the ratifying countries. This was also true for the nonratifiers, but the downward slope was less pronounced. As already indicated, this result may be due to the inappropriateness of the proxy variable used, or to the erosion of the effectiveness of the minimum wage over time.

Average rates of accidents in both manufacturing and construction tended to decline slightly over time, but there was almost no difference in the performance of ratifying and nonratifying countries. Moreover, for both sets of countries a great many of the slope coefficients are not significantly different from zero. This is a disappointing finding, since accident rates are unambiguous measures, and one would have expected ratifying countries to perform better than the nonratifiers. An ILO official has suggested some possible reasons for the failure to secure positive results:

> I am not sure that the two Conventions chosen for relation to accident statistics in manufacturing constitute a valid sample. Industrial safety legislation comprises a great mass of detailed regulations, of which the guarding of machinery and maximum weight are only a small part. This is an area where a substantial part of ILO guidelines have been laid down not in conventions, but in model codes and guides of practice. The need has been increasingly recognized for a "framework" Convention laying down the general obligations and administrative arrangements for establishing and enforcing safety standards (on the lines of the standards which already exist for the maritime sector—Convention No. 134). . . . In the case of construction, the existence of a Convention (No. 62) covering the building industry would seem to provide a firmer base for comparison. However, it is recognized that owing to considerable technological develop-

Table 13. Pattern of *t*-Values for Individual Country Slope Coefficients

	−6 and under	−5 to −5.99	−4 to −4.99	−3 to −3.99	−2 to −2.99
Hours of work					
Ratifying countries	2	2		2	
Nonratifying countries	8		1	1	
Social security					
Ratifying countries					
Nonratifying countries	1	1		1	2
Earnings ratios					
Ratifying countries	12	2	3	1	4
Nonratifying countries	6	1		1	1
Accidents in manufacturing					
Ratifying countries					
Nonratifying countries	11	2	1	2	4
Accidents in construction					
Ratifying countries	2			2	
Nonratifying countries	1	4			4

NOTE: The *t*-values were calculated to show the probability that the estimated slope coefficients were significantly different from zero. Given the size of samples of countries involved, coefficients with *t*-values less than ±1 are not likely to be significantly different from zero, i.e., there appears to be no clear trend over

ments since the adoption of this Convention forty years ago, its standards are no longer adequate and stand in need of revision.[48]

Finally, trend lines for those countries that ratified the conventions with which we are dealing between 1950 and 1975, and for which data are available, were plotted separately, and are shown in Figures 1 to 5.[49] The purpose of this exercise was to determine whether any discernible effects of ratification could be found by looking at the experience of individual nations. In each of these figures the year of ratification is indicated by the letter *R*.

For hours of work, the set includes only two countries, Egypt and Australia. For Egypt, it would be difficult to point to any permanent impact of ratification, but in the case of Australia, hours of work (from 1963 to 1975) peaked at the date of ratification and dropped sharply thereafter (Fig. 1). While one must be

Table 13. *Continued*

− 1 to − 1.99	Less than 1	+ 1 to 1.99	+ 2 to 2.99	+ 3 to 3.99	+ 4 to 4.99	+ 5 to 5.99	+ 6 and over
4	2		1	2		1	
2	3		3	1		1	1
		2	2	2		2	10
1	4	4	4	2	1	2	13
2	10	2	2	1	1		1
2	3			1		2	
4	6	1	2				
7	8	2		2			1
2	3		1				
4	11	1	1	1			

time. Where the coefficients have *t*-values between − 1 to − 2 or + 1 to + 2, the probability of significance is on the borderline between acceptance and rejection. *t*-values greater than ± 2 indicate the probability that the fitted slope is significantly different from zero.

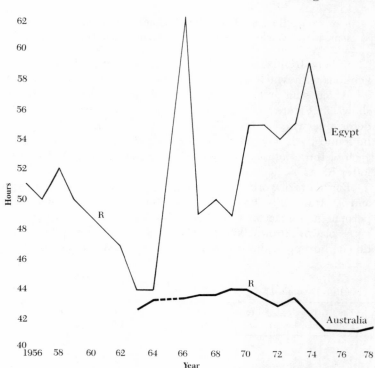

Figure 1: Weekly Hours of Work in Manufacturing—Australia (men only) and
Egypt (men and women)

SOURCE: ILO, *Yearbook of Labor Statistics*, various issues.
R ratified.

cautious in drawing any causal inferences, it is interesting that
Australia chose to ratify a convention dating back to 1937 only in
1970, when average hours of work in manufacturing began to
move down from forty-four hours to the forty-hour target.

Appropriate data for industrial accident rates in manufacturing are available for five countries. Because of differences in the
base against which the accidents were measured, they are shown
in three separate charts. Figure 2 shows the trend for Yugoslavia;
while the accident rate declined after ratification in 1970, there

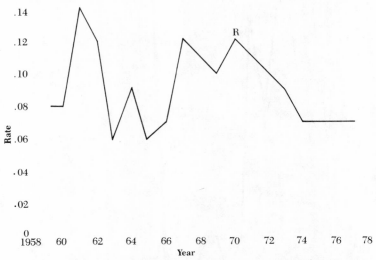

Figure 2: Industrial Accidents Reported per 1,000 Employed in Manufacturing—Yugoslavia

SOURCE: ILO, *Yearbook of Labor Statistics*, various issues.
R ratified.

had been even lower rates in earlier years. For Turkey (Fig. 3),
ratification had no discernible effect. In the case of Norway, the
low rates that had been achieved during the five years before
ratification continued at about the same level in the five years
following ratification, but then declined sharply. The Finnish
rate had been falling sharply since 1963, and the downward
trend continued after ratification in 1969. The Swedish case (Fig.
4) is perhaps the most interesting; from 1956, when the series
begins, to 1964, the year of ratification, the accident rate fell by
about 15 percent, but from 1964 to 1973, it was halved. Whatever the reason, Sweden was a country in which ratification was
followed by action.

There are three countries in the social security set (Fig. 5).
Ireland ratified in 1968, and for the next five years, its social
security expenditures rose sharply. For Belgium and the Netherlands, the correlation between ratification and subsequently

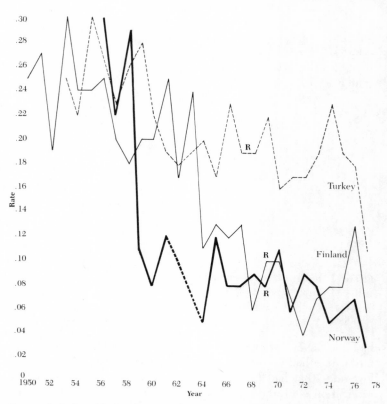

Figure 3: Industrial Accidents Compensated per 1,000 Man-Years of 300
        Days Each in Manufacturing—Finland, Norway, and Turkey

SOURCE: ILO, *Yearbook of Labor Statistics*, various issues.
R ratified.

rising expenditures is striking. If all ILO convention ratifiers be-
haved in this manner, the standard-setting system would have to
be acknowledged a great success.

Taking into consideration the inherent difficulty of relating
ratification of conventions to the implementation of specific social programs, as well as the paucity of suitable data, this exercise
yielded results beyond what might reasonably have been expected. There is evidence that ratification is not a meaningless

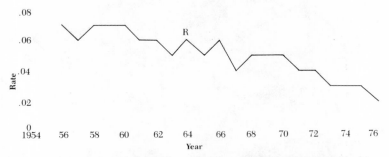

Figure 4: Industrial Accidents Compensated per Million Man-Hours Worked in
          Manufacturing—Sweden
SOURCE: ILO, *Yearbook of Labor Statistics*, various issues.
R ratified.

act, and that many countries are serious in their efforts to conform to the standards they have accepted. If it had been possible
to include among the nations surveyed a larger number of less
developed countries, where good labor standards are difficult to
achieve and where there is a greater temptation to use "paper"
ratifications for internal political purposes, a better test would
have been provided. Nevertheless, the data, imperfect though
they may be, do give some support to the conclusions of the
Landy study quoted above.

This exercise suggests that the ILO should seriously consider
adding a statistical approach to its legal monitoring procedures.
Countries are already required to provide the ILO with a considerable volume of annual information. It would not add much to
their burdens to require them to provide additional statistical
data, much of which is already tabulated and even published in
internal compilations. It would then be possible to have a more
realistic, and perhaps more objective, view of how international
standards are being implemented, and to spotlight both the successes and the failures. This process could also contribute substantially to the setting of new standards and the discarding of
irrelevant ones. It would make it easier to demonstrate that the
ILO has been an effective force for world social progress, if indeed the data were to bear out this conclusion.

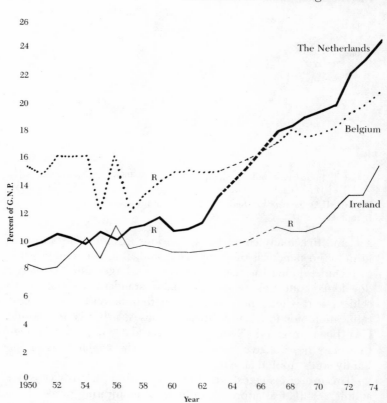

Figure 5: Social Security Expenditures as a Percentage of Gross Domestic
        Product—Belgium, Ireland, and the Netherlands

SOURCE: ILO, *The Cost of Social Security*, various issues.
R ratified.

Human Rights

The work of the ILO in promoting human rights has been of
major interest to the United States. The machinery established
to secure the observance of its conventions in this area is generally regarded as superior to that of any other international organization. It is ironic, therefore, that the withdrawal of the United
States should have taken place during the tenure of a federal

administration that has placed great emphasis on human rights as a basis for its foreign policy.

The key ILO conventions on human rights are No. 87 (freedom of association and protection of the right to organize, 1948), No. 98 (right to organize and collective bargaining, 1949), No. 105 (abolition of forced labor, 1957), and No. 111 (discrimination in employment, 1958). As of January 1, 1977, No. 87 had been ratified by 85 countries, No. 98 by 101, No. 105 by 95, and No. 111 by 90. They are among the most frequently ratified of all conventions.

The ILO machinery has already been described; it remains to consider how effective it has been. The best place to start is with Ernst Haas's study published in 1970 and devoted specifically to this subject.[50] The basis for his work was an analysis of 486 complaints received by the Governing Body Committee on Freedom of Association from 1950 to 1968, involving 87 governments. His rather esoteric terminology and categorization of countries makes it difficult to summarize his results simply. What he found, roughly, was that a disproportionate number of cases had been filed against countries characterized by "reconciliation politics with capitalist institutions and underdeveloped economies" (e.g., Uruguay) and "reconciliation politics with mixed institutions and developed economies" (e.g., the United Kingdom). About one-quarter of the accused states were "convicted" of the alleged violations, but a disproportionate number of these were to be found among governments characterized as having "mobilization" (e.g., the U.S.S.R.), "authoritarian" (e.g., Argentina), and "oligarchic" (e.g., Nicaragua) characteristics.[51]

Haas also found that while the defendants had not improved their records in responding to adverse decisions, they had not grown less cooperative. "Nevertheless," he added, "the rate of full implementation of ILO rulings has declined sharply over the years, and the rate of partial implementation has improved only slightly. . . . we must admit that the regimes most in need of supervision are the least responsive, whereas some of those least in need of it are the most responsive."[52] Overall, the record of implementation was poor, and not much change had occurred over time.

The ILO's own view of its efforts is less cautious. From 1964 to 1976, it reported, there were almost fifty cases in which governments took legislative or other action to comply with the freedom of association conventions. Special mention is made of observations made by the Committee of Experts against the Soviet Union in 1975 and 1976;[53] as we have already noted, however, these complaints did not invoke a conciliatory attitude on the part of the Soviet Union.

In 1979, the Committee of Experts produced a special survey on the abolition of forced labor, but as before, it was confined to an analysis of legislation and to the replies of individual countries.[54] There has never been a systematic attempt to pinpoint the existence and extent of forced labor.

Haas looked at three cases with special care—those involving Spain, Greece, and Japan—and it is useful to see what happened to them after he wrote. The ILO had been pressing Spain for a decade to permit freedom of trade-union association, and in 1969, the government was induced to receive an informal ILO group to discuss its labor situation. The findings of this study group were strong with respect to the lack of freedom of association, but the recommendations were mild.[55] The ILO suggestion that the study group continue to monitor the situation was greeted with indignation by the Spanish government, which demanded that the matter be closed.[56] The ILO acknowledged that "the principles set out in the report of the study group did not find an echo in the new trade union legislation enacted in 1971."[57] Worker representatives in the Governing Body continued to inveigh against the Spanish government for its treatment of trade union leaders,[58] but there is no evidence that ILO pressure had any influence on the course of events that led to eventual liberalization. What led to the establishment of independent Spanish trade unionism was the death of Generalissimo Franco and the emergence of a democratic regime. As soon as the political situation permitted, however, Spanish legislation was put in line with ILO standards, so the ILO can claim some credit for post-Franco developments.

Haas's second case involved Greece. Complaints about lack of trade union freedom had been raised since 1950, brought originally by Communist organizations. With the coming to power of a moderate government in 1963, new charges were made that resulted in referral to a fact-finding and conciliation commission, a rare event in ILO history. After some hearings, the complaining union withdrew its charge, and for a time it appeared that a compromise had been reached. But in 1966, the complaints were renewed, and with the establishment of a military dictatorship in Greece in 1967, the squabbling parties united in a new protest to the ILO.

In 1969 the Governing Body set up a commission of inquiry, the ultimate weapon in the regular enforcement arsenal of the ILO, to look into the allegations. After lengthy hearings, the commission rendered its report in 1970, finding Greece in violation of its obligations under Conventions No. 87 and 98. The Greek government agreed to bring its legislation into conformity with the ILO conventions, to review its limitations on the right to strike, to study its collective-bargaining practices, and to assure the trade union movement of financial independence.[59] The Governing Body expressed general satisfaction with the report and its reception by the Greek government.

But the rejoicing was premature. Three months later, the U.S. worker delegate to the Governing Body castigated the Greek government for its failure to take any action in releasing imprisoned trade union leaders and for not making freedom of association possible. He asserted that a letter to the ILO from the Greek minister of labor "gave the impression that the Commission had simply raised a few technical matters, and it did no more than promise changes in the formulation of certain texts."[60] The reply by the Greek government was standard: the absence of strikes in Greece was due to the country's growing prosperity; the only trade unionists arrested and convicted were guilty of subversive political activities, and their imprisonment had nothing to do with trade unionism.[61]

The Greek government periodically reported progress in meeting its convention obligations, but serious doubts continued to be expressed in the Governing Body as to the effectiveness of new legislative enactments in that country. The reaction of a Belgian trade union representative was typical: "Having himself analyzed both of these [new] texts, he could affirm that their effect was to give the Greek government complete control over the trade unions. They actually supplemented the existing provisions by imposing a number of major restrictions which wiped out any possibility of trade union action. The Governing Body should not imagine that the situation in Greece had improved; it had in fact deteriorated."[62] Little real change was made during the next two years, although the Greek government claimed to have improved matters. The long struggle for trade union freedom in Greece came to an end only with the overthrow of the military government in 1974. Labor legislation was immediately revised in line with the ILO conventions, and a new constitution guaranteed trade union freedom.[63] But it took a revolution to secure Greek compliance with the human rights conventions.

The third case singled out for comment by Haas involved Japan. In 1958, Japanese trade unions, together with the ILO, filed a complaint against the Japanese government about the collective-bargaining rights of public employees. The focal issue was the right to strike, which was barred under Japanese law. Japan had ratified Convention No. 98, but not the more stringent No. 87.

A complaint to the ILO by a trade union in a democratic country is usually a sign of union weakness, since it involves an attempt to use international opinion as a substitute for domestic power. The Japanese labor movement was in fact weak and factionalized. A long skirmish between the ILO and Japan ensued; finally, in 1964, the Japanese government agreed to accept a fact-finding and conciliation commission. For the first time, such a commission made an on-the-spot investigation.

The commission's report was essentially an attempt at conciliation. It warned against strikes for political purposes but suggested that strikes be permitted in public industries, such as the tobacco monopoly, where no public hardship would ensue. It proposed a tripartite negotiating body to consider changes in legislation.[64] Japan ratified Convention No. 87, but the tripartite panel that had been set up failed to make any progress and was disbanded.

This issue continues to bedevil Japanese labor relations.

Short strikes by government-employed railroad workers and teachers, for example, are normally followed by the imposition of penalties involving fines and dismissals. The war of words between the Japanese government and the trade unions continues within the ILO Committee of Experts, which has made numerous observations about Japanese public employee bargaining.[65] Some improvement has been made with respect to the imposition of penalties, and machinery has been established at the ministerial level so that problems can be aired as they arise. Nevertheless, after twenty years, the basic controversy remains very much alive.

In Haas's words, these three cases—Spain, Greece, and Japan—involved "some of the most celebrated complaints in the history of the ILO procedure."[66] We shall now supplement these with five others of more recent vintage, selected according to the level of interest they generated within the Governing Body and the amount of international notoriety they attained.

1. *Chile*. One of the most celebrated human rights cases in the history of the ILO was its action against the Pinochet government of Chile. The report of a fact-finding and conciliation commission which spent three weeks in Chile was one of the most condemnatory ever issued by the ILO.[67] Moreover, to give it maximum publicity, the ILO took the unusual step of publishing the report as a separate book.[68]

Chile has been the target of tremendous international pressure in recent years, despite the fact that it has not ratified Conventions Nos. 87 and 98, and not only by the ILO. In 1977, the Chilean minister of labor wrote to George Meany soliciting the cooperation of the AFL-CIO on the issue of human rights, citing the exchange of the Chilean Communist leader, Luis Corvalán, for an imprisoned Soviet dissident as evidence of Chilean good faith. Meany replied: "I regret to say that we have precious little cause for rejoicing at the alleged efforts of the Pinochet regime to 'safeguard [human] rights.' Your reference to the anti-communist posture of the Chilean government that would disguise the consistent repressing of human rights and trade union freedoms in Chile is immediately transparent. The excesses committed by your government in the name of anti-communism are typical of the most tyrannical fascist regimes of our century."[69]

The Chilean case has continued to wend its way through the ILO enforcement machinery. In November 1977, the Committee on Freedom of Association expressed deep concern at the slowness with which the Chilean government was modifying its labor code to meet ILO objections. It further proposed to look into the government's assurance that all former trade union officials had been released from prison.[70] A few months later, the committee requested information about the reported deaths of several trade unionists and about the fate of others whose names were supplied. It also questioned the forced exile to remote places of seven trade union officials.[71] In June 1978, the committee reported that "the information provided by the Government does not permit it to note that any progress has been made as to the supply of information on the persons in question and requested the Government to continue its investigations in order that these persons might be traced."[72]

2. *Ethiopia*. The overthrow of Emperor Haile Selassie and the installation of a military government created a flurry of activity in the ILO. Ethiopia had ratified only eight conventions, but Nos. 87 and 98 were among them. In September 1974, several worker members of the Governing Body, learning of the arrest of Beyene Solomon, president of the Confederation of Ethiopian Labor Unions and a deputy member of the Governing Body, and other union officials, asked the director-general to take immediate steps to secure their release. The Ethiopian government confirmed the arrests by cable but maintained that the men were to be tried for criminal and political offenses unrelated to their trade union positions.[73] An assistant director-general was dispatched to Addis Ababa to make a personal investigation. He was received with courtesy and assured that the detainees would be given a fair trial. When he reported back to the Governing Body, the worker members demanded more positive action. However, the employer representative of Ethiopia, who was a member of the Governing Body, urged caution, saying that the aim of the new regime was to promote social justice. He pointed out that

the willingness of the military council to receive the ILO representative "was a sign of the high esteem in which the people and the new Government of Ethiopia held the ILO—since similar treatment had been accorded to few other international agencies—and was an excellent omen for future relations between the ILO and Ethiopia."[74]

A few months later, the ILO learned that the headquarters of the federation of labor had been closed. A cable sent by the director-general asking for information about Solomon received no reply. The ICFTU thereupon filed a complaint against Ethiopia.[75] The Committee on Freedom of Association recommended that a tripartite commission be sent there to look into the arrests; again, no reply was received from the Ethiopian government in response to this proposal.[76] The Ethiopian government was then castigated by members of the Governing Body, including the U.S. worker representative. He asserted that not only had Solomon and his associates been arrested but that their successors in trade union leadership posts had also been arrested and tortured. Another member suggested that technical assistance be withheld, but this was not accepted.[77]

Four months later, the only progress made was a notification from the Ethiopian government that Solomon and his fellow trade unionists were to be brought to trial. Otherwise, the government maintained its policy of refusing to reply to ILO communications. This unprecedented action drew a suggestion from the chairman of the Governing Body's worker group that they consider expelling Ethiopia from the ILO, a suggestion that, despite its doubtful constitutionality, was backed by the U.S. worker representative. One member remarked that "this was the sixth session at which the Governing Body had considered the case of Beyene Solomon, and if it did not achieve something soon its impotence would no longer be in doubt."[78]

At the next meeting of the Governing Body, the vice-chairman of the worker group reported the receipt of a letter from Solomon stating that he had been released and hoped to attend the next meeting of the Governing Body. Congratulations were passed all around for the good work of the Office.[79] But Solomon did not attend any of the subsequent meetings, and at the end of

1977, the Governing Body asked for fresh information about his whereabouts.[80] The 1978 and 1979 reports of the Committee of Experts made some pointed observations about Ethiopian non-compliance with the human rights conventions, including its dissolution of the Federation of Employers.[81] All of these criticisms were brushed aside by the spokesman for the Ethiopian government at the 1978 ILO conference, who declared that Ethiopian workers were now organized in the All-Ethiopian Trade Union. This new group, he insisted, was cooperating fully in the formulation of national plans and had "on its own initiative set up armed committees from the workers at each enterprise to defend the Revolution."[82] What had been made clear, in fact, was that Ethiopia had adopted the Soviet trade union model.

3. *Bolivia*. The ILO case against Bolivia has not received the same degree of international attention as those against Chile and Ethiopia, but it has been pursued since 1971, when a new military government gained power. Bolivia had ratified Conventions 87 and 98, so the ILO action could go through normal channels. What was involved was the usual panoply of government actions in such military takeovers: the closing down of trade unions, arrest and banishment of their leaders, and legislation imposing major restrictions on trade union rights. A representative of the ILO visited Bolivia on two separate occasions in 1976 to discuss the situation with the government and trade union leaders.

Bolivia was much more cooperative with the ILO than were Chile and Ethiopia, but it acted very slowly. In 1976, the Governing Body urged the Bolivian government to establish normal union conditions in its mining industry, to reexamine the list of persons dismissed for union activity, and to reconsider the status of union leaders still in prison or exile.[83] A year later, the Governing Body expressed its regret that its suggestions had not been followed. The government's defense was that the trade unions had been engaged in political and subversive activities behind the facade of economic demands. Nevertheless, in October 1977, a number of imprisoned union leaders were released, and others were allowed to return from exile.[84]

Finally, in January 1978, Bolivia announced that, in preparation for a general election, an amnesty had been decreed for all political prisoners and exiles. Moreover, new legislation that would restore freedom of association had been adopted. In June of that year, the Governing Body expressed its satisfaction with the amnesty, but called attention to continuing discrepancies between Bolivian legislation and ILO conventions. Eventually, trade union elections were held, and all political prisoners were released. With that, the Governing Body terminated the case.[85]

It is impossible to say to what extent this happy result can be attributed to ILO action. The Bolivian government had been under pressure from the United States, *inter alia*, to end its suppression of human rights. Still the ILO had pursued the case tenaciously for seven years, and it had provided a forum for close scrutiny of the events in Bolivia. The organization must certainly be accorded some share of the credit.

4. *Uruguay.* ILO involvement with Uruguay, a country once considered the Switzerland of South America, began with a military coup in 1973. ILO complaints conformed to a familiar litany: "restrictions on the exercise of trade union rights, the dissolution of trade union organizations, the detention of trade union leaders and militants, the ill treatment of detained trade unionists and the occupation of trade union premises by the forces of law and order."[86] ILO representatives visited Uruguay in 1975 and 1977, but to no avail. In May 1977, the government was urged to free imprisoned trade unionists, to stop brutal treatment of prisoners, and to restore normal trade union rights. It promised to take remedial steps.[87]

By March 1978, a number of people listed by the Governing Body as having been arrested had either been released or brought to trial, and a committee had been set up to draft a bill concerning trade union organization. The ILO committee complained, however, that the government had supplied no information on the majority of trade unionists the ILO had mentioned in an earlier report. It also expressed concern about the slow pace at which new trade union legislation was being prepared.[88]

Uruguay's Minister of Labor then sent representatives to Geneva to explain what his country was doing to meet the ILO criticism. Joint labor-management committees had been established on a plant basis, but trade unions were still not operating. Guidelines for draft legislation had been drawn up. As for prisoners, "no trade unionist had been arrested because of his trade union activities and if certain were in prison this was for other reasons. These persons were well treated, as foreign scientists had been able to note when they recently visited the country."[89] The ILO committee once again reported its distress at the lack of progress. A draft trade union law was eventually communicated to the ILO, but whether it is operational is not yet clear. Moreover, the Committee of Experts continued to find provisions in the proposed code that were not in conformity with Convention No. 87.

    5. *Argentina*. A similar case was raised against Argentina. In November 1976, the Committee on Freedom of Association listed the names of a number of union officials who had been imprisoned or simply disappeared. The military authorities had taken over various trade union organizations and suspended union meetings, collective bargaining, and the right to strike. The government of Argentina replied that its actions were "a matter of ridding the trade unions of corruption, subversion, and disorder."[90]

    In May 1977, Argentina informed the ILO that ten trade unionists who had disappeared had been released. Another thirty-eight were being held for investigation of subversive activities; eleven were about to stand trial; two had left the country (another was given the opportunity of doing so); three had been tried by military courts and sentenced for possession of arms; and sixty-five were neither in prison nor being sought by the authorities.[91] Six months later, trade union activities were still suspended, and a long list of trade unionists were still allegedly in prison or missing.[92] At a meeting of the Governing Body, the worker vice-chairman declared that freedom of association was in great jeopardy in all Latin America because of the dwindling number of democratic countries. "The Workers put great stock in the work of [the Committee on Freedom of Association and the Committee of Experts] even though their effectiveness was largely limited to countries where breaches of trade union rights were rare, while in countries ruled by dictatorships information from independent sources on which to base charges of violations was extremely difficult to come by."[93]

The dialogue between the ILO and the Argentine government continued in the same vein. The governmental response to ILO entreaties was simply that its actions were essential to eliminate terrorism and to restore economic normalcy and that new legislation was being considered.[94] In August 1978, an ILO representative visited Argentina and reported back that additional trade unionists had been released. How much progress has been made since remains problematic.

These cases represent a small proportion of the workload of the Committee on Freedom of Association, but they were the most prominent ones in recent years. It could also be argued that they were the most difficult cases and that the ILO's performance in monitoring human rights should not be judged by them.

There is some justification for this argument, since the ILO does try to adjust disputes in a great many countries. In 1977, for example, it heard a complaint by the Philippine Airline Pilots Association; by the Post and Telegraph Union of India; by the International Union of Textile and Clothing Workers against Jordan; by the Antigua Workers Union and the Democratic Workers Union of Belize against Britain; by the Colombian aircraft workers' unions; by various Nicaraguan building trades unions against their government; and by the Canadian Workers' Union against the Canadian government. Other countries accused of hampering trade union freedom were Bangladesh, Spain, Guatemala, Benin, Ecuador, Greece, Nigeria, the Dominican Republic, Liberia, Brazil, Paraguay, Peru, and El Salvador. Most of these cases arose out of strikes or local situations that were not of the national scope of the cases outlined above. How successful the ILO was in bringing about satisfactory solutions cannot be determined without conducting an inquiry into each one.

But there is a question whether the ILO should get involved in parochial disputes or should confine itself to major violations of its conventions. For example, should the ILO be ruling on a dispute involving the Ontario Labor Relations Board and a Canadian union over certification of bargaining agents in three steel companies? Or in an allegation of discrimination against the Singer Sewing Machine Company of Colombia? Or on the discharge of a Philippine airline pilot? Such issues are usually complex, and far beyond the competence of a committee in Geneva, meeting briefly, without the benefit of witnesses, and with inadequate resources for investigation. Trade unions like to have an international forum in which to air their grievances. What redress they expect to secure from vague pronouncements by the ILO Committee on Freedom of Association is not clear. Perhaps the ILO procedures make it too easy to bring charges that are best handled at the national level.

The ILO's human rights machinery might be more useful if it concentrated on those parts of the world where trade unions are struggling for independence against government efforts to control them. This situation prevails in much of Latin America, where the ILO has not been very successful when faced with strong military governments. The same holds true for much of Africa and the Middle East. Asia is a mixed bag, although it has a greater proportion of independent labor movements than the other less developed continents. In the Communist world, the ILO machinery has been completely ineffective in bringing about even the semblance of freedom of association, as the ILO defines it. Few cases are brought against Communist countries because it is generally believed that doing so would be a waste of time.[95]

The human rights machinery of the ILO has been instrumental in securing the release of persons imprisoned for trade union activity. Even if this were its only achievement, some might consider it enough to justify the organization's continuance. The ILO shares this role with such organizations as Amnesty International. It has been instrumental in maintaining constant pressure on dictatorial regimes by exposing violations. Moreover, when political changes do occur, the ILO can help in formulating labor codes consistent with its standards.

Whether the ILO can be made more effective in promoting

the spread of democratic trade unionism, which is presumably one of the major labor policy goals of the United States, is a difficult question to answer. Trade unionists in particular have occasionally called for the imposition of sanctions beyond mere publicity, such as the denial of technical assistance or even expulsion from the ILO. As part of its deliberations on future relationships with the organization, the United States should undertake a closer examination of this entire subject, and seek to produce recommendations that can make the ILO human rights machinery more attractive to American workers and employers.

Industrial Committees

The industrial committee system, which is part of the international labor standards mechanism, originated in 1945. The committees are tripartite, with equal representation for all parties. There are ten standing committees, each one covering a specific industry,[96] and additional committees are set up on an ad hoc basis as the need arises.

The schedule of committee meetings is determined by the Governing Body, with the frequency of meetings depending on need and on the status of the ILO budget (the ILO defrays the costs of all attending members.) From 1945 to 1975, the inland transport, coal mining, iron and steel, metal trades, and textile committees held nine sessions each, while the other standing committees met somewhat less frequently.

The one bone of contention surrounding the committees has been access to membership. The number of states nominated to membership has varied between twenty-one and thirty per committee in recent years, which has not been sufficient to satisfy all applicants. Selection is made for each session by the Committee on Industrial Committees of the Governing Body, using a complex system. One-third of the seats are filled by the applicant member states with the largest interests in the industry concerned, as measured by production and employment. The remaining two-thirds are allotted on the basis of the relative importance of a given industry in each country, appropriate geographical distribution, and other relevant factors, for a term of five years. Every country is guaranteed a seat on at least one committee.[97]

This formula assured the United States and the Soviet Union of participation in all committees for which they applied. But other Communist countries have complained that they were not being treated fairly in the distribution of elective seats. In 1970, a Czech representative argued that one-third of all applicant countries had obtained more than half their requests. Czechoslovakia, on the other hand, was being allotted only one seat, even though it had sent observer delegations to almost all committee meetings at its own expense.[98] Discrimination on political grounds was alleged to be the cause. In 1976, the U.S.S.R. indicated that while Israel had received five of the six seats for which it had applied, Czechoslovakia had received only one of eight—and that one was only its third preference.[99] The ILO was under pressure to redress this imbalance, and despite a U.S. desire to maintain the status quo,[100] reform of the electoral procedure seemed inevitable.

Nine months before an industrial committee meets, each member state is asked to send the ILO a report on what has been done to put into effect previous resolutions. This information is presented to the committee in a general report, which also includes a good deal of statistical material relating to the industry in question. Meetings are structured around three or four agenda items, all determined in advance, including at least one of a general, nontechnical nature. The committee meetings generally last for about a week. Employer committee members are briefed by technical specialists from the International Organization of Employers, while the international trade secretariats coordinate the work of the labor group.

The 1977 meeting of the Building, Civil Engineering, and Public Works Committee provides a good example of how the industrial committees operate. The two U.S. government delegates were the New York regional director of the Labor Department and the construction industry coordinator of the Federal Mediation and Conciliation Service. The employers were, respectively, the chairman of the board of Jens Olesen and Sons Construction Company, and the director of labor relations of the

Associated General Contractors of America. The unions were represented by the presidents of the Sheet Metal Workers Union and the United Association of Plumbers and Pipefitters. The principal agenda items were the stabilization of employment in construction and the training of managers and workers.

Out of this meeting came various conclusions having to do with different methods of reducing cyclical and seasonal fluctuations in employment, along with recommendations for improving training. It was suggested, for example, that a modular training system for construction workers developed by the ILO in cooperation with the Swedish aid agency be tested in the field. Both reports were adopted unanimously, as is usually the case.[101] In addition, resolutions dealing with ILO activities in construction were also adopted. These included a recommendation for a construction industry convention and the need for more complete implementation of previous conclusions and resolutions.

In his closing remarks, the president of the U.S. Sheet Metal Workers Union, speaking on behalf of the worker group, noted that all the actions of the committee were limited to the construction industry:

> The Organization could have no higher priority than supporting the Industrial Committees: they were what the ILO was all about, and they constituted the last and best vestige of tripartite, nonpolitical dedication to the interests of the worker. This work of the Committee was the most useful and most meaningful which the ILO could perform. . . . It had been refreshing to participate in an ILO meeting conducted on a tripartite and nonpolitical basis. . . . The politicization of the processes of the organization did not serve the workers: it used them, and in so doing it abused the very ideal for which the Organization had been created. Thus far the Industrial Committee had managed to keep immune from that disease.[102]

The German chairman of the employer group declared that the meetings had demonstrated the loyal partnership that existed between employers and workers in construction and observed that "the session had provided an occasion to renew many old friendships and to make new ones."[103] The latter remark explains a good deal about the continuing popularity of the industrial committees among employers and workers. The people who attend these meetings share a common language in the technical aspects of their industries. Their problems are similar around the world, and there is a common interest in the economic fortunes of the industries. The proceedings are usually conducted in a calm and peaceful atmosphere, without the bitter political divisions that characterize other ILO activities. During the 1977 construction session, for example, the Soviet delegation presented a film dealing with construction and town planning in the Soviet Union without arousing any hostility.

Committee reports are sent to the Governing Body, which submits them to member states for their consideration. Ernst Haas, after evaluating the impact of committee recommendations on actual practice, concluded that the countries reporting the highest degree of compliance were the industrial economies. "In short, ILO authority is strongest in democratic countries whose social and economic conditions are in harmony with the organizational ideology. This finding suggests that the countries requiring *least* persuasion and encouragement to make their national economic life conform with international standards are *most* disposed to obey; conversely, those most in need of persuasion are the least amenable."[104] In its own evaluation, the ILO pointed to specific cases, such as the control of silicosis in coal mining, in which resolutions and conclusions led to concrete action on the part of member nations.[105] But there has been no conclusive analysis of the overall effectiveness of the industrial committees in promoting their objectives, a subject that merits further study.

Industrial committee procedure has occasionally been criticized, generally in the spirit of improving an already satisfactory situation. John Mainwaring, a prominent Canadian government representative, observed that the committees tended to spend too much time adopting conclusions and not enough developing gradual solutions to common problems. He was seconded by a Swedish employer delegate, who felt that committees' results were meager compared with their costs; also seconding was a U.S. government delegate, who feared that the growing size of the committees would impair their effectiveness.[106] But such strictures were unusual.

Of all ILO activities, there is little doubt that industrial committees rate highest with U.S. labor and management. According to the U.S. Chamber of Commerce, practically all the employer delegates who attended committee meetings have been satisfied. Immediate results cannot always be cited, but if nothing else, the employers have been able to take a close look at world technology and labor relations. The information gleaned is of particular interest to multinational corporations. The U.S. trade unions have also expressed their appreciation for the industrial committees. In May 1975, one month before the ILO conference that led to the U.S. notice of intent to withdraw, the U.S. worker representative to the Governing Body made the following statement: "Without doubt, this was one of the most important activities of the Organization, as it was through such meetings that it really reached the labor rank and file in the basic industries at the national level and gave them an idea of what the ILO was trying to do internationally."[107]

Model Codes

Another ILO standard-setting device is the model code, or code of practice. These codes consist of detailed manuals designed to assist drafters of legislation or collective bargainers in the field of safety and health. Before they are released, the codes are discussed and approved by tripartite expert panels.

A number of codes of practice on occupational safety and health have been published thus far. While they are normative in intent, they create no binding obligations. But as evidence of their impact, the ILO points to the fact that some of the codes have been translated into other than the official ILO languages (English, French, and Spanish), as well as to their occasional adoption for legislative purposes.[108]

Conclusions

When he endorsed the decision of President Carter to withdraw the United States from ILO membership, George Meany made the following statement: "The AFL-CIO does, of course, strongly advocate and support the high ideals and principles set forth in the constitution and declarations of the ILO—tripartitism, human rights, freedom of association and the pursuit of humane international standards of life and labor."[109] There has never been any doubt about American labor's support of the ILO standard-setting activities. While a humane attitude toward working people in the poorer countries has certainly been an important factor in shaping labor's views, self-interest is also involved. Raising labor standards abroad is regarded as a way of protecting U.S. workers' jobs from the competition of imports produced by cheap labor.

American employers, on the other hand, have always been skeptical of ILO standard-setting. In supporting the original letter of intent to withdraw, the U.S. Chamber of Commerce said: "For many years, the International Labor Organization has devoted attention toward seeking the ratification of its international instruments (conventions and recommendations) while giving very little attention to the record of implementation of these standards by the States that have ratified them. While it is certainly appropriate to encourage member states to ratify the international instruments developed by the ILO, it is hypocrisy to ignore the demonstrated fact that many member states ratify these instruments without the ability or intent to implement them."[110]

Evaluations to date concerning the effectiveness of ILO standard-setting cannot provide conclusive proof one way or another. The Chamber of Commerce is correct in arguing that, for many countries, ratification is not a very meaningful act. The fact that among the countries that have ratified a large number of conventions are many not known for their advanced working conditions suggests that there, different motives impel ratification.

Nevertheless, the various studies cited above do offer some evidence that, in general, the signing of a convention is a serious undertaking, especially in countries where trade unions are prepared to help in the monitoring process by filing complaints against violations. All in all, it is difficult to escape the conclusion that the 150-odd ILO conventions, plus the various recommendations and model codes, have made a real contribution toward ameliorating the conditions under which people work throughout the world. The United States ought to use its influence to improve the policing of the standards and to require countries that do not honor their obligations to withdraw their ratifications. Standard-setting, with all its faults, should be encouraged and strengthened. It is difficult to imagine any other activity carried on by an international organization that falls more closely in line with the democratic ideals espoused by the United States.

Chapter 7

From Withdrawal to Return:
Developments from
1977 to 1980

There were many dire predictions of what would happen to the
ILO in the event of a U.S. withdrawal: financial bankruptcy;
domination by the Soviet Union; a falling-off of Western European support; a shift of power in the Governing Body, based on
one country–one vote, along the lines of the conference. Thus
far, the ILO has faced some difficulties, but there have been no
major changes. Some structural alterations are inevitable, and
they may transform the ILO into a different organization from
the one the United States left. It is the purpose of this chapter
to explore the developments that have taken place in the period
during which the United States was not a member of the ILO.

Financial Adjustments

The most immediate impact of U.S. withdrawal was on the
ILO budget. Faced with a loss of $42.3 million in income for the
biennium 1978–79, the Governing Body was forced to cut the
budget by $36.6 million, almost 22 percent of the total. It was
hoped that the balance would be made up by additional contributions from member nations.

To achieve this reduction, staffs were reduced, and some pro-

252

grams had to be cut as well. Several ILO publications were discontinued, among them, the *Legislative Series*, which provided information on changes in legislation in various countries, and a recently created newsletter called *Women at Work*. The publication of the *International Labour Review* was reduced from bimonthly to quarterly intervals. The frequency of industrial committee meetings was also reduced, as was the size of delegations at the meetings. Research in general was cut substantially. The largest reductions of all, however, came in the service departments at Geneva, which many members felt were overstaffed.

In terms of the programs previously supported by the United States, the reductions were fairly nominal. Projects involving international labor standards—including human rights, workers' education, and occupational safety and health—suffered less than the average. On the other hand, industrial committees were significantly less active, and a proposed method for evaluating technical assistance projects developed by AID was apparently shelved.

The ILO also suffered from the devaluation of the U.S. dollar, the currency in which member nation contributions are assessed. The budget for the two-year period 1978–79 had been drawn up when the Swiss franc was still selling at 2.5 francs to the dollar. The Governing Body had to approve an additional $30 million in total assessments just to compensate for the further decline of the dollar.

The reactions of the various groups and countries to the adjustments were interesting. Japan, which saw its assessment rise from $5.7 million in 1977 to $10.4 million in 1979, urged that the budget be cut further to compensate fully for the loss of the U.S. share.[1] The Soviet Union, which became the largest contributor ($13.9 million in 1979 compared with $10.3 million in 1977), favored a shorter annual conference and argued for a reduction of "administrative costs while increasing the efficiency of all departments, branches, and officials."[2] When it came time to compensate for the loss of ILO income caused by the decline of the dollar, the Soviet Union voted in opposition, arguing that the resultant deficit should be made good by budget cuts.[3] Nevertheless, the revised budget was adopted by a large majority, with only the Communist bloc voting in the negative or abstaining.

The ILO reported that by August 31, 1978, voluntary contributions of $6.8 million had been either received or pledged. However, a cash-flow problem forced the ILO to borrow $2.5 million from local banks in December 1978.[4]

When the director-general presented his biennial budget for 1980–81, he ran into sharp opposition from the employers' group and some of the larger contributors. It had been generally understood that the shortfall in income resulting from the U.S. withdrawal would not be assessed against other members, and there was some feeling that this commitment was not carried out. The Soviet Union was among the strongest objectors, arguing that "close study of the budget document had shown that full account had not been taken of the reduction of 25 percent in regular budget resources which had followed the withdrawal of the United States."[5] The worker group and the less developed countries, on the other hand, tended to favor even greater expenditures.

In his response, the director-general pointed out that, with 1975 as a base, the staff of the ILO had been reduced from 813 to 713 professionals and from 1,223 to 1,019 service employees. If the 75 percent limitations were taken literally, an additional 75 officials would have to be dropped.[6] The final budget represented a compromise between the conflicting views and caused a drop of 1 percent in the reduced level for the 1978–79 biennium and a further reduction of 25 staff positions.[7]

In general, ILO technical assistance work was not greatly affected because most of the funds allocated for this purpose come from the UNDP and from cooperating nations on a multi-bilateral basis. The organization had to pull in its belt, but there was no evidence of any major deterioration in the technical services it provides. Neither the Soviet Union nor the oil-producing Arab states showed any inclination to secure more power by raising their contributions. The ILO appears to have weathered the financial crisis without substantial harm to its activities.

The 1978 ILO Conference

The major issues that were debated at the 1978 conference were generally resolved in accordance with positions favored by the United States. This was not uniformly true; in some respects, the conference continued to operate in a manner objectionable to the United States. The trend, however, was in a direction heartening to those both in the United States and abroad who favored U.S. reaffiliation.

As in previous conferences, the treatment of Israel continued to be an important criterion by which the U.S. trade unions in particular measure performance. The problem arose in June 1978 in the form of a brief resolution introduced by the Arab bloc calling attention to the "Policy of Discrimination, Racism and Violation of Trade Union Freedoms and Rights Practiced by the Israeli Authorities in Palestine and in the Other Occupied Arab Territories," and instructing the director-general of the ILO to implement the 1974 conference resolution. The Resolutions Committee had before it eighteen other resolutions dealing with issues that were directly germane to ILO interests, including the promotion of economic growth, youth employment, and participation by workers in the administration of social security schemes. Nevertheless, the committee voted to give the anti-Israeli resolution top priority and spent most of the session debating it.

This was a particularly nasty resolution from the Israeli point of view. It clearly implied the nonexistence of the state of Israel. It contained a reference to the fourth Geneva Convention, on the protection of civilian populations in time of war, a matter entirely beyond the competence of the ILO. It neglected four years of ILO activity on charges against Israel, including a special report by the director-general and a personal visit to Israel by the assistant director-general for international standards. A Canadian government delegate termed the resolution "unnecessary, unfortunate and inexpedient," while a Dutch worker representative warned that it "threatened the very existence of the International Labour Organization." The Soviet government representative, however, argued that "further steps needed to be taken to support the interests of Arab workers in the occupied territories," and the resolution was approved by the committee.[8]

In the ensuing debate, spokesmen for the Western industrialized nations were highly critical of the resolution's substantive content. Speaking on behalf of the European community, a Danish government representative stated that it was inadvisable and unhelpful for the ILO to take a position on such matters: "We regret the introduction of this essentially political resolution into the technical forums of the International Labour Conference."[9] The Arab countries argued that the resolution was necessary because the ILO had failed to implement the 1974 resolution; the Soviet bloc followed the same line.

In the final vote, 211 ballots were cast in favor of the resolution, with 139 abstentions. Since the necessary quorum of 236 was not reached, the resolution failed of adoption. The Western nations were solidly against it, while enough less developed countries either abstained or absented themselves.

There was no lack of political speeches irrelevant to ILO jurisdiction at the 1978 conference. Syria mounted a wide-ranging attack on Israel; Cuba denounced the absent "Yankee imperialists" and demanded freedom for Puerto Rico; a representative of the PLO gave a lengthy historical account of Middle East problems without being ruled out of order.[10] On the other hand, some hopeful signs were evident. In selecting employer members of the Governing Body, the employers' group elected no Eastern European despite the enhanced position of the Soviet Union as the largest financial contributor to the ILO. In the workers' group, the ICFTU list, including a representative of the Israeli Federation of Labor as a deputy member, was elected en bloc. This made the ILO the only U.N. agency with an Israeli on its executive board.

The most important development, partly positive and partly negative, was the handling of the long-standing complaint against the Soviet Union. The Committee of Experts, in its observations relating to Convention No. 29 (forced labor), noted that the Soviet Union had still failed to clear up the meaning of its legislation permitting imprisonment of persons who were "leading a parasitic way of life." There was also the possibility that the Soviet penal code might prevent the voluntary termination of employment by collective farm members.[11] In discussing the report of the Committee of Experts in the Conference Committee on the Application of Conventions, representatives of the Soviet government criticized the ILO supervisory machinery and charged that "the Committee of Experts at times adopted an unduly rigid and legalistic approach and that it should exercise greater caution in reaching judgments on the application of Conventions in countries involved in economic and social development."[12] The Communist nations as a group called for abolition of the special list on the grounds that "its application amounted to a condemnation and a sanction, was inconsistent with the atmosphere of international cooperation that should prevail in the Conference Committee, was contrary to the ILO Constitution, had a damaging and not a constructive effect, and was in contradiction with the aim of encouraging and assisting member States, which could be achieved only on a basis of equality, justice and mutual respect."[13] (This plea came from countries that only a few days later voted to condemn Israel without abiding by the ILO constitutional requirements.)

The worker and employer groups were strongly in favor of retaining the special list, and although no action was taken to change existing procedures, a working party was established to review the entire matter. Soviet transgressions of the forced labor convention were noted by the committee report, but in a milder form than in 1977.

When the report came up for debate in the conference plenum, the Soviet Union, despite the downgrading of the charges levied against it, repeated its attacks on the ILO monitoring machinery, which it defined as an "anti-constitutional and in fact unlawful attempt of supervisory bodies to assume competence of a judiciary nature. . . . The ILO does not have and cannot have any possibility of imposing any sanctions whatsoever and the most surprising thing is that there are delegates who do not wish to recognize this and to take this matter into consideration."[14] Argentina and Uruguay, which also came in for criticism, joined in the attack. The Soviet Union must have been aware, however, that a substantial majority was in favor of the committee report;

and so, despite its strictures, the Soviet Union announced that it would vote for acceptance, and the conference adopted the report without a record vote. This was in sharp contrast to what had happened only a year earlier, when the conference had refused to adopt the report.

Representatives of Western nations delivered several pointed warnings to the 1978 conference. A German employer delegate expressed his regret at the U.S. withdrawal, which he said made more difficult the position of those who supported free social systems. He stated that unless the ILO moved back from its path of error, "it may have consequences for the attitudes of other member States."[15] The Canadian employer delegate told the conference that his organization had requested the Canadian government to review Canada's role in the ILO and the direction in which the ILO was headed.[16]

The Structural Problem

The debate on structural change, temporarily sidetracked by the events preceding the 1977 conference, resumed in full force following the U.S. withdrawal. The Working Party on Structure held three meetings between June 1977 and June 1978, and while it was unable to come up with a final recommendation, it did make some progress on the various issues.

Composition of the Governing Body

Some measure of agreement was reached on restructuring the Governing Body. All seats henceforth would be elective, thereby abolishing the nonelective seats held by governments of countries of major industrial importance. The total number of government seats would be increased to 50 or 52 and the distinction between full and deputy membership abolished. The government seats would be distributed on a regional basis.

There were divergent views, however, when it came to the specifics of regional distribution. The larger states sought what amounted to de facto permanent seats, but the smaller countries favored rotation. The Eastern European bloc wanted its own electoral college, separate from Western Europe, with a guarantee of five seats (its present total of voting and nonvoting seats).

Employer spokesmen, however, raised objections to the allocation of seats on an ideological basis: they pointed out that if Communism were recognized as a valid demarcation criterion, other logical classifications might then be in order.[17]

The German government representative expressed serious reservations about the trend of thought embodied in the foregoing proposals. He indicated concern over the proposed enlargement in the Governing Body voting membership, and issued the following warning:

> When it comes to the necessary representativeness of the Governing Body, we feel that the proposals that have been put forward so far do not seem to provide the necessary guarantee. We disagree with persons who simply say "one country, one vote."
> . . . It should be perfectly natural that countries with a particularly high financial burden should have a commensurate share in shaping the destiny of the Organization. . . . The Working Party must aim at finding a balanced solution, because otherwise, I have to say this perfectly frankly, there is a danger that the workers in the large countries might easily lose interest in this Organization, and that could strike a mortal blow to the Organization.[18]

Disagreement continued over the composition of the nongovernmental groups within the Governing Body. The Soviet Union insisted that some provision be made in both the employers' and workers' groups for the election of Communists, and it accused the United States of preventing Communist employer representation as a legacy of the Cold War.[19] The spokesmen for the worker and employer groups replied that they would accept no outside pressure on the manner in which their groups were composed; the employers were especially adamant against any Communist quota. As the chairman of the employers' group stated, "It was not possible for the majority of employers to elect as their representatives those who represented a system whose express vow was to destroy free enterprise."[20]

Amendment of the ILO Constitution

The veto right of a majority of the nonelective Governing Body government representatives over proposed constitutional

amendments would be eliminated by the abolition of the nonelective seats. A consensus appeared to have been reached that
amendments considered important should require approval by a
margin of three-quarters of the votes cast by delegates present at
the annual conference and subsequent ratification by three-quarters of the member states. The purpose of this rule was to make
it more difficult to amend the constitution in any substantial way.
Some delegates expressed the view that this requirement was
too onerous, and it was agreed that further consideration was
necessary.[21]

Article 17 of the Standing Orders

The proposed change in this conference procedural rule,
which would limit the admissibility of extraneous resolutions,
had been one of the principal U.S. demands at the 1977 conference. The Group of 77 and the industrial market economies
reached some degree of consensus on a procedure that would
allow the director-general, in consultation with the officers of the
conference, to bar the introduction of conference resolutions that
condemned member states without any basis in the ILO monitoring procedures. If this rule had been in effect in 1978, the
anti-Israel resolution might not have been placed before the conference.

The Soviet bloc has strong objections to any limitation on the
admissibility of resolutions. A Czech delegate, after claiming
there had never been a case of unjustified criticism of a member
state by the conference, charged that the sole motivation behind
the projected rule change was to persuade the United States to
return to the ILO.[22] A Cuban representative said the proposed
change was antidemocratic, as did representatives from Yugoslavia and Algeria. A Soviet delegate declared that while the Soviet Union was opposed to unfair attacks, its delegation was not
afraid of accusations "because they believed in the collective wisdom of the Conference."[23] The Communists were obviously reluctant to lose the ILO conference as a platform for political
speeches.

The Western nations made it clear that amending Article 17
was part of a package of structural changes and that they would

oppose any agreement that did not provide for it. The final settlement will probably provide for some check on political resolutions that have no relevance to the functions of the ILO.

The Quorum Rule

The present constitution of the ILO provides that at the conference "the voting is void unless the total number of votes cast is equal to half the number of the delegates attending the Conference." Since abstentions are not counted in calculating the quorum, an abstaining delegate can contribute toward the defeat of a motion that might have carried had he voted against it. In recent years, few countries have voted in the negative on any proposition: abstention has become a more effective means of defeating a motion.

The workers' group in the Working Party on Structure proposed an amendment stating that the constitutional requirement of a simple majority would be satisfied by a majority of a minimum of one-fourth of the accredited delegates. Where the constitution required a two-thirds majority, at least one-third of the attending delegates would have to be recorded. Moreover, the voting would be void unless at least half of the accredited delegates had taken part in the voting. Had this proposal been in effect at the 1977 conference, the report of the Committee on the Application of Standards would probably have been adopted. On the other hand, it is likely that the anti-Israeli resolution would have passed in 1978.

The 1979 ILO Conference

This conference again went relatively well from the U.S. point of view, although there were some dark spots. Perhaps the most important positive event was an amendment to the standing orders of the conference allowing secret balloting when requested by at least ninety delegates or by the chairman of one of the tripartite groups.[24] The Communist and some Arab states opposed the change, partly because it gave too much power to group chairmen. After an initial rejection of the proposal by a show of hands, a second vote was called for, and it passed by a very narrow margin. Some forty-four governments of less devel-

oped countries joined with a solid Western bloc, but the critical
margin of victory was supplied by twenty-one employer and
worker delegates from fifteen less developed countries who split
with their governments.[25]

This change could lead to greater employer and worker delegate independence in conference voting and thus strengthen tripartism. Whether the anticipated benefits materialize remains to
be seen, although the pattern of voting at Governing Body meetings (where balloting is secret) offers some hope that there will
be a similar effect at the conference.

There was still no resolution of the structural question. The
Soviet Union continued to press for the division of Europe into
Eastern and Western regions for the purpose of allocating seats
on the Governing Body, even though the Soviets had been
granted a separate electoral college within a unified European
region. Their main concern, however, was to secure some representation in the employer group of the Governing Body, as
well as greater representation in the worker group: "We feel that
the key element here is the question of the formation of the nongovernmental groups in the Governing Body—in particular the
Employers' group. However, to our great regret, it is specifically
within the group that the progress towards a solution of the problems which are of the greatest importance for the Organization
has been the least."[26] The Western nations continued to resist
any infringement of worker and employer group autonomy. To
grant the Soviet demand would mean a further erosion of the
tripartite principle.

There was almost agreement on an amendment to the conference standing orders that would prevent the condemnation
of a state before a proper investigation had been undertaken.
Although the Communist countries continued to oppose any
change, the Western nations and the Group of 77 concurred
upon a new text with only one matter outstanding: the 77 wanted
a time limit of twenty-four months for an ILO inquiry to run its
course before the matter could be debated at the conference,
while the West opposed such a time limit.[27]

The customary litany of complaints was filed against Israel.
The conference was considering a special ILO mission report on

the treatment of Arab workers in the occupied territories. New but predictable events included an Arab attack on Egypt, leading to an immediate Egyptian point of order, and a walkout by Arab and Communist delegates as the Egyptian minister of labor rose to address the conference. None of the delegations from non-Arab less developed countries joined the demonstration, however, and their refusal to do so was a step forward in the quest for depoliticization of the ILO conference.

A further move in the same direction came when the Resolutions Committee failed to adopt an Arab resolution condemning Tunisia for infringing upon freedom of association. This matter was still under investigation by the Committee on Freedom of Association. The chairman of the employer group, in opposing the resolution, asserted that "there should be no double standards"; the terminology of the Kissinger letter was working its way into ILO debate.[28]

The Committee of Experts continued its five-year exploration into Soviet labor legislation and again concluded that "the labor code of the RFSFR, by attributing trade union functions solely to the trade union committee concerned, seems to rule out the possibility of establishing another organization representing the workers of the same category."[29] When the Conference Committee on the Application of Standards considered the matter, a representative of the Soviet government repeated an earlier response: "The Trade unions had freely accepted this leading role [of the Community Party]. It had not been imposed on them and did not involve legislative interference in their affairs. The interests of the Party and of the trade unions were identical."[30] The 1960 ILO report on the Soviet Union was cited to show that "objective observers, even if not sharing the Government's views, recognized the need to consider the real conditions and the historical process of the country."

A companion complaint by the ICFTU accused Czechoslovakia of employment discrimination against participants in the so-called Charter 77, a dissident political group. The Governing Body set up a tripartite committee to investigate the allegations. After considering new information received from the ICFTU and the Czech government, the committee submitted a report in

June 1978 in which the Czech reply was declared unsatisfactory. Annexed to the report was a detailed set of documents that strongly supported the validity of the charges as well as the failure of the Czech trade unions to provide any protection to those members who were involved. On that, the Governing Body decided to publish the full set of documents, a procedure reserved for very serious cases.[31] The matter was discussed at some length by the Committee on the Application of Standards, which expressed the hope that the Czech government would send a detailed report to the Committee of Experts. For the second year in a row, however, the committee failed to cite Czechoslovakia, or any other country, under Criterion 7, which is the most serious category on nonapplication of conventions.

When the committee report was presented to the conference, the worker vice-chairman of the committee recommended that the conference merely take note of the report rather than adopt it. The employer vice-chairman was equally critical. The Swedish worker representative summarized the situation aptly when he said: "This year's report of the Conference Committee is, in our opinion, far from satisfactory. Again this year Criterion 7 on the special list was not used by the Committee. . . . The reason for this is that a majority of the delegates in the Committee feared that the report would not be accepted by the Conference if Criterion 7 were applied. This fear about the Conference's reaction to the report has seriously affected the work of the Committee."[32] The watered-down report was eventually adopted by voice vote. To some observers, it appeared that many delegates had an eye on earlier U.S. reactions of nonapproval of committee reports and wanted to avoid any action that might reduce the chances of U.S. reentry into the ILO.[33]

The Decision to Rejoin

After the fanfare that preceded U.S. withdrawal from the ILO in 1977, reaffiliation in 1980 was something of an anticlimax. There was almost no public discussion of the issues, and it came as something of a surprise when President Carter issued a statement concluding that "a majority of ILO members—governments, workers, and employers—have successfully joined together to return the ILO to its original purposes. Through their efforts, steps have been taken to strengthen the independence of employer and worker delegates, undertake investigation of human rights violations in a number of countries including the Soviet Union, reinforce the principle of due process, and generally reduce the level of politicization in the ILO."[34]

A brief formal statement released by the AFL-CIO was more cautious. It noted that "the AFL-CIO has participated in the discussions leading to the decision to rejoin the International Labor Organization and is satisfied that there is movement toward the goal of returning the ILO to its original principles and purposes. The AFL–CIO will continue to carry on within the ILO the work of keeping secure basic rights and due process for all workers."[35] The U.S. Chamber of Commerce, which had nominated the employer delegate prior to U.S. withdrawal, declined to continue in that role, apparently in the belief that sufficient change had not yet taken place. It was replaced by the U.S. Council of the International Chamber of Commerce, an organization less representative of American business.[36]

How much progress had been made by 1980 in resolving the key issues of conflict that had led to U.S. withdrawal in 1977? On the positive side, an anti-Israeli resolution had gone down to defeat at the 1978 conference, as did a 1979 attempt to condemn Tunisia without prior investigation. The Governing Body had published a long, condemnatory report on some labor practices in Czechoslovakia. There had been no further erosion of the tripartite structure. The most significant gain, from the U.S. point of view, had been the adoption of ILO conference rules permitting secret balloting under certain circumstances.

However, there was little progress on a number of other important issues. The conference rules on resolutions and debates had not been changed, leaving the way open for irrelevant political debate and condemnation without due process. The various charges against the Soviet Union were still being processed by the different ILO committees, with no final resolution in sight. And while no final agreement on structural changes had been reached, it was clear that the Governing Body would be greatly increased in size, with the result that control of ILO policies would shift markedly in favor of the less developed countries and against the developed nations, which were footing the bill.

The Carter Administration had not been enthusiastic about leaving the ILO in the first place, and the strongly affirmative statement of the president suggests that there was no great governmental difficulty in reaching a decision favorable to return. A Labor Department official stated: "It was felt that we gained all we could from withdrawal and that this was a good time to return if we were to retain our influence in the I.L.O." He added that the United States had received pledges from its allies to support its positions in the ILO and had also been promised a number of staff positions.[37]

The AFL-CIO had been the major force for withdrawal in 1977. The reversal of its position was explained by the director of its international department in the following terms: "We got most of what we were demanding. . . . It would have been difficult not to go back at this stage. . . . When we quit we played our last card in trying to change the I.L.O. It was a gamble and we won it. I'm not saying the I.L.O. is perfect. It isn't. But our conditions have been met."[38] In a sense, it was similar to a decision by union officials to call off a strike even though all demands have not been met.

The 1980 Conference

The wisdom of the U.S. decision to rejoin the ILO was soon put to the test. A full U.S. delegation, headed by the Secretary of Labor, attended the 1980 conference. Among the initiatives that were planned in order to present a more positive U.S. image in the ILO were a proposal to look into the possibility of developing minimum international labor standards; the formation of an inter-American consultative group to define ILO programs in the Western Hemisphere; and an inquiry into the use of statistics to help monitor ILO conventions.[39]

Unfortunately, the focus of the conference was shifted to a Jordanian resolution that castigated Israeli settlement in the occupied West Bank; called upon all states "not to provide Israel with any assistance to be used specifically in connection with settlements in the occupied Arab territories"; and asked the Governing Body and the director general to support Arab citizens "in Palestine and the other occupied Arab territories to strengthen their economic and technical capabilities and to counteract the effects of the Israeli occupation and settlement policy".[40]

There were several problems with this resolution from the U.S. point of view. It condemned a member state without any preliminary investigation—a violation of due process. It dealt with matters extraneous to ILO competence. And it was completely political in nature, reflecting current developments in the Middle East. This was pointed out in conference speeches by the U.S. delegation, among others. The U.S. labor delegate stated that the U.S. return was predicated on the assumption that there had been progress on the basic issues and practices that led to withdrawal in 1977, and expressed the hope that "this unpleasant experience will never have to be repeated."[41] The employer delegate remarked: "I must say that in many ways I am delighted that some things remain the same. At the same time I cannot help but express my real concern that some very fundamental matters appear to remain unresolved."[42]

Seventeen resolutions had been submitted to the Resolutions Committee. However, the anti-Israeli resolution received priority, and the committee debate over it consumed nine working days, with the result that all but one of the technical resolutions that were within the ILO sphere of competence could not be considered. The conference vote on it was by secret ballot, a reform that the United States had hoped would prevent a repetition of earlier violations of due process. The resolution was nevertheless adopted.

The conference also witnessed a great many political attacks on member states from the platform, aimed largely but not exclusively against Israel. Among countries that also came under bitter attack were Egypt, Ethiopia, and the United States. When the Syrian minister of social affairs criticized the U.S. position in the Middle East, a U.S. advisor requested the floor and replied: "I can only look on the Syrian representative's statement as the best possible demonstration of why political issues are best left to the competent bodies of the United Nations—that is, the Security Council and the General Assembly. They do not belong in the ILO, and flights of rhetoric, misstatements and unfounded charges will not change that reality."[43]

The Committee on the Application of Standards discussed once again possible violations of the forced labor convention by the Soviet Union but failed to resolve the issue and merely requested the Soviet government to clarify the situation. Czechoslovakia played the role of Soviet whipping boy and was the object of a special paragraph in the committee report for its labor practices.

For the rest, the conference adopted a recommendation on the employment status of older workers and expanded the list of occupational diseases that should be compensable under ILO conventions. But the working party dealing with structural reform was still deadlocked, and its mandate had to be extended once again.

Despite the setbacks, U.S. government and labor representatives expressed some optimism about the future. The secretary of labor, on his return to the United States, stated that the results of the conference were good, on the whole, and that the American delegation was "disappointed but not dejected" at the adoption of the anti-Israeli resolution.[44] The AFL–CIO pointed to preliminary discussions of possible future recommendations dealing with collective bargaining and the prevention of discrimination against workers because of their family responsibilities, as well as the older worker recommendation that was adopted.[45]

The fact remains, however, that the 1980 ILO conference represented serious retrogression from the American point of view. Violation of due process and politicization, two of the major issues that had been cited as part of the rationale for the U.S. withdrawal, persisted. The continued failure of the ILO to reach definitive conclusions on Soviet violations reflected a selective concern with human rights. There is little doubt in my mind that had the U.S. reaffiliation been delayed until after the 1980 conference, the United States would have postponed its return until it could be determined whether the conference represented merely a temporary deviation from what had appeared to be a favorable trend, or whether it was indeed symptomatic of underlying difficulties that were likely to continue into the future.

Chapter 8

The Future Role of the United States in the ILO

The 1980 conference made no progress in resolving structural and procedural changes in the ILO. However, it is clear that when the few remaining issues are resolved, the balance of power in policy-making bodies will shift sharply in favor of the less developed countries. Regionalization of the Governing Body membership and elimination of the power of the Western democracies to veto constitutional amendments will make it more difficult to resist inappropriate practices. It is essential that rules be established which do not yield too easily to the passions engendered by passing political events.

There are a number of constitutional and procedural guarantees that appear necessary in order to meet the minimum requirements of "proper principles and procedures." Unless they are forthcoming, the renewed tenure of the United States in the ILO may not be a long one, judging by past relationships.

1. *Due Process*. No issue is more likely to provoke another U.S. withdrawal than continued disregard of due process. If countries are to be condemned by the ILO without a fair investigation as provided by the ILO's own constitutional machinery,

there is no warrant for the United States to support such action by its presence.

Preventing misuse of the ILO conference is not an easy matter. The various changes in conference procedures that have been under discussion constitute a step in the right direction. There is no guarantee that officials who would be vested with authority to monitor resolutions and debates would be able to prevent the ILO from acting as it has in the past. They should be on notice, however, that the United States will regard transgressions of due process as sufficient condition for withdrawal. The PLO vendetta against Israel will have to be moved to other forums if the ILO is to remain intact.

2. *The Double Standard.* The ILO must treat all member states alike; it cannot accord special privileges to Communist states or to any other group without undermining its credibility. A number of issues are involved, chief among them the selective enforcement of the human rights conventions. The charges against the Soviet Union, which are moving slowly through the ILO enforcement machinery, will provide evidence as to whether or not those who control ILO policy are prepared to dispense justice impartially. It is difficult for anyone in the West to doubt that the Soviet Union is in violation of the conventions on freedom of association, discrimination in employment, and forced labor. A one-sided determination of convention violations undermines the validity of the entire human rights mechanism.

Similarly, the United States should insist on formal elimination, through specific hiring rules, of certain privileges that the Soviet Union and other countries have enjoyed in the past. Selection of all staff members should be done in exactly the same manner. Vacant ILO positions should be advertised, and ILO recruiters should make the selection on competence alone and on a competitive basis. Failure of any government to abide by these rules, which are necessary to ensure a qualified staff, should be the basis for refusal to appoint.

The practice of making it impossible to write objectively in ILO publications about the Soviet Union, or about any other country, should be stopped. The *International Labour Review* is not an appropriate vehicle for propaganda pieces that a country may want to circulate internationally. The basis for the decision to print articles and books in the various ILO publishing outlets should be the quality of the ideas and writing that they embody, not the nationality of the author.

3. *Tripartism.* American trade unions and employers should continue to insist that the ILO give every possible aid to trade unions and employer groups that are trying to secure or maintain their independence. The ILO is an excellent instrument for this purpose, since it is committed by constitution and tradition to such a goal. Tripartism is a slogan that has great popularity within the ILO. The problem is to transform that symbolism into reality through both standard-setting activities and the technical assistance program.

Nothing is more important in the ILO sphere of competence than advancing the cause of free trade unionism and freedom of enterprise. It is all too evident that state-dominated labor fronts and state monopoly of economic activity are incompatible with democracy. There is more labor and management independence in the less developed part of the world than is generally realized, and future U.S. representatives in the ILO should give the highest priority to the sustenance and encouragement of these groups.

Little can be done, unfortunately, about the countries that have already fallen under Communist domination. But it should be made clear that within the ILO context, any further infringement of group autonomy is a step in the wrong direction. If the groups themselves want to rearrange their electoral procedures by majority vote, well and good. The principle of tripartism would be virtually destroyed, however, if Communist or any other workers or employers were forced upon the respective groups. In that case, the ILO might as well abandon tripartism and become simply a governmental body.

4. *Politicization.* It is difficult to specify the precise measures that the ILO can adopt to prevent the introduction of nongermane political issues from intruding upon its processes. How can

visiting dignitaries and delegates who are invited to address the conference be prevented from using the platform to launch political attacks on their adversaries, even though their message has no relevance to the agenda?

Article 14 of the conference standing orders gives the president the power to require a speaker to resume his seat should his remarks prove irrelevant to the subject under discussion. This rule is enforced with varying degrees of severity. It does not seem possible to draft a rule that would require the president to choke off irrelevant discussion. The United States should serve notice, however, that it is prepared to rise to a point of order whenever a speaker exceeds the reasonable bounds of relevancy. The past failure of U.S. representatives to interrupt political attacks directed against the United States may have contributed to the false impression that the United States is a paper tiger.[1]

These basic principles are what would seem reasonable for the United States to espouse in the ILO. The United States should also plan to play a much more active role in the organization than it has in the past. The following recommendations are made with this end in mind.

(*a*) The major governmental responsibility for ILO affairs should be concentrated in the Department of Labor. The State Department does not have the expertise or the interest to play anything but a minor role; in the past, it has intervened only at times of crisis, and the positions it has taken have not been productive. The Commerce Department, too, has shown little interest in ILO affairs. It should have, at the very least, one full-time person who follows the ILO from the employers' point of view. To emphasize the Labor Department's responsibility, the ILO budget should be placed under its control, and not included in the overall State Department budget for international agencies, as it is now. The chief spokesman on all ILO matters should be Labor.

(*b*) The AFL-CIO representative and the new employer representative should be urged to devote closer attention to the ILO than has been true in the past. Both workers and employers have been mainly concerned with the politics of the organization and have paid little attention to its technical activities. If these groups want an organization that is genuinely tripartite, efficiently managed, and carrying on technically sound programs, they will have to allot greater resources to monitor its everyday affairs and not limit their participation to meetings of the Governing Body and the annual conference.

(c) On several occasions the comptroller general has urged the U.S. government agencies involved with the ILO to draw up a statement of U.S. aims in the ILO as a guide to U.S. participation. Several attempts were made, but nothing came of them apart from vacuous generalizations. Additional exercises of this nature are likely to be as futile as those in the past. The continued screening of ILO programs by U.S. experts capable of evaluating them from a technical point of view is required. The U.S. interest in the ILO will become apparent from this type of scrutiny, and the government will then be able to provide the Congress and the public with a much better account of the ILO's relationship with the United States.

(d) The United States should insist upon more meaningful evaluations of ILO technical assistance projects. Experts from the Department of Agriculture, from AID, and from the technical divisions of the Labor Department itself should be called upon to assist in reviewing these evaluations and to make suggestions for improving, terminating, or initiating projects. Labor and management should be invited to participate in the review process. One potential and very important benefit of such evaluative reviews would be that of moving the United Nations Development Program in directions more relevant to U.S. interests than is now often the case.

(e) Similarly, the United States should take the ILO's standard-setting operations more seriously than it has in the past. The United States should begin by ratifying some of the key ILO conventions, particularly those relating to human rights. The fact that the United States has not ratified these conventions handicaps it greatly in advancing the causes of freedom of association and nondiscrimination in employment by means of ILO mechanisms. The obstacles to ratification are political, not legal,[2] and it might require some governmental effort, as well as agreement between labor and management, to secure Senate consent. The effort would be well repaid if it led to greater U.S. effectiveness within the ILO. There is no excuse for failure to ratify conventions on forced labor, occupational health and safety, minimum wages, and social security. These conventions are all well within the federal jurisdiction, and there are no standards involved to which the United States does not already conform.

(*f*) The commonly held view that ILO convention ratifications are little more than pieces of paper without real substance has some validity. The United States should work for a policing process that goes beyond the purely legalistic approach now taken. The use of quantitative data as a monitoring mechanism has already been advocated by the United States. Consideration might also be given to providing the ILO with extended investigative authority, as it already has to some extent in the field of human rights, involving on-the-spot surveys where serious violations of other standards are charged.

(*g*) The United States should pay more attention than it has in the past to monitoring the quality of the ILO staff. Ideally, staff members should be selected entirely on the basis of competence. Since the ILO, and all other international agencies, appear to be addicted to the criterion of nationality, the United States should continue to insist upon getting its fair share of ILO posts. The ILO has complained that recruitment of U.S. citizens is a long and tedious process, in part because the United States requires them to undergo security clearance before they are eligible for posts in international agencies. If the Congress cannot be persuaded to eliminate this demeaning clearance requirement, the Labor Department might consider the establishment of a roster of available potential ILO employees in order to reduce the recruitment lag.

(*h*) The field of human rights is so important that special attention should be given to the relevant ILO operations. A standing U.S. tripartite committee might well be established to work closely with the ILO and to render any assistance that is appropriate. It could also help speed up the ILO's ponderous machinery. Another useful role would be to keep the American public informed of current human rights developments.

(*i*) The United States should maintain much closer liaison with other industrialized nations concerning ILO affairs than it has in the past. Germany and Japan in particular have not, because of historical reasons, played a role in the ILO commensurate with their financial contributions. If the United States could find common ground with them, a formidable bloc would be created. It will be more difficult to cooperate with the French and British; their trade union ideologies cause complications for the AFL-CIO in maintaining good working relationships with them. Canada and Australia have worked very closely with the United States in the past, and this contact should be reinforced.

In terms of U.S. interests, the ILO remains potentially the most important of all the specialized international agencies. Its tripartite character provides contacts for the United States with a much wider range of policymakers than is possible with purely governmental agencies. By its own constitution, the ILO is dedicated to the maintenance of political and economic pluralism. Its major goals—protection of human rights, improvement in the living standards of working people, and facilitation of economic development—are in complete agreement with those of the United States. But if powerful political blocs within the ILO are allowed to subvert the rule of law, the organization's elaborate machinery for protecting human rights will be of little avail. And if the ILO is to assume functions that are beyond its competence and outside its jurisdiction, then its effectiveness in raising standards and furthering development will be seriously impaired.

This is not a counsel of perfection. There are bound to be deviations from what the United States or any other country considers to be sound policy. The Soviet Union and its satellites can be counted upon to oppose tripartism and human rights. The Arab bloc will undoubtedly continue to inveigh against Israel until the Middle East conflict is settled. The question is whether the other nations, the industrial market economies and the less developed countries, are prepared to support the basic values that the ILO has stood for in the past. If they are, the chances are good that the renewal of U.S. membership in the ILO will not be temporary.

The United States has nothing to gain, and a great deal to lose, from a deterioration of working conditions and living standards abroad. The cause of democracy will best be served if people throughout the world, particularly in the poorer countries, begin to see some alleviation of the oppressive and often dangerous conditions under which many of them work. If the member nations can be persuaded to turn the energies of the ILO to this end, instead of dissipating them in fruitless political arguments, it can be an important instrument for furthering the aims that are shared not only by labor and management, but by Americans generally.

Appendices
Notes
Index

Appendix A
The Kilby Studies

Detailed accounts of all the individual Kilby studies could not be secured. Summaries of those that were made available follow. The relevant cost data are shown in Table 5 (see Chapter 5, above).

Project A was undertaken when the wife of the country's president decided that a training scheme in carpet weaving might be appropriate for unemployed women in the capital city. There was, however, no established commercial industry; the local wool supply was insufficient; equipment was slow in coming; there was a great deal of interference with the project by government and women's organizations; and piece rates were set at levels that yielded earnings of more than double the minimum wage, so that labor costs alone were greater than sales value. In the end, only 206 women remained in the industry at a cost of $2,500 per job created in a country where the per capita annual income at the time was about $200.

Project B was a continuation of an earlier project started by the United Nations. Initially, the employees worked at home under a putting-out system, but the ILO expert added on-site production to the original training centers. The end result was 1,000 jobs at a cost of about $1,400 each. Most of the funds, however, were provided by the host country.

Project C was run by the same ILO expert involved in Project A, yet this project proved to be as successful as the other was a failure. In the opinion of the analysts, the circumstances that accounted for its success were (1) the existence of a well-established commercial carpet industry prior to the inception of the project; (2) location of the project far from the capital, thus giving the expert plenty of autonomy; and (3) production facilities that remained largely decentralized. Some 1,450 jobs were created at a reasonable cost of about $200 each.

Projects D and E were similar in purpose and scope. They involved the establishment of regional centers to train craftsmen, produce a variety of artistic goods, and market them. The trainees were drawn from among unemployed youth, with tourists envisioned as the major consumers.

The projects encountered familiar difficulties. Equipment arrived late, and counterpart commitments in personnel and physical facilities were not honored. There were also some problems specific to the individual projects. The scale of Project D was overly ambitious, in disregard of advice given by Geneva headquarters. The UNDP prevented the ILO from monitoring the project, but did not itself conduct a standard project review (presumably in deference to the wishes of the country authorities). The project manager, who was strongly supported by the government, had no taste for business administration, although he did possess the requisite artistic abilities. The experts in Project E were too narrowly specialized in particular crafts, with the result that the product mix was not optimal. Their main goal was to make cooperative centers viable producing units, to the neglect of independent producers. Both projects suffered because earnings were set too low to attract and hold capable people, in one case lower than the local unemployment benefit. A sharp drop in the tourist trade caused a shortfall in anticipated sales. The number of permanent jobs created was very small, making the cost per job astronomically high.

Project F, involving the production of ceramics, suffered from a faulty assessment of the quality of local clay deposits by a geologist, an overestimate of potential tourist demand, and long delays in delivery of equipment. After expenditures of $221,000, only twenty people were engaged in production, working with high-cost imported clay at one-third the average wage. The favorable benefit-cost ratio was based upon the assumption that this level of employment would continue, but the study suggests that the prospects for permanency were bleak.

The leather-tanning project, H, was set up to provide alternative employment for farmers who had been displaced because of a ban on the growing of poppies. The project's original goal was to provide an extension service that would enable existing tanners to improve and increase their product. Instead, attention was centered upon the establishment of a production center, which led to a perverse effect:

> A large production center makes an impressive stop in the itinerary of a visiting dignitary. Ministers love to lay cornerstones and to have their pictures taken "breaking ground" or inaugurating a new building. They also love to claim to the other ministries that their projects are earning money for the public coffers. On the other hand, many small craftsmen, each using simple hand tools and working independently in his own workshop, seem rather undramatic in comparison. Consequently, it is hardly surprising that this project gradually drifted away from

the original "low profile" approach with its relatively poor "PR" return to the sponsoring agencies.[1]

The final results were meager. The same number of entrepreneurial units existed at the end as at the beginning of the project. There is no evidence that new entrants were encouraged. The wage bill rose, but this took the form of a reduction in underemployment rather than in the creation of new jobs. Cooperative enterprises collapsed, and the independent tanners received all the benefit. Cooperation seemed to go against the cultural grain.

Appendix B
Results of Country Survey Visits

The following section includes a summary of the results gained from examining ILO technical cooperation projects in six countries during the spring of 1978. All current and some recent ILO projects were covered in the survey, with certain exceptions. The general conclusions drawn from the survey are found on pages 172–75, above.

Costa Rica
Vocational Training

The ILO's most successful Costa Rican project was apparently vocational training. The project began in 1967, and for 1977–79 was budgeted at $383,000. The National Vocational Training Institute (INA), which is financed by a 1 percent payroll tax, offers courses throughout the country. Four national centers were established, with mobile units set up to serve small communities. Some courses run as short as forty hours, but apprenticeship programs can last for three years. In 1977, some 60,000 students took part thoughout the country, which is a large number for a country the size of Costa Rica. Placement of trainees has not been a problem; in fact, many students were workers with jobs who simply wanted to upgrade their qualifications. All courses are free, and 75 percent of the students in the apprenticeship program receive some financial assistance.

ILO experts drafted the original law creating the institute. From 1967 to 1972, the project concentrated on training the local staff who organized the technical training (the number rose from an initial 50 to 150 in 1972). The ILO provided eleven experts, whose stays varied from a few months to three to four years. The international aid package amounted to $1 million, with Costa Rica providing an additional $5.7 million in counterpart funds. Sixteen institute staff members received ILO fellowships to study abroad, and all its present top executives have held such fellowships.

By 1972, the institute had graduated only 4,000 students, but growth thereafter was very rapid. The objectives of the second phase (1973–76) were to adjust the system more finely to industrial demand, to improve teaching methods, to regionalize, and to bring in fields of study that were not yet covered. Twelve ILO experts served during this period, some for only a few months. The ILO budget was set at $500,000. The most recent phase (1977–79) aimed at the establishment of a skill certification system to improve the status of workers, along with an expansion of the regional centers. The U.S. AID program provided bilateral assistance of $225,000 to help establish a shipbuilding center, and $10,000 was allotted for a study of technical training for women.

The institute staff agreed unanimously that achieving the present level of operation would have taken much longer had it not been for ILO assistance. They pointed to the inferior situation found in neighboring Nicaragua, which has not had any effective ILO aid. A retired UNDP official called the institute the best in Latin America, and he noted that it was providing technical assistance to other Central American countries. There were no dissenting views; apart from some initial problems in recruiting experts, the project functioned smoothly and achieved its objectives. The interest of the government is evidenced by the excellent physical facilities it contributed and by its willingness to finance the institute generously.

Employment-Policy Planning

This project began in 1973 in cooperation with the Ministry of Labor. Scheduled to be completed in 1978 at a cost of $500,000, its objectives were the following:

(a) To design and implement a strategy of development for greater employment and income;

(b) To design and evaluate national programs to assure the attainment of these objectives;

(c) To create the necessary statistical and institutional infrastructure;

(d) To evaluate and design suitable instruments of economic policy;

(e) To design and effectuate the structural changes that would assure the success of the objectives and strategy.[1]

The project's real achievements are difficult to determine. One concrete result has been an excellent system of employment and wage statistics. An institute for labor studies has been established, but it is still too early for its work to be evaluated. The more ambitious goals of the project—to make structural changes in the economic system—have run into problems, however. The plan was as follows:

As the culmination of a development policy with employment

and income distribution objectives, in order to ensure a model of development which would eliminate unemployment and underemployment and achieve a more equitable distribution of income, systematic analysis has been initiated to design the creation of a third sector of the economy—the Labor Economy Sector (SEL)—where, through the establishment of social property,there would be new productive relations. This new type of enterprise would contribute to a policy that would create new sources of employment and a new model of participation in Costa Rica.[2]

It was proposed to finance new enterprises, which were to be owned and managed by the workers themselves, out of an existing fund for the payment of employment termination allowances. Private employers were doubtful about the viability of the scheme and about the ability of the projected enterprises to compete successfully with established firms.

This plan to create a worker-managed sector had the strong backing of the man who was then minister of labor, and while the ILO was somewhat cautious about lending its support, it was difficult to say no to the government. The project was highly political and strongly influenced by a similar Peruvian experiment. To the ILO's relief, national elections in the spring of 1978 brought a new party to power, and the labor economy sector idea was dropped.

In general, this project appears to have been too ambitious. Apart from improving labor statistics, and perhaps the administration of manpower planning, its results were modest.

Rural Development

In rural development, the largest of the ILO's Costa Rica projects, the government established a land colonization institute (ITCO) to buy land for distribution to small farmers and cooperatives in order to improve farming methods and promote rural industry. The role of the ILO was to help in the establishment of cooperatives and to provide a source of farm information.

ITCO had been established in 1976 as a response to rural unrest. It helped avert a political crisis by pledging to redistribute land and set up marketing cooperatives. At the time of the UNDP financial crisis, the president of Costa Rica informed the UNDP that the government gave first priority to this project. When lack of funds made staff cuts imminent, the government itself provided the money necessary to retain all the experts until UNDP was again able to underwrite their salaries. The estimated cost of the project from its inception in 1973 to its conclusion in 1981 is $1.2 million, including a Netherlands contribution of $250,000.

Thus far, there appears to have been no basic change in land tenure. The government bought up little land, partly because Costa Rica is not replete with large landed estates, unlike other parts of Latin America where land reform has long been a burning issue. The ILO's contribution involved the provision of experts on rural industry, marketing, and peasant training and organization. There are two training levels, one for ITCO officials and one for the peasants themselves. All the courses are short, with two weeks being the longest duration.

A local official involved in rural development criticized the ILO project as too vague and beyond the agency's expertise. In his opinion, ILO ideas were grandiose and the experts sent out by the organization, not sufficiently acquainted with local conditions. The whole idea of re-settlement in the Costa Rican context appeared to be more political than economic, and he questioned the desirability of the ILO's getting involved. The change of government may impede realization of the project's objectives.

Other Projects

Several smaller ILO projects in Costa Rica were less controversial. For example, a national council for rehabilitation was created in 1973, on the advice of the ILO, to coordinate the work of twelve public and private institutions engaged in retraining invalids. Costa Rica followed ILO recommendations step by step, including organization of centers, training of personnel, placement, legislation, and campaigns to induce enterprises to hire the graduates. A continuing flow of ILO experts began in 1970, and with one exception, they were highly qualified. According to informed interviewees, the Costa Rican project has become a model for vocational rehabilitation. It established a national register of invalids, and many people are presently being helped. By all accounts, ILO work in this area scores very highly.

Neither labor nor management organizations in Costa Rica appear to be heavily involved in ILO activities. The executive secretary of one employer group professed to have no specific knowledge of any ILO projects. An official of another group expressed the view that some ILO–worker relationships had not always been beneficial to business and that there was some radical political feed-in to the unions through the ILO. This did not imply a deliberate policy on the ILO's part;

rather, he felt, outside forces were using the ILO for their own purposes. The only contact with the ILO he could recall was sending an official of his organization to a six-week course at the ILO Institute for International Studies in Geneva, where the program seemed oriented to the Left. The ILO is apparently not very popular in Costa Rican management circles.

The trade unions are more favorably disposed. The ORIT unions (those affiliated with the ICFTU) have had a good deal of contact with the ILO in workers' education programs, though they complained that ILO seminars tend to be aimed above the heads of the people for whom they are intended. The Catholic-oriented unions thought that the most useful service the ILO performed for them was bringing representatives of different political tendencies together in joint seminars, thus creating some degree of unity in the labor movement. They cited as particularly valuable seminars on manpower policy conducted by CINTERFOR. It has been ILO policy that at all its meetings and seminars in Central America, 60 percent representation should go to ORIT unions (which are favored by the AFL-CIO) and the remaining 40 percent allotted to Catholic unions and the Communists. In practice, this means that the latter two groups normally get 20 percent each.

Of the three regional organizations of the ILO operating in Central America, CINTERFORS, which handles vocational training, appears to be the most effective. PREALC is somewhat less so, while CIAT has been of very little help, since it tends to come in with preconceived programs and then tries to sell them regardless of local conditions.

Despite some deficiencies in two of its major projects, the ILO enjoys a good reputation in Costa Rica. Witness the fact that from 1972 to 1976, the ILO share of total UNDP funds allocated to Costa Rica amounted to 21 percent, far higher than the world average, while the planned program for 1977–81 alloted 32 percent to the ILO. Part of the ILO's popularity may be due to its willingness to participate in politically motivated programs. Apart from employers, however, virtually everyone interviewed, including representatives of the Ministry of Planning, agreed that ILO projects were among the best in Costa Rica. A former country director of the UNDP thought that the ILO had performed well above the average of all U.N. agencies in Costa Rica and that its local representatives had received excellent technical backing from Geneva. All in all, one comes away from Costa Rica with the feeling that the technical assistance work which the ILO is best equipped to handle—that is, vocational training, rehabilitation, and workers' education—reached such a high standard that it overshadowed other less effective programs in rural development and its cooperation in the attempt to effectuate fundamental changes in the social and economic structure of the country.

Peru
Labor Management
The most important recent ILO project in Peru, in terms both of funding and of political importance, has involved cooperation with SINAMOS, an organization created in 1972 as a political arm of the Peruvian revolution of 1968.[3] The ILO spent $1.3 million of UNDP funds on this program, which had as its purpose the installation in Peru of a system of ownership and production modeled upon that of Yugoslavia. The ILO sent in experts on "participation" and helped train their Peruvian counterparts. A research center, in which ILO experts were active, was established to provide the intellectual underpinnings of the new society.

When the Velasco government fell in 1975 following a coup d'état, labor management was abandoned as a social model.[4] The SINAMOS research center ceased to exist, as did the ILO project. The fact that the ILO ever became involved at all is surprising, since both employers and the ORIT labor federation were opposed to SINAMOS and what it stood for. In helping to develop the ideology of labor management through SINAMOS, which had as its goal the elimination of both unions and private employers, the ILO was in effect helping destroy tripartism. There is general agreement that ILO participation was the result of strong government pressure.

This project, and the ILO role in it, are good examples of what a technical agency should not do. In the first place, the ILO had no expertise in the activity upon which it was giving advice. Second, it was not prudent to get involved in a highly controversial political movement, particularly when the ILO's own tripartite constituents were opposed to it. (Both the ORIT unions and the employers' federation fared badly under Velasco: the chairman of the employers' association was exiled for three years; the ORIT federation was opposed to the government. The Communist labor federation, however, basked in government favor.) Third, there is always the risk in a political project that a turn in the wheel of fortune will destroy the project and result in a complete waste of international aid funds.

Vocational Training
ILO cooperation with SENATI, the Peruvian Vocational Training

Institute, began in 1961 when the Institute was created. The first step was to set up an appropriate training methodology. Since the educational level of Peruvian workers was low, some basic elementary instruction had to be provided before these people could absorb skill training. For two years, beginning in 1966, the ILO worked on a program to prepare training personnel. This program was followed by expert advice on apprenticeship and skill testing. The last ILO expert arrived in 1975 for one year to help set up program evaluation techniques. The present director of SENATI and eight other officials attended courses at the ILO Turin Center, as did some of those in charge of training units in large industrial enterprises.

By all accounts, the ILO served a vital promotional function in vocational training. Bilateral aid agencies have now taken over, but the ILO's contribution is highly appreciated.

The Social Property Sector

A substantial government and cooperative sector still exists in the Peruvian economy, in part a legacy of the Velasco experiments. The state sector includes electricity and telephones. The government had taken over the important fishing industry, but this has been restored to private hands after a disastrous period of public operation. Lima's transportation system, some shipping companies, and many large agricultural estates are all run cooperatively.

In 1976, a center for social property research was established to provide managerial training and research support. The ILO provided preliminary assistance in designing courses and helped prepare a project proposal for UNDP support. (The Ford Foundation also provided some funds.) The sum of $800,000 was requested of the UNDP, but its financial crisis during that period intervened. In the meantime, political support for the whole idea appears to have diminished, and it is questionable whether the project will ever get off the ground. The ILO will be fortunate if this occurs, since it would be saved from involvement in what appears to be an ill-defined program.

Training of Mine Workers

About $500,000 of UNDP funds were spent from 1973 to 1976 to establish and operate a school for vocational training in mining, and an additional $400,000 was allocated for the period 1977–79. This school apparently fulfills a vital need in the Peruvian economy, and the government seems quite happy with the ILO contribution to the project.

Rural Development

A government agency has been established to integrate various efforts to promote rural employment. Its purpose is to generate work opportunities in small enterprises through labor-intensive techniques. The project had been in operation for one year at the time of my visit, and at that time only one enterprise had been established. Its principal accomplishment was to identify 350 possible small projects, of which 70 were referred to banks to find out whether financing could be arranged. If these small enterprises can be started, management training will have to be provided, and an ILO expert has been assigned the task of developing the necessary programs. Although political support for the project appears to have declined, the ILO commitment is not a major one.

Other Projects

The ILO has provided other useful technical assistance to Peru. An employment service, considered one of the best in Latin America, was started in 1950 with ILO cooperation. A large manpower-planning project, costing over $1 million, was executed from 1970 to 1976. It led to improved labor statistics, and as a result of the studies it completed, the government moved more actively toward employment-generating policies. The ILO regional employment team, PREALC, has had little impact on employment in Peru. But even the best of programs might have failed under the poor economic conditions that prevailed in Peru at the time.

Peruvian management officials were more positive about the ILO than their Costa Rican counterparts, for the ILO made it possible for them to hold meetings between Peruvian leaders of labor and management. While this was difficult to arrange in Peru, it was feasible in Geneva. Peruvian management officials respect the work of CINTERFOR and CIAT, but they find that PREALC is operating at a theoretical level too remote from actual projects; as a consequence, it is not producing much of any substance. The Peruvian trade unions have not received any assistance from the ILO in recent years, perhaps because of the political situation, although the ILO has been used occasionally as a deterrent against government intervention.

The ILO has done some useful work with the Andean pact nations as a group. ILO experts have acted as technical consultants to the annual Andean conference of labor ministers, advising on labor migration, social security, and the harmonization of labor legislation. Some international trade union seminars have also been highly valued.

In terms of total volume, multilateral technical assistance to Peru has been small compared with bilateral aid received mainly from Canada, Germany, and the Netherlands. But bilateral aid has been aimed primarily at infrastructure, whereas multilateral aid has financed social projects. The government planning office believes that if a specific problem arises in which a potential donor country is interested, particularly where investment resources are involved, bilateral aid works well. Multilateral aid has the advantage of giving the recipient country more control over the selection of experts, and of having no commercial strings attached.

Malaysia

In my first orientation interview with him, a top official of Malaysia's Ministry of Labor stated that the ILO's principal contributions to Malaysia were in the areas of social security and human resources. Beginning in 1958, the ILO had helped to write social security legislation and bring the system into being. In 1976, with ILO assistance, there was an expansion of social security to non–wage earners, and the success of the transition to the new system owed a great deal to the ILO. A large-scale program for human resources began in 1965, when a manpower department was established in the Labor Ministry.

Vocational Training

The ILO has been heavily involved in a number of training projects in Malaysia. An industrial training institute was established in 1964 with Colombo Plan assistance, and ILO cooperation began in 1972. The ILO helped develop a four-year apprenticeship program and prepared training syllabi after making industrial surveys. It also ran a pilot instructor-training project. Although the ILO is no longer involved, there is little doubt about its importance in getting the program started. The World Bank and the Asian Development Bank are now financing regional expansion of training centers in the amount of almost $5 million, so it is clear that the institute is a going concern.

Because of the multiplicity of skill training centers, both public and private, with different curricula, a good deal of confusion developed over qualitative standards. In 1971, the government established a certification system and requested ILO assistance, which terminated in 1975. The certification board sets tests and issues certificates for the attainment of varying skill levels. The ILO presence is regarded as having been crucial in raising the system to its present level of competence.

A third ILO project in vocational training has been less successful.

In 1966, the government of Malaysia founded a nonprofit public corporation, MARA, to promote the social and economic status of the Malays, who make up 65 percent of the population. (The rest of the people are mainly ethnic Chinese, who dominate the economic and commercial life of the country.) The operations of MARA included rural finance and advisory services and training for small entrepreneurs. Small enterprises have been established and sold off to the Malays.

The ILO has been involved in the vocational training aspect of this program. Difficulties have arisen, perhaps because of the imprecise nature of the training required. Whether the ILO should have participated in a racially discriminatory program may also be questioned. MARA is probably not justifiable in economic terms. Its purpose—to help allay discontent among the rural Malay population—may be laudable, but its political character suggests that it should not be financed by international funds. The ILO contribution was not large though, amounting to about $100,000.

A final ILO vocational project involves a training center for the national electrical system. The Electricity Board in Malaysia has 14,000 employees, and the center will be able to offer them a broad range of courses. By 1980, its planned capacity was 400 students, eventually rising to 600. The ILO is to supply six experts at an eventual cost of $800,000 for 174 man-months, with an equal amount coming from bilateral aid. The justification for this special center is that the skills required for work in the country's modern electricity industry cannot be found in the labor market. The center will be modeled upon a similar plan used in France. ILO participation is planned for one year, mainly to train instructors. The Electricity Board, which has found the ILO recruiting machinery to be slow and bureaucratic, believes that it could do a better recruiting job on its own.

National Productivity Center

This center was established in 1962 with ILO assistance. Its functions are training, advising, and consulting in production, accounting, and industrial relations, all at the management level. The average course lasts three to five days, and clients are drawn from both public and private enterprise. A special program of entrepreneurial training has been set up for Malays (3,000 completed such courses in 1977). Currently, 85 percent of the total cost is met by the government, with fees constituting the balance. Although recent assistance has come through bilateral aid, there are still occasional contacts with the ILO Office, which has provided some experts on a short-term basis.

Management Consulting

The purpose of this project was to establish a company to provide management consulting services. From 1973 to 1977, UNDP contributed over $1 million, most of which was used to finance ILO experts. The original consulting team consisted of six ILO experts and thirty Malaysians (who were expected to learn on the job). The original plan called for the company to be self-supporting in five years, but it has never made a profit and owes a great deal of money to the government which it will probably never repay. The main problems were rapid staff turnover and lack of adequate consulting assignments. The project had clearly not met its goals at the time of my visit, and one would be hard put to justify the large expenditures that sustained it.

Social Security

An Indian ILO expert who came to Malaysia in 1965 is regarded as the father of the country's social security system. Through his efforts, social security legislation was enacted in 1969 and implemented in 1971, the first program covering work injuries and invalidity. He left the country in 1973 and was followed by experts on legislation, computers, and actuarial work. Thanks to their efforts, the system has been computerized, and will be expanded to cover sickness insurance and pensions.

The social security administration complains that it has become difficult to obtain ILO assistance because the UNDP does not appreciate the need for this type of aid. The UNDP's priorities are more in economic development; thus, social programs tend to lose out. The Ministry of Labor ranks low in the government hierarchy, and its influence on the allocation of country aid funds is limited. The ILO assistance has been extremely helpful, however, and more is needed.

Manpower Planning

A national manpower coordinating board was created recently to develop, *inter alia*, a national master plan for industrial skills. The ILO contributed the services of several experts and provided six European fellowships at a cost of $107,000. The ILO has also worked with the Ministry of Labor in improving labor statistics; five ministry officials have been attending courses at the ILO Turin Center each year. The ministry expressed general satisfaction with the ILO and indicated that more assistance would be useful.

Other Projects

The Employers' Federation complained that the ILO has not done much for employers. A regional ILO employer representative is now stationed in Bangkok, and in 1977, the ILO ran an employers' seminar for the ASEAN countries.

The Malayan Trade Union Congress indicated that ILO worker education projects had been limited in scope, They did cite an ICFTU-ILO seminar in 1977 on the organization of rural workers, plus a number of fellowships for the Turin Center. Several international seminars were given for trade unionists, and the ILO provided them with teaching aids and documents. The main outside support for the Trade Union Congress comes from the ICFTU and the AFL-CIO.

An official of the economic planning unit, which coordinates all technical assistance in Malaysia, claimed that there is considerable favoritism in the appointment of experts within the UNDP system; as a result, some countries are overrepresented. ILO experts in Malaysia have, moreover, been of uneven quality. The official conceded, however, that there was some truth in allegations that counterpart cooperation had been less than ideal. On the question of bilateral versus multilateral aid, he felt that the former was easier to arrange, if political relationships were good. But some donor countries insist on their own priorities, and multilateral aid may lead to a wider choice of experts.

To summarize, in Malaysia the ILO has remained fairly close to its traditional activities: vocational training, social security, and manpower planning. With one exception, it has managed to steer clear of political projects. By all accounts, it has performed creditably, and its clients would like more assistance. The only project that appears to have failed involved the creation of a management consulting company, an area of work not ordinarily associated with the ILO. The ILO record of achievement also owes much to the restraint shown by the government of Malaysia in not attempting to use the ILO to achieve its political goals.

Thailand
Vocational Training

In 1969, the Thai National Institute for Skill Development became operational with ILO guidance. The first technical assistance phase, which ended in 1973, was financed by the UNDP for $1.16 million, plus a Thai government grant of $2.4 million. The second phase of activity, which extended through 1979, had been budgeted at over $800,000, but the UNDP financial crisis forced cutbacks. Additional assistance was received in the form of a $2.4 million loan from the Asian Development Bank to procure equipment for three new regional vocational training centers. And the Japanese government agreed to provide another regional institute on a turnkey basis—including buildings and machinery, twelve instructors, and twenty-four fellowships—at a cost of $5 million. The German and British governments are considering similar projects.

The ILO assistance project was scheduled to end in 1979. At the time I visited the institute, five ILO experts were on the job. Their role was to conduct courses, train instructors, and help select equipment. Communication was admittedly a problem, since none of the experts could speak the Thai language.

By all accounts, this has been a successful enterprise, and the Department of Labor, which in Thailand is part of the Ministry of the Interior, is well satisfied with the ILO contribution. Recently, however, the ILO has tried to shift the emphasis of its work to curriculum development, something the department believes it is capable of doing on its own. Moreover, the department holds the view that standard ILO-type curricula do not work well under Thai conditions.

The ILO has also worked on a project in cooperation with the Ministry of Education, a rather unusual event. Financed by the Asian Development Bank, the project involves post-secondary vocational training. This type of work is ordinarily handled by UNESCO, but the ILO outbid that organization on cost. Six ILO experts are involved in the project, which is to be completed in 1980. The ILO personnel are training teachers and taking part in curriculum planning and equipment procurement. This project offers a good example of an area in which two international organizations have clearly overlapping jurisdictions.

Manpower Planning

A relatively small project, involving only three man-years of expert assistance, was devoted to manpower planning and the promotion of rural employment. The project, which was terminated several years ago, seems to have left little behind. According to Thai officials, their lack of receptivity to the program had a good deal to do with its failure. Current Thai philosophy in the field of labor generally does not conform to the ILO's; in fact, the government harbors some suspicions about ILO intentions. The ILO's shortcomings lay in its not being able to determine what was appropriate for Thailand. Its experts, moreover, were too academic in their approach.

A case in point is the effort by the ILO to interest the government in labor-intensive projects. An ad hoc committee of government representatives was established at ILO urging to consider the applicability of labor-intensive methods in both agriculture and industry as a means of increasing employment. It turned out that a major constraint was locating a government department willing to sponsor a project. Those responsible for construction, one of the principal targets of this approach, regard labor intensity as a step backward; they wanted the work done quickly, once it was decided upon.

Management Training

Currently, no major ILO projects are under way in this area. Preparatory work for a management consultant training program was completed in 1976, but the UNDP financial crisis intervened. Projects that involve the training of government budget officers and university professors in the consultancy field are under discussion. An ILO-assisted productivity center was established in 1962, and a small business service institute, formerly an ILO project, is now under UNIDO sponsorship. UNIDO has also taken over industrial standardization, formerly within the province of the ILO.

Regional Teams

Since the regional office of ILO is located in Bangkok, it was possible to get firsthand information on the operation of the various teams. The Asian Regional Skill Development Program (ARSDEP) is the largest, since it covers all vocational training. Two-thirds of all ILO projects in Asia fall under its supervision, totaling about fifty projects involving 130 experts. The funds available for the projects—UNDP and bilateral—amount to $50 million.

ARSDEP is now trying to persuade governments to stop institution-building and to concentrate instead on setting up national councils to coordinate the training work being conducted by the various ministries. The time for ILO assistance in setting up vocational training institutions is apparently over; the Asian countries, at least, appear able to do it themselves.

The Asian Regional Team for Labor Administration (ARPLA) has been concentrating on assistance to labor ministries, but it hopes eventually to assist union and employer organizations. The impact of this small unit, which has only three professionals, has been minimal, at least in Thailand.

The Asian Regional Team for Employment Promotion (ARTEP) was established in 1971 with high ambitions but little in the way of staff. Its first activities were concentrated on comprehensive employment strategy missions to Laos and Nepal, which thus far do not seem to have had any significant impact on policy. It was hard hit by the UNDP financial crisis and, according to an ARTEP report, "by this time the project was grappling with staffing problems, lack of continuity in formal leadership, and a steady erosion of credibility. . . . Throughout 1977, ARTEP attempted to revive its credibility by mounting technical cooperation activities at the country level and establishing closer links both with UNDP and other branches of the ILO. But this policy often led to involvement in piecemeal, fragmented activities."[5] A revised program has been developed, and among several new research projects under way is an investigation into the wide differences that exist among countries concerning the intensity of labor input in rice cultivation. Another focuses on the factors that have enabled some countries in Asia to develop labor-intensive industries oriented toward external markets. Whether these and similar projects turn out to be useful remains to be seen. ARTEP is now receiving $250,000 a year from UNDP, plus additional funds from the Danish and Norwegian aid agencies.

Other Programs

Returning to Thai programs, on the labor management front the Thai situation is such as not to permit much in the way of ILO assistance. Trade union membership is small, unions have little power, and what they need is help in organizing rather than seminars on the union role in economic planning and workers' participation in management. The ILO cannot get into the real problems of the unions for political reasons. The AFL-CIO, however, is providing direct assistance, as is the Friedrich Ebert Stiftung, a German foundation that operates with government funds and has been active in many countries. Officials of both these organizations are of the view that the ILO has not been able to offer any meaningful help to the trade unions since October 1976, when the present government took over.

The only ILO contact with organized Thai employers has been in the form of periodic regional meetings, some information from the regional office, and a few fellowships. The Thai Employers' Federation is receiving both assistance and advice from employers of a number of other countries, however, notably Australia, Denmark, and Japan.

Finally there was a consensus among the Thai officials interviewed that bilateral aid is preferable to the present UNDP system. It is easier to negotiate and execute, and more flexible. Donor countries tend to work in areas in which they have expertise. The Thai experience has been that the international agencies have their own programs and targets, which do not always provide what the recipient countries want or need.

Politics are involved in both types of aid, but friction is minimized in bilateral aid because it comes only from friendly nations.

Kenya

From the viewpoint of international aid, Kenya is a model nation. It has had one of the few stable governments in Africa; it has maintained an open society; and it has relied to a large extent on market mechanisms to regulate its economy. The country has a well-functioning government bureaucracy, able to provide the necessary counterpart backing. It has great natural beauty, and its capital, Nairobi, enjoys an ideal climate (this is not an unimportant consideration, for international experts like living there). Development assistance is a thriving industry in Kenya.

Vocational Training

An ILO program to establish a national industrial vocational training scheme began in 1972 and ended in 1975, at a cost of about $800,000. The program is now being coordinated by a national council and nine industry committees, all supported by payroll taxes. Training is being offered in thirty-six skills, and while some assistance is still being received from Canada and the Netherlands, the program is largely self-sustaining. The recruitment of qualified local instructors is a problem, though, since alternative opportunities are available for such persons to practice their skills in private industry. The ILO has continued to give advice on curriculum development and the establishment of uniform skill standards.

As examples of ILO-type projects that individual countries are sponsoring under bilateral aid agreements, several recent Kenyan projects may be cited. The Ministry of Labor signed an agreement with the Dutch government for a project on training for the textile industry, and similar discussions were held with Japan regarding support of training in watch repair. The ministry is currently looking for a donor for training in the printing trades.

Kenya has established a national service corps—a voluntary civilian body under the supervision of the Ministry of Labor—to provide training courses for about 5,000 young people annually. The minimum term is two years, the maximum, five years. About 80 percent of the entrants are said to complete their courses, but the government believes that the most important aspect of the regimen is the instilling of regular work habits and discipline. About twenty people apply for each vacancy, and graduates of the program are in great demand. The ILO did not participate in the project, but Germany and Japan made financial contributions.

Factory Inspection

A joint ILO-Finnish project to train factory inspectors has recently been instituted, to last for a period of three years. Three foreign experts will be involved, and measuring and other equipment will be supplied, plus six fellowships for study in England. There are now eleven factory inspectors in Kenya, and while there should ideally be at least thirty to forty, the goal of the project is to end up with twenty well-trained individuals. The director of the project is a member of the Finnish factory inspection service.

This is the first such project in Kenya, and perhaps in all of Africa. It is also a first for Finland. The initiative came from the Kenyan government, after the UNDP had refused assistance.

Mechanical safety is the main problem to be solved. There is still no inspection at all in construction work. Most of the factory inspectors are young, and as they acquire experience, many are hired away by private firms. Virtually all of them have come from universities, with no previous industrial experience, and the project hopes to recruit nonuniversity personnel who will be more content with permanent government employment. One administrative problem already encountered was the claim made by the Ministry of Health that it had exclusive jurisdiction over all government employees with medical degrees; as a result, it refused to let the Labor Ministry, which controls the factory inspectorate, employ any.

Management Training

In 1966, the ILO helped organize a management training and advisory center for middle management and supervisory personnel. It was originally staffed by twelve ILO experts, each of whom was assigned a local counterpart apprentice. The ILO currently participates only in a special program to train small entrepreneurs. The center is now fully government supported. A large portion of its clientele consists of small businessmen who are financed through government loans and were more or less required to sign up for courses.

By June 30, 1977, total UNDP assistance was about $725,000. Assistance was terminated abruptly, over government objection, because the UNDP believed that the project had not met its objectives. The project appeared to have been designed unrealistically in the first place, for it called upon the Kenyan government to supply forty-six officers to the center by the end of 1976. Since recruits were drawn exclusively (and perhaps mistakenly) from among university graduates with no technical knowledge, and given the financial constraints and the heavy demand for such personnel in the Kenyan economy, it was not surprising that the center had only eleven staff members at the time of my visit, in 1978. After nine years of international assistance, the number of Kenyan nationals is still inadequate, and most of them require further training. Moreover, the objective of developing a management advisory capability has not been achieved.

No one was inclined to deny that this project had failed. The ILO wanted to shut it down several years ago, but the government was against this. The UNDP finally stepped in and brought international participation to an end. It is doubtful that the center can survive.

Rural Access Roads

The rural roads project in Kenya extends beyond the normal range of ILO activities. Its goal is to build 14,000 kilometers of rural feeder roads to provide small farmers with easier access to markets for their products. The idea of building them with labor-intensive methods was an afterthought, the result of a 1972 ILO paper on labor-intensive techniques in construction. The World Bank acquired an interest in the project, and Britain financed three pilot units. Thus far, seven cash donors have appeared, and three more are providing direct technical assistance. By the end of 1977, 450 kilometers of road had been built.

The basic unit of work is an organization that can build 45 kilometers a year using 300 casual workers. Each team of 300 men is split into four groups to minimize the impact on other work activities in the area. The average length of a road is from 5 to 10 kilometers.

Wages have been fixed at the lowest agricultural labor rate in the vicinity to prevent interference with normal farm activities. Time is not a major factor because traffic is expected to be light until farmers adjust to the new opportunities generated by the roads. All labor is local, except for supervising engineers (twelve of whom, including five Kenyans, were in the field). Upon completion, each road is maintained by local farmers, who are paid on the basis of 2 kilometers per man for 12 days a month.

The only equipment each unit has at its disposal is a Land Rover, a seven-ton truck to transport material, a hut for overseers, a storeroom, a shed to manufacture culverts, and six tractors and eight trailers per unit for graveling. There is no equipment for clearing, excavating, or compacting. The finish is not as good as that found on machine-built roads, but the engineers are confident that the labor-intensive roads will prove equally durable.

External economies make it difficult to assess the relative costs of labor- versus capital-intensive modes of construction. Machines need a wider space in which to operate, and many coffee and tea bushes are destroyed in the process. Machine work might be cheaper, but trained operators are difficult to find. Spare parts are a problem, too, and idle time on heavy equipment is an important cost factor.

The project planners are frank to admit that it will take some time before they can determine if the roads are worthwhile in a cost-benefit sense. Much depends on whether there will be consequent changes in land use and cultivation. There is no question about local interest in the project. The fact that compensation is not paid for the right-of-way indicates that landowners are confident enough to donate their land gratis in anticipation of future benefits. In the meantime, some badly needed temporary employment is provided.

During the 1972–74 planning period, the ILO supplied one expert. Since then, it has supported a project supervisor, three man-years of field engineers, and a systems specialist for one year. Bilateral aid has enabled the project to hire thirteen additional construction engineers. The project has aroused widespread interest, and many countries have sent inspection teams to find out whether this type of road building can be applied generally. The ILO became involved in the project because of its interest in employment creation through labor-intensive techniques and because no other agency was prepared to take the project on. If the program should eventually prove successful, the ILO's reputation in technical assistance will be greatly enhanced, for both the planning and execution appear to be imaginative and meticulous.

Other Projects

Kenya was one of the first countries to receive a comprehensive ILO employment mission, and its reaction to the mission report is dealt with in connection with the World Employment Program. Several additional small projects should be mentioned here, however. The World Employment Program is supplying an advisor on labor-intensive technology to the newly created National Council for Science and Technology, which is to provide policy guidance to government ministries. It is hoped that the ILO will be able to steer the choice of technique used in industrial projects in a labor-using direction. There was an ILO-UNIDO struggle for the project which ILO won because of its emphasis on employment.

This project seems to be poorly formulated, and it would be surprising if the results were significant.

The African Regional Labor Administration Center (ARLAC), located in Kenya, began operating on January 1, 1978, under a four-year UNDP grant of $925,000. In the past, the ILO gave a number of short courses for labor department administrators, but the new program will enable it to run residential courses of four months' duration. The program is to cater to the English-speaking countries of Africa; a separate organization (CRADAT) has been set up for the Francophones.

ILO assistance to Kenyan employers has taken the form of information and seminars, the latter about twice a year. The Kenya Federation of Labor has not received much help aside from an occasional seminar.

Several Kenyan government officials expressed a preference for bilateral over multilateral aid, though conceding that ILO technical assistance was good at the operational level. One of them cited as a drawback of international aid the fact that the U.N. approach to development has been subject to changing fads over the years—industrial growth, agricultural development, integrated rural development, population control, basic needs—although Kenya's problems had not changed. There was a strong negative opinion about ILO efforts to promote worker and peasant "participation" projects, on the ground that it is impossible for an outsider to understand Kenyan local traditions, making international advice in this area useless.

The Ivory Coast

The Ivory Coast is one of the few less developed countries that has managed to achieve a satisfactory rate of economic growth through agricultural development. Multilateral aid in this region has been dwarfed by bilateral aid, particularly from France, with which the Ivory Coast has very close connections. During the period 1972–76, only about 15 percent of outside technical assistance was scheduled to come through the UNDP. Consequently, the ILO role has been small.

Vocational Training

The ILO supplied three experts over a two-year period to help organize the National Office for Vocational Training. A new project, involving its reorganization and expansion, is under way with the assistance of five international experts. It coordinates the work of the ten training centers already in existence and will also plan a balance of manpower reserves for the country.

One of the urgent manpower problems of the Ivory Coast is to replace the 40,000 Europeans employed in Abidjan, the nation's capital, both in government and private enterprise. Training facilities will have to be expanded, and the ILO is expected to play an important role.

Rural Development

The rural development project ranks among the most ambitious ever undertaken by the ILO in the Ivory Coast. The National Center for the Promotion of Cooperative Enterprises was established in 1969 with UNDP financing. Starting with six ILO experts, the staff increased to ten in 1972, and in 1978 consisted of three experts and ten associates.

Until 1975, the Ivory Coast cooperatives engaged only in joint marketing, but that year producer co-ops were introduced. Prices of all major crops in the country—including coffee, cocoa, palm oil, and sugar—are determined by state marketing boards. Large producers and the co-ops sell directly to those marketing boards, but independent small producers sell their products through wholesalers. A major purpose of the co-ops is to protect their members against unfair practices—dishonest weighing, for example—by wholesalers. The ILO reasons that small farmers must be organized in order to prevent their exploitation. It is not concerned with the technical aspects of agriculture, merely organization. The experts it sends in are accountants, economists, and sociologists. The Food and Agricultural Organization (FAO) also carries on some co-op activities in the Ivory Coast, but it works primarily with cattle raisers.

The cooperative movement has had its ups and downs in the Ivory Coast. An attempted coup d'état in the 1960s, in which leaders of the movement became involved, led to a negative attitude on the part of the government, but the persistence of ILO technical assistance attests to the evolution of a more favorable view. The co-ops do not receive any special government support, nor is there any effort to impose cooperation on farmers. Cooperative members make up only about 5 percent of the agricultural labor force, although their share of the important coffee-cocoa market runs around 20 percent. They are by no means the dominant form of organization in the country. If the present (or future) government were to decide that agricultural cooperation should become the appropriate national policy, then the ILO will have made a significant contribution toward the training of staff. If not, the ILO project will remain a sideshow.

Social Security

Since 1971, five ILO experts have served in the Ivory Coast helping to organize the social security system, which consists of workmen's compensation, family welfare assistance, and pensions. According to a high official of the Social Security Administration, the ILO experts were much superior to French consultants, who had come into the country under bilateral aid. The ILO project is finished, but the administration would like more aid in staff training. There was no doubt about the enthusiasm that the name ILO invoked here.

Other Activities

In 1973, a World Bank–ILO mission studied the Ivory Coast's employment problems, but its report had little impact, and its findings were never incorporated into the national plan. Local officials expressed the view that employment-creation activities through ILO teams created goodwill for the organization but that their analyses were not sound. The government does not perceive labor-intensive technology as being applicable to the Ivory Coast, since private entrepreneurs make all technological decisions without government participation. As for the "basic needs" approach to development advocated by the ILO, the government feels that it is already satisfying the basic needs of the population.

The Ivory Coast Federation of Labor has apparently enjoyed satisfactory relations with the ILO. It sent people to Turin Center courses, and the ILO has operated seminars in Abidjan for some 120 union officials. Trade union approval of the ILO is important in the Ivory Coast context, inasmuch as the general secretary of the federation is a member of Parliament and works closely with the governing political party.

Notes

Copies of many of the documents issued by the ILO that are referred to in these notes are in the possession of the author and will be made available to interested scholars. The *Record of Proceedings* of the ILO and *Minutes* of the ILO Governing Body are available at the ILO libraries, in New York City and Washington, D.C., as are many of the other ILO materials cited. Reports issued by various departments of the U.S. government may be obtained by writing to the specific department; material issued by various congressional committees can be found in the same way if the reader does not have access to a central library that carries such materials.

In addition to the abbreviations used in the text, the notes contain the following shortened forms:

GB	Governing Body
ILC	International Labor Conference
Provisional Record	*Provisional Record of Proceedings*

Chapter 1: Introduction

1 The title was changed to director-general after World War II.
2 The U.S. role in the ILO during this period is described in some detail in John B. Tipton, "Participation of the United States in the International Labor Organization" (Ph.D. diss., University of Illinois, 1959).
3 Quoted in Torsten Landelius, *Workers, Employers, and Governments* (Stockholm, 1965), p. 305.
4 Tipton, "Participation of the United States," p. 47.
5 Antony Alcock, *History of the International Labour Organization* (New York, 1971), p. 159.
6 Quoted in Tipton, "Participation of the United States," p. 70.
7 Press release, Nov. 1, 1977.

8 *New York Times*, Aug. 14, 1977, p. 16.

9 ILC, *Provisional Record*, 63rd sess., 1977, p. 5/13.

10 This is, of course, also true of other international organizations, including the General Assembly of the United Nations, and has given rise to similar problems.

11 ILC, *Standing Orders*, 1975 ed., Article 14(12).

12 Prior to the exclusion of Taiwan from the United Nations, Taiwan held the Chinese seat.

13 ILO, *Director-General's Program and Budget Proposals for 1980–81*, GB. 209/PFA/7/1, 1978, Annex No. 2.

14 ILO, GB, Position Paper for the United States Delegation, 202nd sess., Agenda Item 13, Feb. 7, 1977, p. 29 (mimeographed).

15 The Governing Body debate on this issue is of interest. The then director-general of the ILO, C. Wilfred Jenks, was anxious to consummate transfer of the seat to the People's Republic in the interest of "universality," though he admitted that he had had no contact with the Chinese government regarding its intention to participate in ILO activities. The U.S. government delegate argued that the decision should be made by the conference, not by the Governing Body, while the U.S. trade union delegate opposed the immediate switching of the Chinese seat and favored a two-China policy, which would have preserved Taiwan's membership. The U.S. employers were firmly opposed to change, while the U.S.S.R. supported it. The Governing Body voted 36 to 3 in favor of seating Communist China, with 8 abstentions. ILO, GB, *Minutes*, 184th sess., Nov. 1971, pp. 7ff.

By 1978, China was about $9 million in arrears in its dues payments.

16 ILO, GB, *Draft Minutes*, 202nd sess., March 1977, pp. 1–2.

17 The vote on a structural question was 132 to 2 for the Western side, but 212 abstentions invalidated the resolution for lack of a quorum. On the second issue, involving ILO standards, the vote was 135 to 0, with 197 abstentions, which again meant no quorum. These issues are considered in greater detail in Chap. 2, below.

Chapter 2: The United States and the ILO

1 G. A. Johnston, *The International Labor Organization* (London, 1970), p. 53.

2 U.S., Senate, Committee on Government Operations, *U.S. Participation in International Organizations*, 1977.

3 A recent case in point was a proposed UNESCO declaration that

American newspapers considered inimical to freedom of the press. The *Wall Street Journal* called the watered-down version that was eventually adopted "a piece of thoroughly pernicious claptrap about the press's obligation to promote the UN's approved political agenda." The *Journal* pointed out that after the vote, "the U.S. chief delegate to the meeting called the compromise 'a triumph of spirit, good will and international understanding.' In fact it was no such thing, and it was galling to see our representative behaving as U.S. diplomats have too often done at these gatherings, exhibiting a kind of crazed cheerfulness in the face of yet another erosion of liberal values." The *Wall Street Journal*, Dec. 5, 1978. Other leading newspapers, including the *New York Times*, which even stated that the United States might better withdraw from UNESCO rather than accept the original declaration, reacted in the same way. If the newspaper industry or U.S. educators (who have had other problems with the organization) were an official part of the U.S. representation at UNESCO, U.S. withdrawal would undoubtedly be a real possibility.

4 Interview with Irving Brown, June 1977.

5 See Tipton, "Participation of the United States," pp. 18–67; D. P. Moynihan, "The United States and the International Labour Organization" (Ph.D. diss., Massachusetts Institute of Technology, 1960).

6 Quoted in Tipton, "Participation of the United States," p. 88.

7 Quoted in Alcock, *History of the International Labor Organization*, p. 286.

8 Ibid., pp. 286–88.

9 Quoted in the report of a committee appointed by the Departments of State, Commerce, and Labor to advise them on U.S. participation in the ILO, p. A3 (mimeographed copy in my files). Part of the report of the committee, which was chaired by Joseph E. Johnson, was published in the *Annals of the American Academy of Political and Social Sciences*, March 1957. Herein referred to as the Johnson Committee Report.

10 Alcock, *History of the International Labor Organization*, pp. 307–8.

11 Quoted in Tipton, "Participation of the United States," p. 99.

12 Johnson Committee Report, pp. B–19, B–22, and B–17.

13 Ibid., p. B–39.

14 Ibid., p. B–46.

15 "Measures to Be Taken by the Departments of State, Commerce,

and Labor to Improve US Participation in the ILO," Feb. 28, 1957 (typewritten copy in my files).

16 Among the latter were such countries as Guatemala, Haiti, Nicaragua, Paraguay, China, Iran, Liberia, and Thailand.

17 Staff memorandum submitted to the Johnson Committee, Johnson Committee Report, Appendix I.

18 The worker members of the committee were split 3 to 2. All five government representatives, including those of the United States, voted in the negative.

19 This report appears in ILO, GB, *Minutes*, 83rd sess., April 1938, pp. 94–95.

20 The U.S. worker delegate apparently voted with the majority to show solidarity with the workers' group at the conference. He gave no explanation for his vote.

21 Alcock, *History of the International Labor Organization*, p. 289.

22 ILO, GB, *Minutes*, 125th sess., May 1954, p. 23.

23 Ibid., 127th sess., Nov. 1954, p. 42.

24 For the text of the McNair Committee Report, herein referred to as the McNair Report, see ILO, *Official Bulletin*, 1956, no. 9, p. 475.

25 McNair Report, p. 584. The key phrase in this paragraph is "information supplied by the U.S.S.R." Presumably the three members of the committee, all lawyers, did not have the expertise to reach an independent conclusion on this highly technical problem.

26 Ibid., p. 584.

27 ILC, *Record of Proceedings*, 39th sess., 1956, pp. 133, 134. In the last sentence quoted, the delegate refers to the withdrawal of the democratic trade unions from the Communist-dominated World Federation of Trade Unions in 1949. They then proceeded to form the International Confederations of Free Trade Unions at a conference in London.

28 Ibid., p. 187.

29 ILO, GB, *Minutes*, 133rd sess., Nov. 1956, p. 22.

30 Ibid., p. 29.

31 ILC, *Record of Proceedings*, 43rd sess., 1959, p. 52.

32 ILO, GB, *Minutes*, 143rd sess., Nov. 1959, p. 31.

33 In recent years, P. T. Pimenov, a secretary of the All-Union Central Council of Trade Unions, represented Soviet workers on the Governing Body.

34 For the full text, see ILC, *Record of Proceedings*, 56th sess., 1971, pp. 485–87.

35 Ibid., p. 700.
36 Ibid., p. 702.
37 Henry A. Kissinger to the director-general of the ILO, Nov. 5, 1975, files of the U.S. Department of Labor.
38 Statement of Charles H. Smith, Jr., Nov. 6, 1975, files of the U.S. Department of Labor.
39 Statement of George Meany, Nov. 6, 1975, files of the U.S. Department of Labor.
40 Memorandum of conversation, Nov. 26, 1975, files of the U.S. Department of Labor.
41 Ibid.
42 Kissinger to the director-general of the ILO, Nov. 5, 1975.
43 For example, Earl Warren was a member of the Committee of Experts from his retirement as chief justice of the U.S. Supreme Court until his death.
44 ILO, GB, *Minutes*, 133rd sess., Nov. 1956, p. 21.
45 Ibid., p. 53.
46 Ibid., 135th sess., May–June 1957, pp. 75–76.
47 Ibid., p. 20.
48 Ibid., 137th sess., Oct.–Nov. 1957, p. 31.
49 Ibid., p. 46.
50 Ibid., p. 58.
51 Ibid., p. 74.
52 Ibid., p. 76.
53 Ibid., 138th sess., March 1958, p. 17.
54 Ibid., 139th sess., May–June 1958, p. 27.
55 Ibid., 140th sess., Nov. 1958, p. 48.
56 For a good account of the early history of Soviet trade unions, see Isaac Deutscher, "Russia," in Walter Galenson, ed., *Comparative Labor Movements* (New York, 1952), p. 480.
57 Emily Clark Brown, *Soviet Trade Unions and Labor Relations* (Cambridge, Mass., 1966), p. 319.
58 The reasons for Shelepin's removal and his subsequent fate have never been revealed.
59 There has been a recent unsuccessful attempt, however. See below, Chap. 7.
60 International Labor Office, *The Trade Union Situation in the United States* (Geneva, 1960).
61 ILO, *The Trade Union Situation in the U.S.S.R.* (Geneva, 1960).
62 *AFL-CIO News*, Feb. 25, 1961, p. 2.
63 Ibid., p. 30.

64 Ibid., p. 36.

65 Ibid., p. 84.

66 Ibid., p. 134.

67 Ibid.

68 ILO, GB, *Minutes*, 154th sess., March 1963, p. 50.

69 See Carl Gershman, *The Foreign Policy of American Labor*, The Washington Papers, no. 29 (New York, 1975), p. 30.

70 Ibid., p. 29.

71 Stephen Haseler, "Visas for Soviet Trade Unionists," AFL-CIO *Free Trade Union News*, Feb. 1978, p. 13.

72 See below, Chap. 4.

73 ILO, GB, *Draft Minutes*, 193rd sess., May–June 1974, p. II/5.

74 Ibid., p. II/3.

75 Ibid., p. II/6.

76 See ILC, *Record of Proceedings*, 59th sess., 1974, pp. 538–43.

77 Ibid., pp. 735–36.

78 Ibid., p. 752.

79 Ibid., p. 758.

80 Ibid., p. 753.

81 Ibid., 60th sess., 1975, p. 700.

82 ILO, *Report of the Committee of Experts on the Application of Conventions and Recommendations*, 1976, p. 128.

83 ILC, *Record of Proceedings*, 61st sess., 1976, p. 186.

84 ILO, *Report of the Committee of Experts on the Application of Conventions and Recommendations*, 1977, p. 98.

85 Ibid., p. 135.

86 ILC, *Provisional Record*, 63rd sess., 1977, p. 25/24.

87 Ibid., p. 25/36.

88 Ibid., p. 25/9.

89 See below, pp. 80–81.

90 ILC, *Provisional Record*, 63rd sess., 1977, p. 35/12.

91 Kissinger to the director-general of the ILO, Nov. 5, 1975.

92 This episode is recounted in detail in Alcock, *History of the International Labor Organization*, pp. 318–37. There was an earlier case involving Hungary. In 1958, the conference, under the impact of the Soviet invasion, invalidated the credentials of the Hungarian delegation, despite the plea of the chairman of the Credentials Committee (an Israeli) that this action violated the rule of law.

93 ILC, *Record of Proceedings*, 45th sess., 1961, p. 616.

94 Ibid., 47th sess., 1963, p. 145.

95 "Mr. Borisov, Government delegate of the USSR, gave the signal

for the walkout as Mr. Hamilton mounted the rostrum, amid yells, boos, table pounding and other noises. . . . The noise continued as the Africans, Arabs, Communists and all Worker delegates departed. Many of them went outside the hall, but a number remained in back of the hall, creating a disturbance throughout the South African Employer Delegate's speech." U.S., Department of Labor, report of the U.S. Government Delegate to a Meeting of the International Labor Organization, June 5–26, 1963, p. 17.

96 Alcock, *History of the International Labor Organization*, pp. 324–25.

97 ILC, *Record of Proceedings*, 47th sess., 1963, p. 169.

98 Ibid., p. 263.

99 Alcock, *History of the International Labor Organization*, p. 331.

100 ILO, GB, *Minutes*, 156th sess., June 1963, p. 25.

101 Ibid., 157th sess., Nov. 1963, p. 23.

102 Ibid., 158th sess., Feb. 1964, p. 10.

103 Ibid., 159th sess., June–July 1964, p. 147.

104 ILC, *Record of Proceedings*, 48th sess., 1964, p. 506.

105 A specific provision for this procedure appears in Article 26 of the ILO constitution.

106 For the full report, see ILO, *Official Bulletin*, 1962, no. 2.

107 ILO, GB, *Minutes*, 151st sess., March 1962, p. 16.

108 ILC, *Record of Proceedings*, 49th sess., 1965, p. 697.

109 Ibid., p. 445.

110 Ibid., 57th sess., 1972, p. 707. In this, as in the South African case, the AFL-CIO was apparently motivated by a desire to seem even-handed in condemning totalitarian practices of the Right as well as of the Left. But in doing so, it violated a basic principle of procedure and reduced the effectiveness of its protests in subsequent cases.

111 U.S., Department of Labor, unpublished study, 1976, pp. 15–16 (mimeographed copy in my files).

112 ILO, GB, *Draft Minutes*, 191st sess., Nov. 1973, p. IX/6.

113 Ibid., 192nd sess., Feb.–March 1974, p. V/3.

114 Ibid., p. V/7.

115 ILC, *Record of Proceedings*, 59th sess., 1974, p. 487.

116 Ibid., p. 488. In the ILO context, this was tantamount to a negative vote.

117 Ibid., pp. 713–14.

118 Ibid., p. 702.

119 ILO, GB, *Draft Minutes*, 194th sess., Nov. 1974, pp. IV/7–9.

120 Ibid., 195th sess., March 1975, p. IV/5.
121 Ibid., 196th sess., May 1975, p. IV/1.
122 Ibid., pp. IV/2–4.
123 ILC, *Record of Proceedings*, 60th sess., 1975, pp. 803, 807, 823.
124 ILO, GB, *Draft Minutes*, 198th sess., Nov. 1975, pp. VIII/20–24.
125 Ibid., 200th sess., May–June 1976, pp. III/4–6.
126 Ibid., 202nd sess., March 1977, p. VI/3.
127 Ibid., p. VI/3.
128 The question of the role of the Palestine Liberation Organization at the ILO is a separate one; it is treated below, in the section on "politicization."
129 ILC, *Record of Proceedings*, 58th sess., 1973, pp. 653–54.
130 Ibid., p. 651.
131 Ibid., p. 707.
132 Ibid., 59th sess., 1974, pp. 477–78.
133 ILO, GB, *Draft Minutes*, 194th sess., Nov. 1974, p. VII/4.
134 Ibid., 195th sess., March 1975, pp. I/6–10, and 196th sess., May 1975, pp. IV/16–18.
135 Ibid., 199th sess., March 1976, p. VIII/13.
136 Ibid., p. 15.
137 Ibid., p. 16.
138 For the details of Office action, see ILO, *Report of the Director-General to the International Labor Conference*, 1977, pt. 2, pp. 42–59.
139 ILO, GB, *Draft Minutes*, 202nd sess., March 1977, p. V/11. This action was regarded by U.S. representatives as a very encouraging sign. The U.S. government member was quoted as saying that the vote represented an "important step toward the return to basic principles," a view shared by both labor and employer representatives. *New York Times*, March 6, 1977, p. 8.
140 The Soviet objections were based on a misinterpretation of international law. The committee was merely recognizing the presence of Israel in the occupied territories and never referred to Israel as having sovereignty over the area.
141 ILC, *Provisional Record*, 63rd sess., 1977, pp. 25/52–62.
142 Ibid., p. 31/18.
143 For the text of the proposed amendment, see ILC, *Provisional Record*, 63rd sess., 1977, p. IV/1.
144 ILO, GB, *Draft Minutes*, 202nd sess., March 1977, p. IV/1.
145 Ibid., p. III/5.
146 See below, Chap. 3.

147 ILC, *Provisional Record*, 63rd sess., 1977, p. 7/16.

148 Ibid., pp. 7/22–23.

149 Ibid., p. 35/5.

150 Kissinger to the director-general of the ILO, Nov. 5, 1975.

151 ILC, *Record of Proceedings*, 59th sess., 1974, p. 385.

152 Ibid., 60th sess., 1975, p. 236.

153 Ibid., pp. 259–60.

154 Ibid., pp. 256–58.

155 See below, Chap. 5.

156 *New York Times*, June 17, 1976, p. C12.

157 AFL-CIO *Free Trade Union News*, Nov. 1975, p. 13.

158 Files of the U.S. Department of Labor.

159 *Report of the U.S. Delegation to a Meeting of the International Labour Organization*, ILC, 51st sess., June 1967, pp. 58–61.

160 Ibid., ILC, 52nd sess., June 1968, p. 40. The reference was to the Soviet invasion of Czechoslovakia.

161 ILC, *Record of Proceedings*, 54th sess., 1971, pp. 463–64.

162 Ibid., 57th sess., 1972, p. 99. The tougher line adopted by the U.S. government was undoubtedly connected to the imbroglio surrounding the U.S. withholding of its contribution to the ILO in 1970. The change of the federal administration in 1969 and the replacement of George L. P. Weaver as the principal U.S. government representative to the ILO were other contributing factors.

Chapter 3: Structural and Operational Problems of the ILO

1 For a tabulation of Governing Body members by country, see Landelius, *Workers, Employers, and Governments*, pp. 127–35.

2 Since 1963, 60 percent of the total weight has been based on national income, 30 percent on budget contribution, and 10 percent on economically active population. A heavier weight to the population factor might have resulted in a considerable reallocation of seats, with some of the larger less developed nations—Indonesia, Pakistan, and Brazil, for example—replacing the smaller Western European nations.

3 ILC, *Report of the Working Party on Structure*, 61st sess., 1976, pp. 58–59.

4 Ibid., 60th sess., 1975, p. 28.

5 Ibid., pp. 27–28.

6 Ibid., p. 35/2.

7 Ibid., p. 23.

8 ILO, GB, *Minutes*, 183rd sess., May–June 1971, p. 32.

9 ILC, *Structure of the ILO*, Report IX, 59th sess., 1974, p. 55.

10 *Report of the Working Party on Structure*, 1975, p. 33.

11 *Structure of the ILO*, 1974, p. 57.

12 *Report of the Working Party on Structure*, 1976, pp. 54, 72.

13 ILO, GB, *Minutes* 182nd sess., March 1971, pp. 30–31.

14 ILC, *Record of Proceedings*, 58th sess., 1973, pp. 664–67.

15 *Structure of the ILO*, 1974, pp. 30–36.

16 *Report of the Working Party on Structure*, 1975, pp. 16–18.

17 ILC, *Record of Proceedings*, 62nd sess., 1976, p. 244.

18 U.S. labor and employer delegates did respond in kind to Soviet attacks on U.S. policy, but they attempted to concentrate on freedom of association and other relevant issues—as, for example, their criticism of the appointment of a former head of the KGB as chairman of the All-Union Central Council of Trade Unions. For a good summary of these responses, see the annual reports of the U.S. delegation to the ILO from 1964 to 1970.

19 ILC, *General Review of the Reports of the Working Party on Program and Structure*, 53rd sess., 1969, pp. 178–80.

20 Ibid., p. 209.

21 ILC, *Record of Proceedings*, 54th sess., 1970, p. 133.

22 Ibid., p. 144.

23 Ibid., p. 219.

24 Ibid., p. 244.

25 Ibid., pp. 464–65.

26 This change of policy coincided with a change in government personnel representing the United States and an obvious switch to a tougher line after the stoppage by Congress of U.S. funds for the ILO.

27 ILO, GB, *Minutes*, 185th sess., Feb.–March 1972, pp. 151–53.

28 ILC, *Record of Proceedings*, 58th sess., 1973, p. 8.

29 *Report of the Working Party on Structure*, 1975, p. 43.

30 U.S., House of Representatives, Committee on Appropriations, *Hearings Before the Subcommittee for the Department of State*, 1973, p. 634.

31 U.S., Senate, Committee on Government Operations, *U.S. Participation in International Organizations*, 1977, pp. 117–21.

32 See, for example, John T. Fishburn, "A Report on the International Labor Organization," 1970, p. 56 (mimeographed), files of the U.S. Department of Labor.

33 Comptroller General of the United States, *U.S. Participation in the*

International Labour Organization Not Effectively Managed, 1970, p. 22.

34 See ILC, *Record of Proceedings*, 63rd sess., 1977, p. 23; *U.S. Participation in International Organizations*, pp. 52–54.

35 *U.S. Participation in International Organizations*, p. 52.

36 *U.S. Participation in the International Labour Office Not Effectively Managed*, pp. 23–24.

37 *U.S. Participation in International Organizations*, p. 55.

38 Ibid., p. 57.

39 Fishburn, "Report on the International Labor Organization," p. 55.

40 *U.S. Participation in International Organizations*, p. 52.

41 U.S. House of Representatives, *Hearings Before a Subcommittee of the Committee on Appropriations*, Pt. 5, 1970, p. 57. A few years later, when the ILO was seeking a list of Americans from which the ILO might choose a deputy director-general, Meany refused to let the U.S. government submit more than one name.

42 *New York Times*, July 22, 1979, p. 1.

43 *Hearings Before a Subcommittee of the Committee on Appropriations*, p. 48. The article in question was written by a Russian, and certainly does not represent the attitude of the ILO staff; the publication of this piece of pure propaganda in the official ILO journal was a political error.

44 Interested readers are invited to examine the following articles, *inter alia*, that have appeared recently in the *International Labour Review*: V. Poliakov and A. Selen, "Personnel Management in Soviet Undertakings," Dec. 1972, p. 527; M. Lantser, "Progress in Social Security for Agricultural Workers in the USSR," March 1973, p. 239; S. V. Ivanov, "New Codification of Soviet Labor Law," Aug.–Sept. 1973, p. 143; Alexander Kotlyar, "Problems of Younger Workers in the USSR," April 1974, p. 359; L. Khitrov, "The Role of Management and Workers in Raising the Efficiency of Soviet Industry," June 1975, p. 507; Svetlana Turchaninova, "Trends in Women's Employment in the USSR," Oct. 1975, p. 253; L. P. Yakushev, "Old People's Rights in the USSR and Other European Socialist Countries," March–April 1976, p. 243.

45 Fishburn, "Report on the International Labor Organization," p. 58. This characterization of the distribution of honors as the "single greatest Russian threat" is extreme. Other Soviet activities obviously create equally serious problems for the United States.

46 In 1966, however, a Polish government delegate was elected to the presidency of the conference.

47 Memorandum of conversation, Geneva, Nov. 26, 1975.

Chapter 4: The U.S. Decision to Withdraw

1 This certainly was the perception held by David Morse, former ILO director-general. In a conversation with Joseph Sisco, a high State Department official, he expressed the view that the threat of labor's nonparticipation gave the AFL-CIO a veto on U.S. foreign policy in the ILO. Memorandum of conversation, Sept. 29, 1965, Morse Papers, Princeton University Library.

2 Comptroller General, *U.S. Participation in the International Labour Organization Not Effectively Managed*, passim.

3 See U.S., House of Representatives, *Hearings Before a Subcommittee of the Committee on Appropriations*, 1970, p. 66.

4 Memorandum of luncheon meeting at Ambassador Tubby's residence, Nov. 14, 1967, Morse Papers, Princeton University Library.

5 Memorandum of meeting in the director-general's office, April 17, 1970, Morse Papers, Princeton University Library.

6 Ibid.

7 Statement of George H. Hildebrand, *Hearings Before a Subcommittee of the Committee on Appropriations*, p. 71.

8 Jenks first raised the issue with the officers of the Governing Body on June 24, 1970. He told them that "Mr. Morse indicated that he envisioned making such an appointment in August." The chairman of the employer group expressed his opposition to the appointment, while the chairman of the workers' group accepted the appointment, "with no great enthusiasm," because the workers were split. ILO, GB, *Minutes of the Meeting of the Officers of the Governing Body*, June 24, 1970.

9 *Hearings Before a Subcommittee of the Committee on Appropriations*, p. 1.

10 Ibid., p. 58.

11 Ibid., p. 69.

12 ILO, GB, *Minutes*, 181st sess., Nov. 1970, p. 56.

13 Ibid., 182nd sess., March 1971, p. 73.

14 "The United States and the ILO: The Problem and a Plan of Action," Feb. 16, 1971 (mimeographed), files of the U.S. Department of Labor.

15 U.S., House of Representatives, *Hearings Before a Subcommittee of the Committee on Appropriations of the Departments of State, Justice, and Commerce*, 1972, pp. 1118–37.

16 Bert Seidman, "Hopeful Developments and 1972 Conference at ILO," AFL-CIO *Free Trade Union News*, Aug. 1972, p. 4.

17 The ILO had been obliged to cancel meetings and freeze office staff vacancies. The working capital fund of the organization was drawn upon and almost depleted. Because of U.S. budgeting procedures, it was not until 1976 that the United States was fully paid up.

18 Bert Seidman and Michael Boggs, "Keeping the ILO on a True Course," AFL-CIO *Free Trade Union News*, July 1973, p. 1.

19 ILO, GB, *Minutes*, 190th sess., June 1973, p. 67.

20 Ibid., pp. 68–71. The charges were not made specific, and there is no evidence that the allegation was true.

21 Michael Boggs, "The ILO's Rocky Road," AFL-CIO *Free Trade Union News*, Sept. 1974, p. 1.

22 ILC, *Record of Proceedings*, 59th sess., 1974, p. 658.

23 Bert Seidman, "The Future of the ILO," AFL-CIO *Free Trade Union News*, Jan. 1975, p. 10.

24 AFL-CIO *Free Trade Union News*, Oct. 1975, p. 1.

25 This and subsequent references are to a report termed "ministudy," completed in September 1975 and available in the files of the U.S. Department of Labor.

26 Memorandum of William B. Buffum to Joel E. Segal, July 28, 1975, ibid.

27 Comptroller General of the United States, *Need for U.S. Objectives in the International Labour Organization*, Document B–168767, May 15, 1977, p. 18.

28 Ibid., p. 14.

29 Ibid., p. 14.

30 Interview with James Steiner, U.S. Chamber of Commerce, June 1977. Mr. Steiner also noted that he had been devoting only half his time to ILO affairs.

31 *Need for U.S. Objectives*, p. 23.

32 Ibid., p. 17.

33 Ibid., p. 24.

34 AFL-CIO Department of Public Relations, press release, Nov. 6, 1975.

35 U.S. Chamber of Commerce, press release, Nov. 6, 1975.

36 AFL-CIO *Free Trade Union News*, Feb.–March 1976, p. 1.

37 Lane Kirkland, in AFL-CIO *Free Trade Union News*, July 1976, p. 3.

38 *Washington Post*, June 29, 1977, p. A16.

39 *New York Times*, Oct. 12, 1977, p. A24.

40 Text of speech by Charles H. Smith, Jr., Sept. 13, 1977, in files of U.S. Department of Labor.
41 *New York Times*, Oct. 5, 1977, p. D7.
42 AFL-CIO *Free Trade Union News*, March 1978, p. 4. The article was written by Jorgen Schleimann and had originally appeared in *Jyllandposten*, Nov. 7, 1977.
43 *Department of State Bulletin* 78, no. 2011:48.
44 *Need for U.S. Objectives*, p. 39.

Chapter 5: The ILO's Technical Cooperation Program

1 Comptroller General of the United States, *Need for U.S. Objectives in the International Labor Organization*, p. 3.
2 The U.S. Agency for International Development (AID) has devised an elaborate evaluation system. The question of whether it is effective in the sense of revealing defects in project design and execution merits much closer attention than it has received.
3 ILO, *Technical Cooperation: New Prospects and Dimensions*, Report of the Director-General to the International Labour Conference, 1977, pp. 88–89.
4 This is the opinion of Peter Kilby, an experienced development economist, who wrote as follows: "Evaluating technical assistance is a tough business. Comparatively speaking, I think the ILO does a good job." Kilby to the author, Nov. 11, 1977.
5 In preparing the draft budget for 1978–79, the ILO used the same exchange rate as that adopted for the 1976–77 budget: Sw. fr. 2.51 to $1. It was estimated that each centime of reduction in the relative value of the dollar would cost the ILO $320,000 over the entire biennium. Thus, the decline in the dollar to about Sw. fr. 1.80 in 1978 would have meant a real loss of almost $23 million over the biennium, or about 14 percent of the total budget. See ILO, *Director-General's Program and Budget Proposals for 1978–79*, Dec. 1976, pp. 21, 36.
6 The problems posed for the ILO by UNDP financing are discussed below.
7 The project number was JAM/72/004, and the document containing the Project Findings and Recommendations, issued in Geneva, was dated 1975.
8 Ibid., p. 18.
9 The project was designated as CYP/63/504 and CYP/71/514, and the Project Findings and Recommendations documents were dated 1974.

10 Ibid., p. 14.

11 ILO, GB, *Report of the Committee on Operational Programs*, GB. 184/14/26, 1971, p. 3.

12 Ibid., GB. 191/19/41, 1973, p. 5.

13 Ibid., GB. 198/17/38, 1975, p. 4.

14 Ibid., GB. 201/17/37, 1976, p. 4.

15 The annual summary reports of the Office to the Governing Body are considered below.

16 ILO, GB, *Report of Tripartite Evaluation Teams*, GB. 201/09/3/3, 1976, App., p. 8.

17 ILO, GB, *Report of the Tripartite Team*, GB. 199/6/5, 1976, App., p. 7.

18 Quoted in Peter Kilby and Paul Bangasser, Jr., "Evaluating Technical Assistance: The Case of Rural Industry," ILO World Employment Program Working Paper, Geneva, July 1977, pp. 3–4.

19 The 1967 data are from ILO, *Technical Cooperation: New Prospects and Dimensions*, p. 8.

20 ILO, GB, *Minutes*, 190th sess., June 1973, p. 28.

21 ILO, *Technical Cooperation: New Prospects and Dimensions*, p. 31.

22 The standard costing figure of $55,000 a year per expert was reportedly being used in Malaysia in 1978. This figure, however, was gross of a 14 percent agency overhead. At the same time, the poverty line for Malaysian households was drawn at $295 a year, and it was estimated that more than 45 percent of all households were below that level.

23 See, for example, ILO, GB, *Report of the African Advisory Committee on Its Sixth Session*, GB. 199/6/4, 1976, p. 21.

24 ILO, GB, *ILO Technical Cooperation Activities in 1974*, GB. 198/OP/1/2, 1975.

25 ILO, GB, *ILO Technical Cooperation Activities in 1975–76*, GB. 201/OP/1/1, 1976.

26 ILO, GB, *In-Depth Review of the Management Development Program*, GB. 191/PEA/8/5, 1973.

27 ILO, GB, *ILO Technical Cooperation Activities in 1975–76*, pp. 39–40.

28 ILO, GB, *In-Depth Review of Rural Development*, GB. 201/PFA/13/1, 1976, p. 13. "Other" includes training of managers of rural development projects, support to rural workers' organizations, and action to improve conditions in rural areas.

29 For a statement of the program's purpose by its director, see Jef

Rens, "The Development of the Andean Program and Its Future," *International Labour Review*, Dec. 1963, p. 547.

30 See P. Mueller and K. H. Zevering, "Employment Promotion through Rural Development: A Pilot Project in Western Nigeria," *International Labour Review*, Aug. 1969, p. 111.

31 It is just as important to analyze project failures as successes if future mistakes are to be avoided. The practice among international agencies is to give considerable publicity to new programs and to let them slip into obscurity when the expected results do not materialize. This practice greatly adds to the difficulty of evaluation.

32 ILO, GB, *In-Depth Review of Rural Development*, 1976, p. 2.

33 Ibid., p. 18.

34 Ibid., GB 201/PFA/11/12, 1977.

35 ILO, GB, *In-Depth Review of the Social Security Program*, GB. 185/FA/12/9, 1972, p. 25.

36 ILO, GB, *Second Report of the Administrative and Financial Committee*, GB. 186/7/22, 1972, p. 7.

37 ILO, GB, *In-Depth Review of the Social Security Program*, GB. 186/FA/11/11, 1972, p. 6.

38 ILO, GB, *In-Depth Review of the Workers' Education Program*, GB. 188/PA/9/4, 1972.

39 ILO, GB, *Report of the Tripartite Team*.

40 See ILO, GB, *Draft Minutes*, 199th sess., March 1976, p. IV/3. He may have been referring to the fact that the report criticized the government, in mild terms, for not having given "as much importance to employers' and workers' organizations as to government authorities."

41 ILO, GB, *Report of Tripartite Evaluation Teams*, p. 9.

42 Ibid., p. 11.

43 Ibid., p. 11.

44 Kilby and Bangasser, "Evaluating Technical Assistance." A somewhat abbreviated version of this report appeared in the *International Labour Review*, May–June 1978, pp. 343–53, and subsequent quotations are from this version. Only three of the case histories were made available to me by the ILO.

45 United Nations Development Program, *Why What How Where* (New York, 1978), p. 15.

46 Kilby and Bangasser, "Evaluating Technical Asistance," Working Paper, pp. 11–12.

47 ILO, GB, *ILO Technical Cooperation Activities in 1975–76*, p. 25.

48 See Alcock, *History of the International Labor Organization*, pp. 346–51, for a history of the ILO–UNIDO negotiations.

49 I was present at a meeting of ILO regional and local officials in an Asian city, convened at the request of a UNDP representative from New York. He explained that the UNDP was evaluating all labor and manpower programs in Asia and, without preliminary warning, asked the ILO officials to prepare, within three days, detailed descriptions of all projects under way and precise estimates of future needs for everything in the manpower field, including projections of manpower requirements by detailed occupation and skill categories. The discussion became quite heated when the ILO people protested that they could not possibly secure the information in so short a time, and perhaps not at all. In the end, they agreed to meet the request. One wonders what use UNDP bureaucrats in New York could possibly have for such information, and how it could help them in programming Asian manpower projects.

50 See ILO, *Report of the Director-General to the International Labor Conference*, 1978, p. xi.

51 See Appendix B.

52 ILO, *The World Employment Program* (Geneva, 1969), p. 7.

53 Ibid., pp. 122–23.

54 ILC, *Record of Proceedings*, 53rd sess., 1969, p. 119. That there was some confusion in Washington about the program is suggested by the use of the word "continues." The program had just begun, and no one had yet been offered any "practical solutions."

55 Ibid., p. 125.

56 Ibid., pp. 393–95.

57 Ibid., p. 80.

58 ILO, *Towards Full Employment* (Geneva, 1970).

59 A few recommendations that were adopted led to interesting results. The abolition of licensing for taxicabs to permit greater employment for "gypsy" cab drivers caused an increase in the accident rate; as a result, the restoration of licensing became necessary.

60 Martin Godfrey, "The ILO Kenya Report and Basic Needs," Kenya Seminar, Nairobi, April 18–23, 1977, p. 8 (typewritten).

61 ILO, *World Employment Program: Research in Retrospect and Prospect* (Geneva, 1976).

62 Erik Thorbecke, "A Comprehensive Evaluation of the Research Component of the World Employment Program of the ILO," Oct. 1976 (mimeographed).

63 Among them might be mentioned Amartya Sen, *Employment,*

Technology, and Development (Oxford, 1975); Mark Blaug, *Education and the Employment Problem in the Developing Countries* (Geneva, 1973); A. S. Bhalla, *Technology and Employment in Industry* (Geneva, 1975); H. F. Lydall, *Trade and Employment* (Geneva, 1975).

64 ILO, GB, *Draft Minutes*, 195th sess., March 1975, p. II/3.

65 Ibid., 196th sess., May 1975, p. II/3.

66 Advisory Panel of Consultants, Tripartite World Conference on Employment, Aug. 1975.

67 ILO, GB, *Draft Minutes*, 198th sess., Nov. 1975, pp. VIII/5–11.

68 U.S., Department of Labor, Summary of Meeting with Mr. Louis Emmerij, Dec. 17, 1975.

69 Edward B. Persons to Louis Emmerij, Jan. 8, 1976, files of the U.S. Department of Labor.

70 C. H. Smith, Jr., to Louis Emmerij, Dec. 18, 1975, files of the U.S. Department of Labor.

71 C. H. Smith, Jr., to Francis Blanchard, Dec. 18, 1975, files of the U.S. Department of Labor.

72 ILO, *Employment, Growth and Basic Needs* (Geneva, 1976), p. 49 (italics supplied).

73 Ibid., p. 48.

74 Walter Galenson, "Economic Growth, Poverty, and the International Agencies," *Journal of Policy Modeling* 1, no. 2 (1979):251.

75 This view received some confirmation in a speech by Sri Lanka's minister of labor at the 1979 ILO conference. Sri Lanka was a pioneer of the basic needs approach in distributing free rice rations, among other things. He said: "The impressive advances in welfare and the quality of life that characterize this approach have, however, not been achieved without cost. They have indeed been achieved at high cost: economic growth has been foregone, and there has been a steady deterioration in Sri Lanka's terms of trade over the years, leading to the pursuit of an inward looking economic policy by the previous Government. Such policies involved the imposition of stringent controls and irksome restrictions which further inhibited economic growth." ILC, *Provisional Record*, 65th sess., 1979, p. 15/17.

76 For a good description of these events, see the articles by A. H. Raskin in the *New York Times*, June 18, 1976, p. 1, and June 19, 1976, p. 1.

77 U.S. Delegation Report, *World Conference on Employment* (Geneva, 1976), p. 29.

78 The instructions to the delegation included a mandate to secure the removal of this phrase, which was generally recognized as a code word for a Marxist solution. A majority of the Western European nations, however, declined to back a U.S. initiative to this end, although Germany and Japan, among others, were willing to push for such an amendment.

79 For the text of the report, see ILO, *Meeting Basic Needs* (Geneva, 1977).

80 ILO, GB, *Draft Minutes*, 201st sess., Nov. 1976, p. II/7.

81 U.N. General Assembly, Doc. A/33/206, Sept. 6, 1978, pp. 76–77.

82 *New York Times*, June 19, 1976, p. 28.

83 ILO, *Follow-Up of the World Employment Conference: Basic Needs*, ILC, 65th sess., 1979, p. 10.

84 Ibid., p. 107.

85 Ibid., p. 38.

86 ILC, *Provisional Record*, 65th sess., 1979, p. 42/15.

87 ILO, GB, *Minutes*, 153rd sess., 1962, p. 33. There was also some fear that the trainees might fall under the influence of the Communist trade union movement of Italy, which was strong in Turin.

88 Ibid., 155th sess., 1963, p. 9.

89 U.S., Department of Labor, "The United States and the ILO,"

Chapter 6: The Setting of International Labor Standards

1 ILO, GB, *In-Depth Review of International Labor Standards*, GB. 194/PFA/12/5, 1974, p. 15.

2 The ILO classifies the conventions into the following categories: basic human rights, labor administration, employment policy and human resources development, industrial relations, general conditions of employment, employment of children and young persons, employment of women, industrial safety and health, social security, migration, seafarers, social policy, and plantations.

3 ILO, GB, Reply of U.S. Government, in *In-Depth Review of ILO Programs*, GB. 198/PFA/11/22, 1975, p. 67.

4 Johnson Committee Report, pp. B24–29.

5 ILO, GB, Statement by Edwin P. Neilan, *In-Depth Review of the General Conditions of Work Programs*, GB. 189/WP/GCW/1, 1973, pp. 18–19.

6 ILO, GB, Statement by Bert Seidman, in *In-Depth Review of International Labor Standards*, GB. 194/12/48, 1974, p. 2.

7 See Paul F. Power, "American Employer Behavior in the Interna-

tional Labor Organization," *Midwest Journal of Political Science*, May 1968, p. 274.

8 ILO, GB, *In-Depth Review of International Labor Standards*, GB. 194/12/48, 1974, p. 4.

9 Ibid., p. 3.

10 For an exception to this rule, see below, note 16.

11 U.S., Department of Labor, "The United States and the ILO'," pp. 49–50.

12 U.S., Department of Labor, *U.S. Interests in the ILO*, p. 35.

13 The question of ratification still remains an issue with the return of the United States to the ILO.

14 ILO, GB, *In-Depth Review of ILO Programs*, 1975, p. 67.

15 ILO, GB, *In-Depth Review of International Labor Standards*, GB. 199/9/22 (rev.), 1976, pp. 9–11.

16 Actually, any *conference* delegate, including a government representative, may raise a complaint of noncompliance regardless of the ratification status of his own country, under Article 26 of the ILO constitution. However, use of this avenue would have opened the United States to counterattack for failing to ratify.

17 For a detailed account of how the machinery evolved, see E. A. Landy, *The Effectiveness of International Supervision* (London 1966).

18 Frank McCulloch, an American who has been very active on the committee, was reappointed to a three-year term in November 1977.

19 ILC, *Report of the Committee of Experts*, 64th sess., 1978, pp. 27–29.

20 Ibid., pp. 147, 87, 93, 98.

21 Ernst B. Haas, *Beyond the Nation-State* (Stanford, Calif., 1964), p. 257. To reduce the bulk of the annual reports, the committee has adopted the practice of sending about two-thirds of its observations directly to the countries concerned and limiting its published report to the more serious cases.

22 ILO, *The Impact of International Labor Conventions and Recommendations* (Geneva 1976), pp. 66–67.

23 See Landy, *The Effectiveness of International Supervision*, p. 66; and Haas, *Beyond the Nation-State*, p. 269.

24 Ernst B. Haas, *Human Rights and International Action* (Stanford, Calif., 1970), p. 29.

25 ILO, GB, *In-Depth Review of International Labor Standards*, GB. 194/PFA/12/5, 1974, p. 32.

26 ILO, *The Impact of International Labor Conventions and Recommendations.*

27 "Where human rights are concerned, the contribution of ILO standards has been immense" (Ibid., p. 7); "A genuine world community has begun to take the place of what had previously been purely a society of States—and the ILO has made a significant contribution to this change" (ibid., p. 4).

28 Ibid., p. 30.

29 ILO, GB, *In-Depth Review of International Labor Standards*, GB. 199/9/22 (rev.), 1976, p. 2.

30 U.S. Chamber of Commerce, press release, Nov. 6, 1975.

31 ILO, *The Impact of International Labor Conventions and Recommendations*, p. 33.

32 One of the reasons for choosing this as an illustration is that I was a member of the expert group charged with drafting the last minimum wage convention and am therefore familiar with its background.

33 ILO, *Minimum Wage Fixing and Economic Development* (Geneva, 1968), pp. 157–59.

34 For the full text of the convention, see ILC, *Report V(1)*, 54th sess., 1970, p. 38.

35 The reality of the minimum wage program is well illustrated by comments made by the government of Zambia about an ILO program review. It pointed out that in some developing countries excessive minimum wages may have reduced employment and widened the gap between the earnings of urban and rural workers. In other countries, enforcement is lax, and workers accept much lower wages simply to keep themselves alive. "These problems are serious in the developing countries where lack of reliable or even basic statistics on wages, productivity levels, etc., makes it very difficult to implement the concept of Convention No. 131." ILO, GB, GB. 189/WP/GCW/3, 1973, p. 6. One should not infer that minimum wage legislation is always inappropriate for less developed countries. On the contrary, there are circumstances where it may be of great help to lower-paid workers without unduly affecting employment. In such cases, the influence of ILO standards may be quite positive.

36 ILO, GB, *In-Depth Review of International Labor Standards*, GB. 199/PFA/7/12, 1976, p. 8.

37 ILO, GB, *Report of the Working Party on the In-Depth Review of*

the General Conditions of Work Programs, GB. 192/10/1, 1974, p. 7.

38 Landy, *The Effectiveness of International Supervision*, p. 83.

39 In the case of some less developed countries, particularly in Africa, conventions were ratified for them by colonial powers prior to their independence. Very few have been renounced subsequently, however.

40 Landy, *The Effectiveness of International Supervision*, p. 210.

41 Haas, *Beyond the Nation-State* pp. 259–65.

42 Ibid., p. 291.

43 ILC, *Report of the Committee of Experts on the Application of Conventions and Recommendations*, 64th sess., 1978, pp. 31, 224.

44 ILO, *The Impact of International Labor Conventions and Recommendations*, p. 43.

45 Ibid., p. 50.

46 Ibid., p. 45.

47 Nicolas Valticos, assistant director-general of the ILO, to Walter Galenson, Nov. 22, 1977.

48 Ibid.

49 Where ratification occurred less than three years from the end of the period covered, the country was excluded. This allowed some time for the ratification to take effect.

50 Haas, *Human Rights and International Action*.

51 Ibid., pp. 44–46.

52 Ibid., pp. 91–92.

53 ILO, *The Impact of International Labor Conventions and Recommendations*, p. 52.

54 ILO, *Abolition of Forced Labor*, (Geneva, 1979).

55 For the text of the report, see ILO, *Official Bulletin*, 1969, no. 4.

56 ILO, GB, *Minutes*, 176th sess., June 1969, p. 71.

57 ILO, *The Impact of International Labor Standards and Recommendations*, p. 74.

58 ILO, GB, *Minutes*, 181st sess., November 1970, p. 38.

59 Ibid., p. 33.

60 Ibid., 182nd sess., March 1971, p. 9.

61 Ibid., pp. 10–11.

62 Ibid., 184th sess., November 1971, pp. 75–76.

63 ILC, *Record of Proceedings*, 60th sess., 1975, pp. 94, 329.

64 For an account of the commission and its work, see Morris Hand-

saker and Marjorie Handsaker, "The ILO and Japanese Public Employee Unions," *Industrial Relations*, Oct. 1967, p. 80.

65 ILC, *Report of the Committee of Experts*, 64th sess., 1978, Report III, Part 4A, p. 142.

66 Haas, *Human Rights and International Action*, p. 100.

67 See International Labor Office, *The Trade Union Situation in Chile* (Geneva, 1975).

68 This had also been done for the study group report on Spain.

69 AFL-CIO *Free Trade Union News*, Feb. 1977.

70 ILO, GB, *Report of the Committee on Freedom of Association*, GB. 204/13/18, 1977, pp. 2–7.

71 Ibid., GB. 205/11/12, 1978, pp. 31–37.

72 Ibid., GB. 206/6/18, 1978.

73 ILO, GB, *Draft Minutes*, 194th sess., November 1974, p. II/2.

74 Ibid., 195th sess., March 1975, pp. III/9–11.

75 Ibid., 196th sess., May 1975, pp. I/1–2.

76 Ibid., 198th sess., November 1975, pp. I/1–2.

77 Ibid., pp. VI/3–6.

78 Ibid., 199th sess., March 1976, pp. V/5–7.

79 Ibid., 200th sess., May 1976, p. I/3.

80 Ibid., 204th sess., November 1977, p. I/4.

81 ILC, *Report of the Committee of Experts*, 64th sess., 1978, Report III, Part 4A, pp. 138–39; ibid., 65th sess., 1979, Report III, Part 4A, pp. 123–24.

82 ILC, *Provisional Record*, 64th sess., 1978, p. 14/21.

83 ILO, GB, *Report of the Committee on Freedom of Association*, GB. 206/6/15, 1978, p. 2.

84 Ibid., GB. 204/13/15, 1977, p. 5.

85 Ibid., GB. 206/6/15, 1978, pp. 1–4. The military takeover in July 1980 may lead to a reopening of the matter.

86 Ibid., GB. 205/11/14, 1978, p. 2.

87 Ibid., GB. 204/13/16, 1977.

88 Ibid., GB. 205/11/14, 1978.

89 Ibid., GB. 206/6/16, 1978, p. 7.

90 Ibid., GB. 202/8/11, 1977, p. 35.

91 Ibid., GB. 203/12/23, 1977, pp. 10–11.

92 A particularly unfortunate case concerned Antonio Vitaic Jakasa, for many years a member of the ILO Governing Body representing the Argentine employers. When he failed to appear at a meeting of the Governing Body in May 1977, inquiries were made as to his whereabouts. It was subsequently revealed that he disappeared on the

eve of his departure for Geneva. Although some believe that his disappearance was somehow connected with his ILO position, no additional information was forthcoming from the Argentine government or from any other source.

93 ILO, GB, *Draft Minutes*, 204th sess., November 1977, p. VI/7.

94 ILO, GB, *Report of the Committee on Freedom of Association*, GB. 205/11/15, 1978; ibid., GB. 206/11/15, 1978.

95 See Chap. VII, however, for the cases brought against the U.S.S.R. and Czechoslovakia subsequent to the U.S. withdrawal from the ILO.

96 The industries are inland transport, coal mining, iron and steel, metal trades, textiles, petroleum, construction, chemicals, salaried employees and professional workers, and plantations.

97 For a good discussion of the problem of allocating industrial committee seats, see ILO, GB, *Minutes*, 181st sess., November 1970, pp. 108ff.

98 Ibid., p. 84.

99 ILO, GB, *Draft Minutes*, 201st sess., November 1976, p. VIII/25.

100 For strong statements by U.S. government, worker, and employer delegates in favor of the prevailing system, see ILO, GB, *Draft Minutes*, 190th sess., June 1973, pp. 138–40.

101 See ILO, Building, Civil Engineering, and Public Works Committee, *Note on the Proceedings*, 9th sess.. 1977, pp. 47–53, 79–82.

102 Ibid., p. 14.

103 Ibid., p. 13.

104 Haas, *Beyond the Nation-State*, pp. 310–11.

105 ILO, *The Impact of International Labor Conventions and Recommendations*, p. 80.

106 ILO, GB, *Minutes*, 174th sess., March 1969, pp. 20–21.

107 ILO, GB, *Draft Minutes*, 196th sess., May 1975, p. IV/12.

108 ILO, *The Impact of International Labor Conventions and Recommendations* p. 79.

109 AFL-CIO *Free Trade Union News*, Dec. 1977, p. 6.

110 U.S. Chamber of Commerce, press release Nov. 6, 1975.

Chapter 7: From Withdrawal to Return

1 The real impact of this increase was cushioned by the sharp increase in the value of the yen with respect to the U.S. dollar.

2 ILO, GB, *Draft Minutes*, 204th sess. [GB. 204/PV,] Nov. 1977, pp. III/4–5.

3 ILC, *Provisional Record*, 64th sess., 1978, p. 13/5.

4 Speech of Francis Blanchard to the ILO staff, Jan. 8, 1979.

5 ILC, *Draft Program and Budget, 1980–81*, Report II, p. 23.

6 Ibid., p. 95.

7 *ILO News*, March 12, 1979.

8 ILC, *Provisional Record*, 64th sess., 1978, pp. 31/1–9.

9 Ibid., p. 35/11.

10 Ibid., pp. 12/18–19, 14/32, and 14/35–38.

11 ILC, *Report of the Committee of Experts*, 64th sess., 1978, Report III, Part 4A, pp. 98–100.

12 ILC, *Provisional Record*, 64th sess., 1978, p. 29/3.

13 Ibid., p. 29/5.

14 Ibid., p. 34/7.

15 Ibid., p. 24/6.

16 Ibid., p. 28/31.

17 Ibid., pp. 2/1–40 and 35/1–28.

18 Ibid., p. 36/12.

19 Ibid., p. 2/15.

20 Ibid., p. 33/15.

21 Ibid., pp. 33/12–13.

22 Ibid., p. 33/25.

23 Ibid., p. 33/27.

24 Record votes will still be required for some decisions, including adopting conventions and recommendations and amending the constitution.

25 ILC, *Provisional Record*, 65th sess., 1979, p. 29/7.

26 Ibid., p. 41/10.

27 Ibid., p. 2/3.

28 Ibid., pp. 40/11–15.

29 ILC, *Report of the Committee of Experts*, 65th sess., 1979, Report III, Part 4A, p. 145.

30 ILC, *Provisional Record*, 65th sess., 1979, p. 36/39.

31 ILO, GB, *Minutes*, 206th sess., June 1978, GB. 206/5/8, App., pp. 1–64.

32 ILC, *Provisional Record*, 65th sess., 1979, p. 43/6.

33 U.S., Department of Labor, Bureau of International Labor Affairs, "Report of the 65th Session of the International Labor Conference", 1979, p. 7 (mimeographed).

34 Office of the White House Press Secretary, press release, Feb. 13, 1980.

35 AFL–CIO, press release, Feb. 13, 1980.

36 At a meeting sponsored by the U.S. Council, two representatives

of European employers had strongly urged American employers to back U.S. reaffiliation. Raphael Lagasse, secretary general of the International Organization of Employers, argued that while the U.S. withdrawal had greatly improved the situation within the ILO, "a prolonged absence of the United States would blunt its effectiveness in achieving more progress. . . . The active presence of United States employers would reinforce free employers' efforts in maintaining the results obtained and in tackling the very difficult issues still remaining, such as helping employers to maintain their autonomy and be free to keep the employers from communist countries outside the Governing Body of the ILO—as they have done for more than 25 years—or helping the employers to maintain an effective procedure of control of the application of ILO conventions." Memorandum, United States Council of the International Chamber of Commerce, October 1, 1979.

37 Statement of Dean K. Clowes, *New York Times*, Feb. 12, 1980, p. A9.

38 Statement of Michael Boggs, ibid.

39 U.S., Department of Labor, scope paper, ILC, 66th sess., May 13, 1980.

40 ILC, *Provisional Record*, 66th sess., 1980, p. 39/31. This was the text of the final resolution submitted to the conference. The text originally submitted was much tougher.

41 Ibid., p. 26/10. The speech was actually delivered by a labor advisor due to the indisposition of the delegate.

42 Ibid., p. 36/7.

43 Ibid., p. 20/9.

44 *New York Times*, June 28, 1980, p. 2.

45 *AFL–CIO News*, July 5, 1980, p. 6.

Chapter 8: The Future Role of the United States

1 Probably nothing can be done at this point about paragraph 12 of Article 14, which gives "representatives of liberation movements" the privilege of addressing the conference with the permission of the president. It is difficult to see how the remarks of such representatives could be anything but political.

2 The office of the solicitor of the Department of Labor has recently determined that ratification of the human rights conventions "is within the constitutional power of the federal government, that each convention may be found appropriate for federal action, and that it is unnecessary, as a matter of law, to submit any of these

conventions to the states for action on their part." *Task Force on International Labor Standards*, App. 7–1. The problem areas relate to such matters as the right of public employees to strike, minimum conditions laid down by federal legislation that labor unions must meet in their constitution and operation, the establishment of trusteeships over local unions by their national bodies, and a few similar matters. Apart from the status of public employees, none should cause any great difficulty.

Appendix A: The Kilby Studies

1 Paul Bangasser, "An Anatomy of Technical Assistance: The Case of the Charicar Tannery," ILO Technology and Employment Branch, p. 62 (mimeographed).

Appendix B: Results of Country Survey Visits

1 E. Lederman, "Costa Rica: Proyecto de Planificacion y Promocion del Empleo," Nov. 1977 (mimeographed).
2 Ibid., p. 12 (translated from Spanish).
3 SINAMOS has been described as follows: "An army-staffed propaganda and public works agency. . . . SINAMOS was run by General Leonidas Rodriguez, one of the army's most prominent radicals, and was meant to proselytize for the revolution at the same time as it was building roads and sewage systems in the shanty towns. But as the government grew more unpopular, SINAMOS became an instrument of repression. In 1975, some 70 people were killed in widespread rioting in the South against the offices of SINAMOS, after which the agency quietly faded away." *The Economist*, Sept. 2, 1978, p. 71.
4 Among other things, the Velasco regime had nationalized the oil industry; the Lima power company; the major airline; the telephone system; the railways; the cement, chemical, and fishing industries; some copper mining firms; insurance companies; and three commercial banks.
5 "The Role of ARTEP," an appraisal prepared by ARTEP, Feb. 1978, p. I–3 (mimeographed).

Index

Administration of technical assistance. *See* Technical assistance, International Labor Organization administration of

AFL. *See* American Federation of Labor

AFL-CIO. *See* American Federation of Labor-Congress of Industrial Organizations

Africa, 72, 86, 87, 133, 146, 176, 245. *See also* Organization of African Unity; Technical assistance, to Africa

African Regional Labor Administration Center for English-Speaking Africa (ARLAC), 151, 303

African Regional Labor Administration Center for French-Speaking Africa (GRADAT), 151, 303

Agency for International Development (AID), 194, 195, 253, 274, 285

Ago, Roberto, 46, 109

Agricultural assistance, 303, 304. *See also* Food and Agricultural Organization; Rural development

Agriculture Department. *See* United States Agriculture Department

AID. *See* Agency for International Development

Alba, Pedro de, 38

Albania, 18

Algeria, 88, 260

All-Union Central Council of Trade Unions (AUCCTU), 35, 48–49, 53, 54, 58

American Federation of Labor (AFL), 4, 5, 7, 58

American Federation of Labor-Congress of Industrial Organizations (AFL-CIO), 181, 288, 295, 298

attitudes toward communism, 42, 55, 58–59, 89, 115, 120

attitudes toward International Labor Organization, 30, 45–46, 117, 118, 121–22, 135–37, 200–201, 250, 265, 266, 268

participation in International Labor Organization, 24, 55, 71, 75, 119, 126, 131–32, 238. *See also* Labor representatives, American

support for Israel, 78, 86, 120, 136

Andean Indian project, 155

Andean pact countries, 291

Angola, 72

Antigua, 244

Apartheid. *See* South Africa

Arab countries, 88, 89, 128, 135, 254, 261, 263. *See also* League of Arab States

attacks on Israel in the International Labor Organization, 65–66, 78, 79, 80–81, 84, 86, 133, 255–56, 263, 266–67, 276

Argentina, 34, 161, 233, 257. *See also* Trade Unions, Argentine

ARLAC. *See* African Regional Labor Administration Center for English-Speaking Africa

ARPLA. *See* Asian Regional Project for Strengthening Labor and Manpower Administration

ARSDEP. *See* Asian Regional Skill Development Program

ARTEP. *See* Asian Regional Team for Employment Promotion

Asia, 146, 176, 198, 245

JACKET DESIGNED BY GARY GORE
COMPOSED BY GRAPHIC COMPOSITION, INC., ATHENS, GEORGIA
MANUFACTURED BY INTER-COLLEGIATE PRESS, INC.
SHAWNEE MISSION, KANSAS
TEXT AND DISPLAY LINES ARE SET IN CALEDONIA

Library of Congress Cataloging in Publication Data
Galenson, Walter, 1914–
The International Labor Organization.
Bibliography: pp. 307–333
Includes index.
1. International Labor Organization. 2. Labor
policy—United States. 3. United States—Foreign
relations—1945–.   I. Title.
HD7801.G3   341.7′63   80–52295
ISBN 0–299–08540–6
ISBN 0–299–08544–9 (pbk.)